WHO *was* WHO
in the
ROYAL MILE
EDINBURGH

DAVID DICK

Published by Clerkington Publishing Co. Ltd.,
West Lodge Clerkington, Haddington,
East Lothian EH41 4NJ, UK.

Tel: (0162) 082 5341
E-mail: 113300.3557@compuserve.com

The moral right of the author has been asserted.
A catalogue record for this book is available from the British Library and the National Library of Scotland.

ISBN 0 9530274 1 4

Printed by Kelso Graphics, The Knowes, Kelso TD5 7BH.

The photographs are by the author except where otherwise acknowledged.

WHO *was* WHO
in the
ROYAL MILE
EDINBURGH

This Royal Mile walk downhill from the Esplanade of Edinburgh Castle to the Palace of Holyroodhouse has been split into four walks. There are four street plans and each walk will take about half-an-hour, but this depends on how long you stop at any point. For example, you could spend an hour at Lady Stair's House Museum, another hour in St Giles Cathedral and yet another in John Knox House, but assuming that you stop only long enough to gaze in admiration and to read the numbered summaries contained in the first few pages of each walk, it should be a fairly leisurely and certainly a thoroughly enjoyable stroll.

Closes which are numbered in the text contain the brief biographies of eminent residents of the past and those Closes shown in parenthesis no longer exist but have interesting stories.

4

Primarily, my gratitude is to my wife, **Muriel**, whose forbearance and unfailing interest in this project is the reason for its completion. Her patience, her many suggestions, her help with my photography and her accuracy in proof reading is a true blessing.

My daughter **Mrs Pamela Armstrong** for her marketing expertise, her unfailing interest and her infectious enthusiasm.

Miss Agnes Hamilton for her interest, help, encouragement and in lending me several volumes of Edinburgh books.

Mr Alan Hughes for his continuous and unfailing interest in this project during many conversations. His help in proof reading is greatly appreciated.

Miss Margaret Pringle of Haddington's History Society whose interest, encouragement and help in proof reading are greatly appreciated.

Leslie Spoor MA(Hons), BA(Hons) retired Senior Lecturer of History, Napier University, Edinburgh, retired Visiting-Professor of Modern European History at Colorado College and at the University of Maryland USA; he checked the historical accuracy of the text. To Leslie, a dedicated historian, I am eternally grateful for many interesting and informative conversations about the history of Scotland.

My daughter, **Dr Moira Catherine Watson** of Napier University, for her patient interest, her excellent suggestions and for proof reading the text.

Neil Wilson of Neil Wilson Publishers Ltd., for permission to reproduce the biographies of William Ewart Gladstone, George Drummond, Henry Dundas, George Heriot, Dugald Stewart and David Hume from my book: *Capital Walks in Edinburgh - The New Town*

Doreen Grove of **Historic Scotland** for permission to reproduce my photograph of Edinburgh Castle.

Lieutenant Colonel David Anderson, Superintendent, Palace of Holyroodhouse for permission to reproduce my photographs of the Abbey, the Palace and the statue of Edward VII

Lastly to a long line of overseas visitors with whom I have toured the Royal Mile many times and whose many questions I have tried to answer in this book.

Dedication

To my five daughters, Brenda, Sandra, Linda, Pamela and Moira who will, I hope, read some of this in the years ahead to my eleven grandchildren - Christopher, Jane, Karen, Scott, Jack, Moira, Andrew, Sam, Billie, Katie and Sarah.

Introduction

Edinburgh, the Capital City of Scotland, consists of the Old Town (the Royal Mile), the New Town and many villages which have merged with the city.

The Old Town - the Royal Mile, so named because in ancient times Scottish Kings and nobles of Scotland lived in or near the Castle. Queen Margaret, wife of Malcolm Canmore, took refuge in the Castle where her little chapel was built in her memory by her son David I. Edinburgh was the 'King's Burgh' when David I (r.1124-1153) granted the Charter of Holyrood Abbey in 1128.

Two hundred years later, on 29th May 1329 to be exact, Edinburgh's Royal Charter was granted by King Robert the Bruce only a few weeks before he died. The Royal Mile became the central place of residence for the nobility, leading churchmen, jurists, academics and politicians who lived side by side with the ordinary people.

Overcrowding, the absence of drains and the poverty and misery which followed the Union of Parliaments of 1707 caused disease and abominable smells in the Old Town. A New Town was the dream of the Lord Provost, George Drummond (1687-1766) and he lived just long enough to see the winning design of a young architect, James Craig.

This is a walk through the Old Town - the Royal Mile. It is an exploration of its history through the lives of many of the eminent inhabitants of the old Closes and Wynds and deals with many of the luminaries of the 'Scottish Enlightenment' who socialised in hostelries and as members of their clubs.

Incidentally, the difference between a 'Close' and a 'Wynd' is simply explained - a Close is a passage or entry just wide enough to take a sedan chair and could be closed at night, whereas a Wynd is an alley, an open thoroughfare wide enough for a carriage. A Pend is an arch; a Bow is the bend in a street; a Port is a gate; a Land is a house of several storeys; a Toll is a turnpike; a Tolbooth is a jail and a Tron is a weigh-beam. The names of Closes and Wynds have changed many times over the centuries but those which have stood the test of time tell us of the exciting history of the Royal Mile and of Scotland.

David Dick

Tour Walk 1 - The Castle Esplanade, Castlehill and Lawnmarket

1. Edinburgh Castle
2. King Robert the Bruce
3. Sir William Wallace
   Obelisk to the 72nd Duke
   of Albany's Own Highlanders
   Ensign Charles Ewart
4. Frederick, Duke of York
   Three Celtic Crosses
5. Earl Haig equestrian statue
   The Witches Fountain

Castlehill
6. Ramsay Garden
   - Allan Ramsay
   Cannonball House,
   Castlehill School
   (The Scottish Whisky Centre)
   Boswell's Court
7. The Outlook Tower
   - Patrick Geddes
   Sempill's Close,
   Assembly Hall of the
   Church of Scotland
   The Tolbooth Church,
   Johnstone Terrace,
   [Stripping Close]

Lawnmarket
   Mylne's Court
8. James's Court
   - David Hume
9. Riddle's Court
   - Bailie Macmorran,
   - David Hume,
   - Patrick Geddes,
   - Major Thomas Weir.
10. Brodie's Close
    - Deacon Brodie
11. Lady Stair's Close
    [Baxter's Close],
    Wardrop's Close
    [Old Bank Close],
    Bank Street
12. George IV Bridge
    St Giles Street

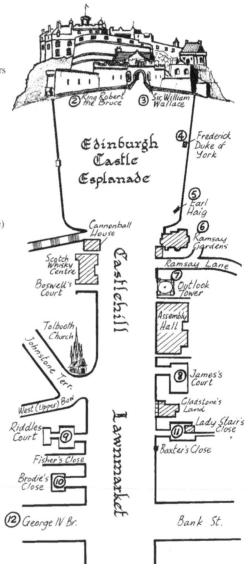

Tour 1 - Summary

The Castle Esplanade forms part of this walk but before describing some of its monuments and statues, a little of the history of the Castle itself cannot be omitted.

1. Edinburgh Castle is the major tourist attraction of Scotland. The Edinburgh Military Tattoo, held on the Castle Esplanade, is a prime attraction of the annual Edinburgh International Festival.

There was an early settlement on the Castle rock during the 1st century and a fortress existed even before St Margaret's Chapel was built prior to her death in 1093. The Castle therefore became the origin of the Burgh of Edinburgh. It was the residence of several kings and was attacked many times by English invaders. It was the scene of murder, it was a prison and it was destroyed and rebuilt many times during its long history. St Margaret's Chapel, where St Margaret, the only British female Saint, was said to have worshipped, has survived every onslaught. There is much to see of great interest:

- Chapel of St Margaret,
- King's Lodging, the birthplace of James VI,
- Scottish National War Memorial,
- Regalia Room with the 'Honours of Scotland' - the Scottish
  Crown Jewels and the 'Stone of Destiny',
- Great Hall with its early 16th century timber roof,
- United Services Museum,
- Half Moon Battery built in 1573-88 by Regent Morton on the
  lower part of David II's tower, from which the one-o'clock gun
  was fired; it is now fired from Mills Mount Battery,
- Mons Meg, the great cannon used by James III at the Siege of
  Dumbarton Castle,
- Dogs' Graveyard for Regimental pets,
- Argyll Tower, built in 1574 with dungeons and Portcullis.

On either side of the entrance arch of the Castle are two statues: Sir William Wallace, on the right (north side), and King Robert the Bruce, on the left (south side). They were unveiled in 1929 by George V to commemorate the 600th anniversary of the granting of Edinburgh's Royal Charter by Robert the Bruce.

2. King Robert the Bruce (1274-1329) was crowned king of Scotland in 1306. He was the victor of many battles, the greatest of which was the Battle of Bannockburn in 1314 when he defeated Edward II's army to make Scotland free of English dominance.

3. Sir William Wallace (1274-1305) was the victor of the Battle of Stirling Bridge in 1297 when he expelled the English from Scotland and was elected Governor of Scotland. He was beheaded, hanged, drawn and quartered at Smithfield in London following his betrayal in 1305. This fired the anger of the Scots.

Monuments on the Esplanade

Before the Esplanade existed, some wooden houses sheltered by the Castle entrance. After their removal the space was used as a drill ground and was called the Esplanade. It was formed in 1753 from the stone and rubble of the old tenements which were demolished to make way for the new Royal Exchange (now the City Chambers in the High Street). It was on this ground that Charles I (1625-49) honoured eminent Scots with the Knighthood of Scotland and Nova Scotia and this little part of Old Edinburgh was considered, by means of a legal fiction in 1621, to be part of the colony of Nova Scotia; Canadian visitors must feel specially welcome. The sentry boxes and turrets were added in 1816. The memorials on the Esplanade include:

- **The Obelisk to the 72nd Duke of Albany's Own Highlanders**, by R.Rowand Anderson, 1861. This regiment, raised by the Earl of Seaforth in 1778, served valiantly in India (1781), Ceylon (1796), Cape Colony (1806), Crimea (1854-56)) and in the Afghan Campaign (1878-80).
- **Ensign Charles Ewart**, by W.H.Kininmonth.1938; Ensign Charles Ewart heroically captured the French colours at the Battle of Waterloo (1815). His remains, having been transferred from Salford, were buried at the North side of the esplanade

4. Frederick, Duke of York, second son of George III (1763-1827); by Thomas Campbell, 1939. *The Grand Old Duke of York* won very few battles but he gave the Duke of Wellington a well-trained officer corps.
- **Three Celtic Crosses** - one to the 78th Highlanders with an elephant at its base, another to Colonel Douglas Mackenzie by John Steell in 1875; and another to the Scottish Horse by Stewart McGlashan & Co., 1905.

5. Statue of Earl Haig; he was Commander-in-Chief of the British Army during the Great War; by G.E.Wade 1922-3.

- **The Witches Memorial** on the wall of the north-east corner is a plaque, gifted by Sir Patrick Geddes, by John Duncan at the place where over 300 women were strangled and burned between 1479 and 1722.

6. Ramsay Garden, at the foot of the Esplanade, is the attractive, colourful, almost Continental, group of houses in one of which lived Allan Ramsay (c1685-1758), the wig-maker who became a well-known poet. He designed the octagonal Ramsay Lodge about 1740 and was not a little annoyed when it was nick-named the "Goose-pie". He started the first lending library in Britain and wrote *The Gentle Shepherd*. He was buried in Greyfriars Churchyard and his monument of white Carrara marble (by Sir John Steell) stands above the floral clock in West Princes Street Gardens. His eldest son, also Allan Ramsay (1713-84), became a distinguished portrait painter and was appointed painter to George III. However Ramsay Garden and Lane take their names from an earlier owner, Ramsay of Dalhousie who was *The Laird O' Cockpen*, immortalised by Lady Nairne. His 17th century mansion occupied the site of the Outlook Tower. In 1847 Thomas Guthrie DD (1803-73) started his "Ragged School" for seven child beggars at Ramsay Lane.

Castlehill

Cannonball House is the 16th century house, at the top of Castle Hill; it has an inscription 'AM. MN. 1630' on its west facing dormer window (Alexander Mure a furrier and his wife). The house was named from the fact that two cannon balls are embedded in its west wall. They were said to have been fired from the Castle during the 1745 siege when Prince Charles Edward Stuart's Jacobites took over the city. However, the cannon balls, placed neatly side by side, simply mark the water level of Comiston springs near the Braid Hills for the laying of water pipes by a Dutch engineer, Bruschi, in 1681. No water appeared when the valve was first turned on and he made a hasty exit, imagining that his scheme was a failure. He need not have worried, the flow of water was rather slow.

The 2 million-gallon (9.1 million litres) ashlar block **Castlehill Reservoir** on the north side of Castle Hill was constructed in 1849-50 and the wells of the Royal Mile were supplied from it in 1851. A recent £2-million transformation has been carried out to form a huge five-storey tartan weaving mill with sixteen weaving machines. Visitors entering from street level can see for themselves the full process of transforming sheep's wool into beautiful tartan weave. An ancient weaver's cottage complete with its water-wheel powering a small Hattersley loom is an additional exhibit.

Castlehill School was built in 1896 on the site of the Gordon Mansion, the residence of the 1ˢᵗ Duke of Gordon who was the Captain, Constable and Keeper of the Castle from 1686 to 1689. The Baird family of Newbyth owned the mansion during the 18ᵗʰ century when Baird's Close (previously Blair Close) existed. Sir David Baird (1757-1829) who became the hero of Seringapatam and Corunna was born and spent part of his boyhood here.

The school has been converted into the **Scotch Whisky Heritage Centre** and unveils some of the magic in the distillation of Scotch Whisky in its 300-year history.

Boswell's Court was built in 1630 and was originally called Lowthian Close after its original owner Thomas Lowthian, a rich merchant. His initials and the inscription: "O LORD IN THE IS AL MI TRAIST" are barely discernible over the moulded doorway at the side. A later owner, Dr Boswell, was an uncle of the famous man-of-letters, James Boswell (1740-95), the biographer of Samuel Johnson (of *Dictionary* fame). The mansion was said to have been occupied by an Earl of Bothwell.

Arms of the Biggars of Woolmet –
'Giving and Forgiving'
(above the doorway of the Outlook Tower)

7. The Outlook Tower is just below Ramsay Lane, opposite Boswell's Court; it was originally a 17th century mansion of Ramsay of Dalhousie. Two floors were added in 1853 for Maria Short's Camera Obscura. **Professor Patrick Geddes** (1842-1934), the father of town planning, redesigned it as an Outlook Tower with a planetarium. His globes, showing the world's vegetation and geology, explained the fundamentals of conservation. The 'Geddes Trails' commemorate his work in rejuvenating the Royal Mile.

Sempill's Close was the grand mansion of the Barons Sempill (whose title was granted in 1489). The two surviving doorways, dated 1638, have inscriptions;

'Praise be the Lord, My God: My Strength and My Redeemer' and *Sedes Manet Optima Coele* (The choicest seat remains in Heaven).

The mansion was occupied by Grizel, sister of the 1st Earl of Rosebery and widow of Francis, 8th Lord Semple in 1734 and, in 1743, Hugh, 11th Lord Semple. His son, the 12th Lord Semple, commanded the left wing of the Royal Army against the Jacobites at Culloden in 1746; he too lived in the house. In 1755 Sir John Clerk of Penicuik became the new owner. He, a learned and talented man, was thwarted in his bid for the hand of Susanna Kennedy who chose the much older (and richer) Earl of Eglinton, she having been told to "bide a wee...my wife's very sickly!"

The Assembly Hall of the Church of Scotland, by David Bryce in 1858-9, was built on the site of the 'Guise Palace' occupied by Mary of Guise, wife of James V and mother of Mary, Queen of Scots, who took up residence there in 1544 when Holyrood was sacked by the English under the Earl of Hertford. The Hall extends from Castlehill northwards to the quadrangle of New College.

The Tolbooth Church, on the corner of Johnston Terrace and Castle Hill, was designed in Gothic detail by James Gillespie Graham and Augustus W. N. Pugin in 1839-44; it has the highest spire in Edinburgh. As well as a church for Gaelic speaking Highlanders, it was the meeting place for the General Assembly of the Church of Scotland.

When the Western Approach Road was completed in 1836 it was firstly called Castle Place but it was renamed **Johnston Terrace** in 1852 to mark the end of Sir William Johnston's Lord Provostship in 1851. This construction and that of the Tolbooth Church necessitated the demolition of old buildings and Closes. One of these old Closes was **Stripping Close** which was named from the fact that prisoners from the Old Tolbooth Jail, near St Giles Church, were brought here to be stripped to the waist, regardless of sex, in readiness for their punishment at one of the nine whipping posts in the Royal Mile. This practice continued until July 1822.

Lawnmarket

The **Lawnmarket** was named from the fact that 'lawn-merchants' were permitted by an Act of the Scottish Parliament of 1477 to sell their cloth there. It was called the 'Landmarket' early in the 18th century when the Wednesday market for the sale of produce from the land took place.

Mylne's Court (formerly Cranston's Court) on the north side of Lawnmarket is named after **Robert Mylne** of Balfargie (1633-1710), the King's Master Mason (the 7th generation of master masons of his family). He designed this, the first open square in Edinburgh, to give a new meaning to spacious living. He built the extension of Holyrood Palace in 1671 for Charles II and was hereditary master-gunner of the Castle where Mylne's Battery was named after him. He sculpted the statue of George Heriot in the quadrangle of George Heriot's School.

His son, **Robert Mylne**, was the architect who designed St Cecilia's Hall (1761-63) at the foot of Niddry Street. He designed Blackfriars Bridge in London and surveyed St Paul's Cathedral.

Above the entrance to Mylne's Court, the year '1690' is engraved. In 1745 some of Prince Charles's officers occupied the houses of the Court during his siege of Edinburgh. The Court was restored between 1966 and 1970 and is now a students' residence with halls commemorating Edward Salveson, Philip Henman and Patrick Geddes .

8. James Court (formerly Brownhill's Court), built in 1725-7, is named after James Brownhill, a wright and builder. The north-west section was burned down in 1857 and rebuilt by David Bryce, the architect of Fettes College. It was a fashionable address for Lords and Ladies and other eminent people such as David Hume (1711-1776), philosopher and historian, who let his house to Dr Hugh Blair, Professor of Rhetoric and Belle Lettres of the University. Another resident was James Boswell (1740-95) biographer of Dr Samuel Johnson (1709-84) of *Dictionary* fame, who as a guest of Boswell, was heard to remark, "I smell you in the dark." He was referring to the lack of sanitation in Edinburgh and not to his host! But Boswell's wife thought Johnson to be an ill-mannered boor. Other residents included Lord Bankton, the judge who wrote *Institutional Law of Scotland,* Sir John Clerk of Penicuik and Ilay Campbell, Lord President of the Court of Session.

9. Riddle's Court (formerly Macmorran's Court, Shaw's Court) on the south side was also known as Royston's Close after Sir James Mackenzie of Royston. However, the Court is now named after George Riddell who rebuilt it in 1726, but the buildings inside probably date from 1591 when the wealthy **Bailie John MacMorran** built his house in which James VI and his Queen, Anne of Denmark, dined in courtly style.

MacMorran was shot and killed by a High School boy when, with the City Officers, he attempted to negotiate the end of the schoolboy 'strike' in 1595 for additional holidays. The culprit was never brought to trial even though James VI was informed; MacMorran had been in the service of Regent Morton and was a man of influence but the boys were sons of the nobility.

David Hume (1711-76), the greatest philosopher and historian in Europe, lived here from 1769. He started his *History of England* in six volumes when he lived at Riddles Court. The University's Hume Tower, in George Square, is named after him.

Patrick Geddes opened the first summer school in Riddle's Court which was a students' residence. The motto in stone above the inner archway was chosen by Professor Geddes, 'Vivendo Discimus' (we learn by living together).

The house nearest the street remained unoccupied for over one hundred years. It was a house of horror and thought to be haunted. The infamous **Major Thomas Weir** and his sister, **Grizell**, a self-confessed witch, lived there. Towards the end of his life the Major confessed his horrendous deeds and the couple were executed and burned.

Fisher's Close (formerly Hamilton's Close), next to Riddle's Court, takes its name from Thomas Fisher, the first Chamberlain of Edinburgh. Built in 1699 and restored by the Carnegie United Kingdom Trust in 1953; it is now the headquarters of the Scottish Central Library. It was the site of the Duke of Buccleuch's 18th century house, part of which was demolished to make way for the construction of Victoria Street. The 3rd Duke had as his tutor the famous father of economics, Adam Smith, during his grand tour of Europe when the Duke's young brother, Hugh Campbell Scott, was murdered in Paris.

10. Brodie's Close (formerly Baker's Close, Cullin's Close, Little's Close) was the venue for the first meetings, in 1785, of the Masonic Lodge, Roman Eagle No. 160 (the year of its charter). The ceiling of the hall is dated 1645. The Close was the home and work premises of **Francis Brodie**, a well-respected Deacon of Wrights, whose playboy son **William** took over the successful business after the death of his father. His drinking, gambling and cock-fighting habits together with his two mistresses and their five children led to his double life and his debts. He was a respectable member of the Edinburgh bourgeoisie, a Deacon of Wrights by day and a reprobate robber by night. He was caught in Amsterdam and hanged at the Tolbooth in 1788. Brodie's double life inspired Robert Louis Stevenson to write *Dr Jekyll and Mr Hyde*.

Gladstone's Land, almost opposite Riddle's Court, is a 16th century town house as it would have been during the visit of Charles I to Edinburgh in 1633. The original house was bought by Thomas Glaidstones, a city burgess, in 1617 who extended it towards the street by about twenty feet (6 m). The 16th century interior, the first floor segmental arch, the doors, windows and oriel-shaped balcony are all beautifully preserved. The building was taken over by the National Trust for Scotland in 1934.

11. Lady Stair's Close and **House** (formerly Lady Gray's Close and House) was originally built in 1622 for Sir William Gray of Pittendrum, a rich merchant who died in 1648.

Today it is the **Writers' Museum** of memorabilia of Scotland's great literary figures: Robert Burns (1759-96), Sir Walter Scott (1771-1832) and Robert Louis Stevenson (1850-94). The shield above the doorway is dated 1622 with the inscription: 'Fear the Lord and Depart from Evil'.

The house takes its name from one of its owners, Elizabeth, Dowager Countess of Stair who inherited it in 1719. Her daughter-in-law, Eleanor is sometimes erroneously assumed to the be the source of naming this Close and house. Eleanor was a lady of strong character who cut a fine figure and with her good looks and her black servant she was often seen in her sedan chair in the High Street in the first half of the 18th century.

The house was the gift of the 5th Earl of Rosebery (1847-1929) to the City of Edinburgh in 1907. He purchased it in 1895 and restored it to save it from demolition.

[**Baxter's Close**] was demolished in 1798 to make way for Bank Street and was named from the property of the baxters or bakers. It was adjacent to Lady Stair's Close and was the house in which Scotland's great poet, Robert Burns, found lodgings on his arrival for the first time (28th November 1786) in Edinburgh. He shared a small room with his friend John Richmore with whom he shared the rent of three shillings per week. During this visit his portrait was painted by Alexander Nasmyth (1758-1840) who lived almost opposite in **Wardrop's Court** (formerly Henderson's Court) named after a wright or carpenter and burgess, John Wardop, who built the close in 1790 and where William Scott, the first Professor of Greek of the University, had his home.

[**Old Bank Close**] was situated on the site of the Lothian Regional Council Headquarters where Gourlay's House was demolished. The latter was the residence of Robert Gourlay, a messenger-at-arms of Holyroodhouse and a favourite of James VI; the former resided there in 1593-94. The Bank of Scotland was founded in this Close in 1695.

Bank Street was cut through the Closes on the north side of the Lawnmarket in 1798 and two years later the north site was purchased by the Bank of Scotland whose first bank, built in 1802-06 to a design by Robert Reid and Richard Crighton, was not admired. In 1863 David Bryce completed a redesign of the north frontage with sculptures by John Rhind.

12. George IV Bridge was built between 1829 and 1834 as a southern approach to the city and was named in honour of the king's visit to Scotland in 1822. This was a grand affair master-minded by Sir Walter Scott; it was the first visit of a monarch since that of Charles II on 1st January 1651 for his Coronation at Scone (the last to take place in Scotland).

St Giles Street commemorates the patron saint of cripples, lepers and nursing mothers and was so named because of its proximity to St Giles Cathedral. The name was originally intended by James Craig for the New Town's Princes Street but George III vetoed it on the grounds that St Giles was a disreputable area in London. St Giles Street marks the boundary between the Lawnmarket and the High Street.

1. Edinburgh Castle

Edinburgh Castle dominates the Edinburgh skyline; it gives the Capital City its romance and valour of centuries past. It is undoubtedly the great tourist attraction of Scotland and from its Esplanade the Edinburgh Military Tattoo during the Edinburgh International Festival is a superb and colourful pageant of world wide military music, history, marching and gymnastic skill.

There was a settlement of sorts on this volcanic plug in the 1st century AD. A hill fort existed in the 2nd century when the Romans occupied Inveresk. The first siege took place after the death of the king, Malcolm Canmore, in 1093 when his brother, Donald Bane attacked; Queen Margaret died shortly after her husband. The earliest building, still in existence, is Queen Margaret's Chapel which is said to have been built early in the 12th century by her youngest son, David I, who lived in the Castle when he signed the Charter for Holyrood Abbey in 1128.

The English took the Castle for the first time in 1174 and in 1291 Edward I, 'hammer of the Scots', lived at the Castle when he was asked to decide, from thirteen claimants, who should sit upon the Scottish throne. He chose John Balliol, the first born of the earliest ancestor of David I, who was the easiest to manipulate. In 1296, Edward besieged the Castle and held it for the next seventeen years.

In 1314 the Earl of Moray, a nephew of Robert the Bruce, scaled the Castle rock and cunningly took it from the English. He destroyed it, except for St Margaret's Chapel, to prevent its future use by the enemy. The Castle remained ruined for the next twenty-one years; Edward III rebuilt it in 1335 but the Scots destroyed it again six years later.

In 1357 **David's Tower** was built over a period of ten years by David II. Richard II devastated Edinburgh in 1385 and the Castle was destroyed and refortified several times afterwards.

The **Great Hall** was built for James I in 1433-4; it was used by the Scottish Parliament. The **Banqueting Hall** was the scene of the 'Black Dinner' when, in 1440, the two Douglas boys - the 6th Earl of Douglas and his young brother - were beheaded on a trumped up charge of treason by the two Regents, Sir William Crichton and Sir Alexander Livingstone; the weeping, ten-year-old James II being a reluctant participant.

The Castle was the principal residence of the Stuart kings. On the south side of Crown Square stands **Register House**; the monogram 'IR4' on one of the corbels dates it to James IV (r.1488-1513). The mother of Mary Queen of Scots, Mary of Guise, died in the Castle in 1560 during the 'Siege of Leith'. Mary, Queen of Scots gave birth to her son, James VI, in the **Palace** or **King's Lodging** in 1566 and Sir William Kirkcaldy defended the Castle for Mary against English guns in 1573. James VI built the northern half of the 1434 **Great Chamber** in 1615 as a Royal Lodging.

The Covenanters held the Castle in 1640 and Cromwell captured it in 1650. In 1661 the Marquis of Argyll, in spite of paying homage to Charles II, was sent for trial to Edinburgh Castle for his previous support of Cromwell. He spent the eve of his execution in the **Argyll Tower** (then called Constable's Tower). The last siege took place when the Duke of Gordon held the Castle for the deposed James VII (II of England) and the last defence of the Castle was against Bonnie Prince Charlie (Prince Charles Edward Stuart) in 1745. Jacobites of the '45 Rising were imprisoned in the Castle as were French soldiers of the Napoleonic wars. The kitchens for the Great Hall were built in 1708 and now accommodate the **United Services Museum**.

Today, Edinburgh Castle is the major tourist attraction; there is a wealth of historical interest.

The **Chapel of St Margaret**, the oldest building in the Castle, dates to c1100. It was 'rediscovered' in 1845 and restored in 1851-2; it had been used as a storehouse. St Margaret was the beloved Queen of Malcolm Canmore. Her Chapel has survived every onslaught of the Castle over many centuries. Queen Margaret died in the Castle in 1093 on learning of the death of her husband. Her body was taken secretly to its last resting-place at Dunfermline Abbey. Her son David I, who founded Holyrood Abbey, is said to have built the Chapel in her memory. She converted the Scots from their outdated religious usages to the Church of Rome and was canonised in 1251.

The **Scottish National War Memorial**, designed by Robert S. Lorimer 1924-7, is the National Shrine commemorating the dead of the World Wars 1914-18 and 1939-45 whose names are inscribed in the Rolls of Honour so often inspected by relatives and friends.

The **Crown Room** or Regalia Room houses the 'Honours of Scotland' and the Stone of Scone popularly known as the 'Stone of Destiny'; these are spectacular exhibits of the Crown jewels of Scotland which remained hidden from Oliver Cromwell after the Battle of Dunbar in 1650. They were used at Scone for the coronation of Charles II after which they were hidden firstly at Dunotter Castle and then smuggled to Kineff Church by the minister and his wife. After eighty years they were returned to Edinburgh Castle where they lay in a locked chest. After the Union of Parliaments of 1707 they were hidden again to be 'rediscovered' by a group of distinguished men including Sir Walter Scott on 4th February 1818.

The **Scottish United Services Museum**, on the west side of Crown Square, was built in 1708 and features military memorabilia of Scottish Regiments

Mons Meg is the name given to the ancient cannon which was forged in 1486 in Flanders in Belgium. There is a story that Mons Meg was forged in the Castle and was first fired on the birth of James V (10th April 1512); another story gives the place of its manufacture as Galloway where it was used by James II (r.1437-60) at the siege of Threave Castle. The great cannon burst when fired from the Castle in a salute to the Duke of York (who became James VII) on his arrival in 1682. It was taken from the Castle in 1758 but returned from the Tower of London in 1829 after a plea by Sir Walter Scott.

The **Dogs' Graveyard** is a poignant commemoration of Regimental pets.

The **Half Moon Battery** was built by Regent Morton in 1547 (ref. 30 Blackfriars Street) over and around David's Tower and the 'one-o'clock gun' was fired from here each weekday. Firing the one o'clock gun started in 1861 shortly after the formation of the 1st Edinburgh Volunteers who practiced their gunnery on the Argyll Battery in preparation for a French invasion feared to be imminent. The gun is now fired from **Mills Mount Battery** facing Princes Street.

2. Robert the Bruce Statue, Edinburgh Castle

The statue to Robert the Bruce, King of Scotland, guards the south side of the entrance arch to the Castle with the statue of Sir William Wallace on the north side. Both statues are set into canopied niches; that of Bruce is by Thomas J. Clapperton.

The Scottish hero of the War of Independence, Robert the Bruce, was crowned King of Scotland in 1306 and by 1313 the English were swept out of Scotland except for Stirling Castle, the English defence of which led to the famous Scottish victory in the Battle of Bannockburn on 24th June 1314.

Robert the Bruce was born in 1274 at Lochmaben near Lockerbie. He was the eldest son of Robert de Bruce (1253-1304) and through his mother Marjory, Countess of Carrick, his father became the Earl of Carrick, but he resigned the title to his son Robert in 1292. Robert's grandfather, also Robert de Bruce, was 5th Lord of Annandale and his claim to the vacant Scottish throne, on the death of Margaret the Maid of Norway in 1290, was lost when Edward I of England declared in favour of the weak John Balliol (nicknamed 'Empty Jacket'). The illustrious Bruce family dates back to the Norman Conquest when Robert de Bruis accompanied William the Conqueror at the Battle of Hastings in 1066. The name

Bruis derives from the French domain of Bruis near Cherbourg.

Edward I had forced the Scottish nobles to plead their allegiance personally at Westminster. Balliol's weakness was scorned after he surrendered the Scottish Crown at Montrose and the nobles of Scotland expelled the Englishmen from their Court. Edward had gone too far after Balliol's renunciation of allegiance; he took the 'Stone of Destiny' from Scone Palace, where Scottish kings were crowned, and his treasurer, Cressingham, greedily took everything he could.

Scotland was poised for action. Young Robert, as Earl of Carrick, was forced to swear fealty to the English king but soon afterwards he joined forces with Sir William Wallace against the English in 1297. Wallace razed Lanark and killed the English Sheriff, Hazelrig, as an act of revenge. Then followed Wallace's great victory, the famous Battle of Stirling Bridge, where the numerically superior army of Edward I was totally routed. But the following year, 1298, when Edward returned from Flanders he personally commanded the greatest army ever to leave England and Wallace was forced into battle at Falkirk. Edward's archers overwhelmed Wallace's infantry. Wallace's cavalry deserted him and he fled to France to raise another army. Meanwhile, Bruce lost his lands for his allegiance to Wallace.

In 1299 Bruce was one of four Regents in Scotland and with Sir John Comyn he was Guardian of Scotland. However, they were competitors for the throne of Scotland. In 1305 Wallace was betrayed to the English and was arrested by the Sheriff of Dumbarton. He was tried at Westminster and condemned to the most heinous death at Smithfield - disemboweled when half dead and then beheaded and quartered. As a lesson to any would-be rebels, his quarters were sent to Newcastle, Berwick, Stirling and Perth to be displayed. The effect on Bruce was exactly the opposite of that intended; he left the Court of the ruthless Edward, 'Hammer of the Scots', to meet his hereditary enemy, Red Comyn, in the church of the Minerite friars in Dumfries on 10th February 1306. Sir John Comyn, the nephew of Balliol, considered his claim to the throne superior to that of Bruce. They argued so bitterly that Bruce drew his dirk and stabbed Comyn. According to legend, he left the church in a confused state and said, "I doubt I ha' slain Comyn." His squire, Sir Neil Kilpatrick finished the job.

Bruce had to act quickly. Remembering the sight of Wallace's head on London Bridge, he decided to lead Scotland against the English. He collected his support from south-west Scotland and from Lochmabon to Glasgow and he made his way to the ancient Moot Hill of Scone. On 25th March 1306 he was crowned by the Bishop of St Andrews in the presence of the Bishops of Glasgow and Moray and the Earls of Lennox, Athol and Errol. On 29th March, Isabella, Countess of Buchan repeated the ceremony as the right of her family, the MacDuffs, Celtic Chiefs of Fife.

Bruce, however, was in a precarious position; he had brought a blood feud with an exceedingly powerful family on his head. Most of Scotland was controlled by the English and Bruce was accused of murder and sacrilege but he was absolved of his sins by the Bishop of Glasgow and sermons supporting him were preached throughout Scotland.

The first year of his reign was disastrous: at Methven the English easily defeated his band of followers and at Dalry in Ayrshire the Comyn family wrought their revenge. Edward ordered the capture of Bruce's family. His wife, Elizabeth, and his sisters were incarcerated and the Countess of Buchan was caged from a wall of Berwick Castle. Bruce fled to the Isle of Rathlin on the coast of Ireland and was almost on the point of giving himself up when he saw the legendary spider continuously spinning its web, never giving up. It was said to have inspired him to 'try, try and try again.' After avoiding his pursuers he increased his guerrilla attacks ruthlessly harassing small English outposts but his two brothers were captured and executed. Edward I was now quite old and unwell and Bruce had won a decisive victory in 1307 at Loudoun Hill in Ayrshire. Edward died bringing his army over the Solway to counter attack. This was a turning point. Edward II was not half the warrior of his father. Bruce now had time to plan: his first objective was to deal with the Comyns and the followers of Balliol who still had aspirations to the throne. He attacked them at each of their strongholds and castles - in Galloway, Inverlochy, Nairn, Elgin and finally at Inverurie. After the Lord of Argyll was put down at Pass of Brander in 1308, Bruce controlled two-thirds of Scotland.

Edward II brought his army north in 1310 but Bruce easily eluded him for several months. Edward gave up the chase and the following year Bruce invaded the North of England, gained funds and cattle and returned to Scotland to expel the last of the English. In 1312 he took Dundee and Perth. Only a few castles remained in English hands and at Stirling Castle the English Commander agreed to surrender to avoid a long and bloody siege, but only if no reinforcements arrived by Midsummer's day. Bruce decided to use the delay by taking the remaining castles at Linlithgow, Edinburgh and Roxburgh.

Edward II, stirred into action, decided to relieve Stirling. His army was almost twice that of Bruce who initially intended to retire, as he usually did when facing superior numbers. However, he was told that English morale was low and that they had positioned themselves in soggy ground between the River Forth and Bannock Burn. Bruce knew that this victory would give Scotland its independence. His position on high ground with good cover gave his forces the advantage. They were well trained and itching for the fight and fight they did, as never before.

The 24th June 1314 was a damp, 'dreich' day which suited Bruce well. He led the attack with four battalions. The English, having approached from Falkirk, found all roads blocked except that through marshy ground across the Bannock. They had little room for manoeuvre and following Bruce's assault they found themselves trying to recross the Bannock. They slithered and slipped; they fell on top of each other and many were drowned in the mud.

Their famous and feared longbows proved ineffective and their arrows were deflected by the cover of trees. The Scots pressed home their attack and routed the English. Victory was total; Edward escaped to his waiting ship at Dunbar. Bruce captured his belongings including the privy seal and the subsequent ransom money was a handsome bonus to the Scots.

At last Scotland belonged to the Scots. However, it took another fourteen years before Scotland gained its full independence during which time Bruce avenged all of Edward I's previous gains. He took Berwick and York and so ravaged the north of England, it was exempted from paying taxes but Bruce's brother, Edward, had been killed in Ireland.

With the Declaration of Arbroath in 1320, signed by the Scottish nobles, the Pope was now asked to recognise Scotland's independence and Bruce as rightful King, but the Pope remained unconvinced. In the peace negotiations of 1324, Edward II would not accept Bruce but a truce was agreed.

Edward's Queen divorced and deposed him and she married her lover Roger Mortimer. After Edward was found incompetent in 1327 Mortimer ruled in place of the young Prince who was crowned Edward III in February 1327. On that day Bruce attacked Norham Castle and by July, after the revolt in Ulster, a truce was declared. Bruce proceeded to claim Northumberland, defeating Mortimer who, unable to raise another army, had to agree the peace treaty which was signed at Holyrood and two months later at Northampton - this was the 'Peace of Northampton' of 4th May 1328 which gave Scotland its independence and sovereignty under King Robert the Bruce. The new peace was confirmed through the marriage of Bruce's son, Prince David, to Edward's sister, Joan, and Bruce was taken back into the Church of Rome after Edward's intercession to the Pope.

Bruce, now fifty -five, was suffering from leprosy from which he died in June 1329 at Cardross Castle on the River Clyde. Only six days after his death a Papal Bull was issued; it gave final recognition of the independence of the Kingdom of Scotland. Bruce's last wish was to have his heart taken to the Holy Land. Lord James Douglas took it but he was killed in a crusade against the Moors in Spain. The heart was brought back to Scotland to be interred at Melrose Abbey, his body being interred in Dunfermline Abbey. He is forever remembered in Scotland's history as the person who hath restored the people's safety in defence of their liberties.'

The Scots quickly exercised their right to crown and to anoint the five-year-old son of Bruce on 24th November 1331 as David II confirming Scotland as an independent nation.

3. Sir William Wallace

The statue of Sir William Wallace, by Alexander Carrick, stands in a canopied niche on the north side of the entrance arch of the Castle. On the other side of the arch is the statue of King Robert the Bruce. They were unveiled by George V in 1929 in celebration of the 600th anniversary of the granting of Edinburgh's Royal Charter by King Robert the Bruce.

Sir William Wallace, the Guardian of Scotland in 1298, was the charismatic champion of Scotland's independence when Scotland was completely subdued by Edward I, 'the Hammer of the Scots'. Edward was successful in his subjugation of Scotland partly because many nobles of Scotland were imprisoned and others knew that if defeated they would lose their estates; they vacillated, delayed action and changed sides often. John Balliol (r.1292-96) had been made king of Scotland by Edward and, instead of raising taxes and an army to help Edward in his fight against France, he formed the 'Auld Alliance' with the French against the English.

In 1296 Edward attacked Berwick killing men, women and children until the Tweed flowed red with blood. Many Scottish nobles joined Edward who now continued to slaughter all before him – Dunbar Edinburgh, Perth and as far north as Elgin. Balliol's submission was humiliating and he surrendered Scotland to the English king. The Earl of Surrey, having won the Battle of Dunbar (1296), was Guardian of Scotland. Hugh de Cressingham was Treasurer who taxed the people mercilessly and another Englishman, William Ormsby, administered the law. The principal Scottish castles were garrisoned by the English troops, who took food from the people and rarely paid for it.

This was the state of Scotland in which William Wallace found himself as a young man. It was brought home to him when he and his friends were continuously scorned by Englishmen merely for their dress and bejewelled daggers. After many taunts, one of them made the fatal mistake of touching Wallace's sword - the ultimate insult - for which he paid with his life. The story, as told by the poet Blind Harry, some two hundred years after Wallace's death, continues with Wallace's escape from Hazelrig, the governor of the garrison of Lanark, who sought revenge by burning Wallace's house and killing his wife. From that day Wallace was a sworn enemy of the English; he killed Hazelrig and decided to devote his life for the freedom of Scotland.

Wallace was not alone in leading the revolt, others were: Robert Wishart, Bishop of Glasgow, James Stewart who, when Alexander III died, became one of six Regents of Scotland, MacDuff, son of the Earl of Fife and the Earl of Carrick whose son, Robert the Bruce, was to be crowned King of Scotland in 1306. The real rising took place in the north led by Andrew Murray who with Wallace became the true commanders in the fight for independence.

Not a great deal of accurate information is known about Wallace and many of the Blind Harry's stories are exaggerations; others are simply untrue, but his versions of oral testimony bear witness to the great esteem in which Wallace was held.

William Wallace was born about 1274, the second of three sons of Sir Malcolm Wallace of Ellerslie near Paisley. He was a natural leader of men, tall, handsome, enormously strong and exceedingly brave. He collected about him those, like himself, who had been outlawed and others whose wish it was to see Scotland free again. At first his victories were more in the nature of commando raids than battles. His reputation grew and several Scottish nobles accepted his leadership even though he was not of noble birth. Prominent among them was Sir William Douglas ('William the Hardy') whose son 'Black Douglas' was to become the faithful captain of King Robert the Bruce, Sir John Graham who became Wallace's most trusted friend and Andrew Murray who led the rising in the north. Some of the others deserted when the Earl of Surrey arrived with a sizeable, well-disciplined army.

Unlike Balliol, Wallace was a confident man and a master strategist who knew the country well. He had held Dundee under siege and the English Guardian, the Earl of Surrey and the Treasurer, the greedy Cressingham, decided that enough was enough; Wallace had to be stopped. The battle-ground was near Stirling on the north side of the river Forth. Two friars were sent to tempt Wallace with a pardon if he submitted. Wallace answered that a pardon from the English king was valueless and that he had come not for peace but to fight for Scotland's freedom.

The English attacked, but they had to advance over a narrow wooden bridge and were easy targets for the Scots. Wallace cleverly allowed Cressingham with his vanguard to cross and when the bridge was crowded Wallace attacked with his whole force. A terrible slaughter took place and most of those who crossed, about half of the English army, were killed, others drowned and the rest fled for their lives. Cressingham was killed and, such was the barbarity of the day, he was flayed so that bits of his skin could be displayed as a reminder of the Scots' revenge for his greed in stripping Scotland of its riches.

Scotland was free at last and Wallace, in a letter to Lübeck and Hamburg of October 1297, invited the Germans to trade. However, his troubles began when he was chosen as Guardian of Scotland. Some nobles considered this to be too great an honour for one who was not of noble birth. Some deserted him and his army diminished in size. Edward I had been preoccupied in fighting the French in Flanders and Wallace, reverting to hit-and-run tactics, now attacked Cumberland and Northumberland. His men burned and sacked towns and villages unmercifully but Wallace did try to prevent the killing of those who were unarmed and offered protection to priests in Hexham, but his men were almost out of control. Wallace could not afford to pay them and they took payment in booty. As in all wars, the ordinary people suffered terribly.

Edward I, on his return to England, was furiously angry. He took command of a massive army and marched into Scotland. Wallace was his target, but after some weeks he could not find him and was on the point of returning home when two Scots nobles sent word to Edward that Wallace was at Falkirk. Edward immediately went there to find Wallace's much smaller army well arranged in 'schiltrons' - circles of men armed with long pikes between which were archers. Behind were the horsemen but they fled almost as soon as the fighting began. The English lancers charged on mail clad horseback. The Scottish archers stood their ground but were cut down by the English horse soldiers. However, they could do nothing against the Scottish spearmen in the schiltrons; they stubbornly held fast and Edward now used his Welsh and French six-foot bows from a safe distance. Wallace saved part of his army by retreating into nearby woods.

Wallace was now without an army and he gave up his Guardianship of Scotland, but he continued to fight using commando tactics of old.

A large reward was offered for his capture, dead or alive, but he continued to harass his enemy for another seven years. His end came with betrayal, supposedly by Sir John Mentieth. He was handed over to the English, taken to London and put on trial as a traitor. Wallace rightly maintained that the charge was false - he had never taken the oath of allegiance, and had never agreed to be a subject of the English king. All this was to no avail, he was treated simply as a rebel and accused of killing and burning towns and castles. He agreed wholeheartedly that he had done this against the English oppressors and only regretted that he not killed many more of them. He held that it was his duty in defence of his native land. In 1304 he was found guilty and given the traitor's death - hanged, disemboweled, beheaded and quartered. His head was stuck on a pike and displayed at London Bridge. His quarters were displayed at the Castles of Newcastle, Berwick, Stirling and Perth as a lesson to others. This served only to harden the determination of the Scots to be free of English rule. Wallace became a cult hero and is still honoured in Scotland. The immensely popular film *Braveheart* has revived his glory.

4. Frederick, Duke of York Statue

The bronze statue, on the Castle Esplanade, of **Frederick, Duke of York**, by Thomas Campbell in 1839, commemorates a largely unsuccessful general of the French Revolutionary and Napoleonic Wars (1793-1815). He was George III's second son born in 1763. His mother, the Queen, was Charlotte of Mecklenburg-Strelitz after whom Charlotte Square is named. She had nine sons and six daughters.

Frederick, although educated in England was trained for a military career in Germany as was the custom with Hanoverian Royalty. Aged twenty-eight he married Frederica, Princess Royal of Prussia.

This was a period of revolution and Europe was in turmoil. The Bastille had been stormed in July 1789, the Belgians had revolted, Louis XV1 fled from Paris in July 1791 and France declared war on Britain and Holland on 1st February 1793 offering aid to all freedom-seeking peoples by eliminating all anti-revolutionary forces.

Following the execution of Louis XV1 in January 1793 the Duke of York, in command of an army against the revolutionary forces, was initially successful in Flanders when he captured Valenciennes. He was hailed as 'King of France' but his glory was short-lived, he was badly defeated at Dunkirk and at Flanders in Belgium. By 1794 he had been driven back to Hanover but he could not be faulted for lack of courage and energy; his lack of tactical experience was against him. He failed to follow up his successful siege of Valenciennes near the Belgian border and his campaign collapsed.

The acrimony in Parliament threatened Prime Minister Pitt and he withdrew the command from the Duke who was publicly lampooned as:

The Noble Duke of York
He had ten thousand men,
He marched them up to the top of the hill,
And he marched them down again

However, a Commander-in-Chief of the British army in 1798 he tackled discipline by examining its root cause - the system of recruiting was disorganised and considered unfair by the regular soldiers who, being enlisted for life, found themselves much less well off in comparison to the more highly paid, short-term militia men. His first step was to improve the status and pay of the regulars; he then started the first Staff College to formalise the training of officers. The Duke of York therefore deserves the credit for giving Wellington disciplined, efficient and well-trained officers with which he defeated the French. Wellington, however, was less than pleased, the Duke had appointed staff officers without consulting him. The Duke's letter of apology weakly explained that he could not countermand their orders as they had 'indulged in expensive equipment'. In 1799 he was again given command of the British Army but his link up with the Russian army was another disaster; Wellington was to say of it: "at least I learned what not to do."

In 1809 the Duke of York's personal 'affairs of the heart' caught up with him. He had discarded several mistresses and one of them, Mrs Mary Ann Clarke, encouraged by some Radicals, was coerced to give evidence against the Duke in relation to the sale of army commissions. On the day after he had signed the report on the Convention of Cintra (20th January 1809), Colonel Wardle M.P., in the House of Commons, moved for an enquiry into the conduct of the Duke of York as Commander-in-Chief: "did the Duke of York knowingly allow Mrs Clarke to indulge in the criminal sales of commissions to augment her income?"

Lord Melville had already been impeached for 'gross malversation and breach of duty' as treasurer of the Navy (he was cleared of guilt), George III's mental state had worsened and the horrifying prospect of the irresponsible Prince of Wales becoming Regent led to general disgust. There was agitation in the press, the trade unions and in parliament - the monarchy was at its lowest ebb. However, the Duke of York was exonerated from any involvement in trafficking army commissions and Mrs Clarke was imprisoned for libel having gone too far in her accusations by implicating the Duke of Wellington.

Such was the doubt and disgust of the people, effigies of the Duke were burned in Suffolk and in Yorkshire; he resigned his office but he was reinstated in 1811. He died in 1827 with no family, his memory smeared with scandals.

5. Earl Haig's Statue - Castle Esplanade

Earl Haig, the Commander-in-Chief of the British army during World War I was pleased to attend the unveiling of his equestrian bronze statue by George E. Wade in 1923. The plaque on its base of rock reads:

EARL HAIG
This statue was presented
to the City of Edinburgh
by Sir Dhunjibhoy Bombani
of Bombay
in admiration of the services
rendered to the British Empire
by the Field Marshal

He was born at No.24 Charlotte Square, Edinburgh on 29th June 1861. As a boy Douglas Haig must have sensed his ambitious mother's disappointment in his intellectual backwardness and, in his anxiety to please her, he strove to prove himself in her eyes. This was a family of very successful entrepreneurs which had made its fortune from its distilleries of 'Haig's Whisky' and the young Douglas Haig was conscious that he was the dunce of the family. At school his academic record was poor and he only just managed to pass, with the aid of a crammer, the entrance exam for Sandhurst. He sought social approval and showed 'traits associated with pathological achievement-motivation.' [34]

Having been passed over for promotion, his elder sister, Henrietta, who knew the Duke of Cambridge, ensured his entry into the Staff

College. His appointment as ADC to the King, in spite of his poor record during the Boer War, seemed not to affect his promotion and his marriage to one of Queen Alexandra's maids of honour along with his tendency to denigrate his subordinates as well as his Chief of Staff led inexorably to his ascent.

As Commander-in-Chief of the greatest ever British Army, Haig seemed well fitted for high rank. His credentials were considered impeccable: public school - Clifton and Oxford; at Military School he was head boy; commissioned at age twenty-four in the 7th Hussars; active service as a Squadron Leader and a Staff Officer; polo player; Staff College graduate; fought in the Omdurman campaign in 1898 with the Egyptian army; service in the South African War at Ladysmith; Chief Staff Officer in the Cavalry division under Lord Roberts in the Transvaal victory; aide-de-camp to King Edward VII in 1902; high level service in India; Commander of the first and only Army Corps at Aldershot.

At the outbreak of the Great War in 1914, Haig was the undisputed choice to take command of the 1st Army. He bore the pressures of his generalship with a strange detachment which could have been mistaken for arrogance. He had been offered no sinecure; the British Expeditionary Force had been hastily assembled and was quite unprepared for what was to come. First to Flanders in Belgium and then to France to suffer heavy losses at Ypres, the retreat from Mons and beaten back at Loos with 50,000 casualties.

Haig blamed Sir John French claiming that his officers commanding corps had lost confidence in him whilst letting it be known to the King that French ought to be removed and adding, 'I personally am ready to do my duty in any capacity.' But unimaginably worse was to come after Sir John French was removed from command and Haig became Commander-in-Chief.

Compulsory conscription was introduced in May 1916 and within a month the British tried an offensive at the Somme - 60,000 men were killed on the first day. British casualties totalled 418,654, French 194,451 and German 650,000 in that offensive in which 'advance' was measured in yards per 1000 men.

Lloyd George and Churchill imagined that they could alleviate the stalemate of the Western Front by a strategic peripheral action to the east through the Dardanelles in Turkey. The military mismanagement of this disastrous expedition ruined Churchill's reputation for years.

Field Marshal Haig never publicly commented upon or in any way criticised his political masters although in his diary he described Lloyd George as 'a real bad 'un'', Milner as 'a tired dyspeptic old man', Lord

Curzon as 'a gas-bag', Wilson and Rawlinson as 'humbugs', Marshal Foch as 'most selfish and obstinate' and Pershing as 'very obstinate and stupid'.

In 1917 even with the horrors of Passchendale under the superior strength of the German attack, the unreliability of his ally and the British Government at home seeking to replace him, never once did he change his firm resolve - AJP Taylor makes reference to 'a total lack of imagination' and Churchill in his *Great Contemporaries* describes him as 'inflexible, rigorously pedantic.....cool and undaunted.' 17

In 1917 the Canadians beat off a German offensive at Vimy Ridge. This was one of three badly needed successes. In desperation the German offensive at Amiens was halted - that was in March 1918. General Foch was given command five months later and through sheer stubbornness, at last came the breakthrough at a terrible cost of lives - from Amiens to Mons and from the Somme to Selle; the German resistance was finally overcome - a victory credited to Haig. The cost in lives was three-quarters of a million killed and 2.5 million injured mostly with permanent disability.

After this so-called 'war to end all wars' Haig returned home to almost total obscurity. He was fifty-eight, experienced and energetic but he was given no offer of work, no advice or consultation was sought, no committee membership; he was left to his fireside. He remained silent and aloof from the debates and writings of criticism or praise of his generalship. He devoted the rest of his life to the welfare of ex-servicemen by organising work for the blind and disabled and by the building of factories and homes.

The Earl Haig Fund is a well-known and highly respected charity that gives help to ex-servicemen, their widows and ex-servicewomen in need or distress through the distribution of poppies which are made by disabled service men and women. An American lady, Mrs. Moina Michael, inspired by a poem written by a Canadian Medical Officer, Colonel John McRae, first thought of the sale of Remembrance Poppies to keep faith with those who had sacrificed their lives.

In Flanders' fields the poppies blow
Between the crosses, row on row,
That mark our place; and in the sky
The larks, still bravely singing, fly.
Scarce heard amid the guns below.
We are the dead. Short days ago,
We lived, felt dawn, saw the sunset glow,
Loved and were loved, and now we lie
In Flanders' fields.
Take up our quarrel with the foe,
To you from failing hands we throw
The torch: be yours to hold it high.
If ye break faith with us who die
We shall not sleep, though poppies grow
In Flanders' fields.

On his sudden death on 29th January 1928 he was mourned throughout the British Empire. He is the only individual honoured in the National War Memorial in Edinburgh Castle that commemorates the 200,000 Scots who died in the Great War and those who died in World War II.

He was buried at Dryburgh Abbey where his simple gravestone, similar to those of his compatriots in endless cemeteries scattered across northern France, is inscribed:

DOUGLAS HAIG
Born in Edinburgh June 19th
1861: Departed out of this
World Sunday Jan. 29th 1928

He trusted in God
and tried to do the right

6. Ramsay Garden, Lane, Lodge - Allan Ramsay

Just below the Castle Esplanade, off Castlehill, is Ramsay Lane leading to picturesque Ramsay Garden, Nos. 13-16 of which were designed by

Henbest Capper in 1892 for Professor Patrick Geddes. Ramsay Lodge, built about 1740 with its stepped buttresses, was the home of Allan Ramsay, the Scottish poet, who designed the octagon-shaped house himself and, much to his annoyance, it was nick-named the 'goose-pie'; an extension added to the house in 1856, by Robert W. Billings, caused a sensation when it collapsed and fell into the valley below.

The **Allan Ramsay Monument**, of Carrara marble by John Steell (1858) is in Princes Street Gardens above the floral clock. Ramsay Garden, however, is named after Ramsay of Dalhousie - the *Laird o' Cockpen* immortalised by Lady Nairne.

Allan Ramsay the elder (his eldest son was a distinguished painter) was born at Leadhills in Lanarkshire in 1686. His father was a mine manager for Lord Hopetoun and his mother, Alice Bower, was an English lady from Derbyshire. Allan was apprenticed in Edinburgh to a wigmaker when he was eighteen and after his five-year apprenticeship he opened his own shop in the Grassmarket, but his main interest was in literature and in writing poetry and satire.

He founded the Easy Club in Edinburgh in 1712 and within a few years he had become well-known in literary circles.

He wrote two cantos to the Scots poem *Christ's Kirk on the Green and Tartans or the Plaid*. He was known to have been secretly sympathetic to the cause of the Jacobites and hoped for the success of the 'Rising' of 1715. From his shop, opposite Niddry Street, in the High Street he wrote and published *The Gentle Shepherd* and other poems. About this time, 1718, he started his bookselling business from which he lent books - he has the distinction of starting the first lending library in Scotland (1725) - and his shop became a meeting-place for the 'literati' who enjoyed Ramsay's wit and his stories.

From his shop in the Luckenbooths he wrote and printed his poems each day and many a youngster clutching a penny was sent for 'Allan Ramsay's last piece'. He remained in business there until 1752 and became known affectionately as 'honest Allan'.

His collected edition of *Poems* made a profit for him of 400 guineas in 1721 (about £70,000 today) and in the years to 1737 his works included *Fables and Tales, Fair Assembly, Health, a Poem*, four volumes of songs - *The Tea-table Miscellany* which ran to twelve editions. This was followed shortly afterwards by *The Evergreen*, a collection of old Scottish poems written in 1600, and was his best work. *The Gentle Shepherd, a Pastoral Comedy* was published in 1725 and dedicated to the astonishingly beautiful Susanna, Countess of Eglinton. In this year he opened his circulating library but the magistrates, fearing that the spread of fictional literature would somehow corrupt the young, tried unsuccessfully to close it down.

He became comparatively rich and again, aggravating the authorities, he ignored convention and built a theatre at the foot of Carrubbers Close in 1736. He was in love with theatre and was keen to encourage drama to a wide audience, but soon after the opening of his theatre an Act was passed by the Town Council which required theatres to be licensed. He was refused a licence and had to close his theatre - to the satisfaction of the clergy and heavy financial loss to Ramsay.

Allan Ramsay was a man of many interests who revived the awareness in Scottish national culture. He was a bright and interesting conversationalist; any who met him parted with a feeling of well-being. He played golf on Bruntsfield Links and was well-known during the convivial evenings in taverns of the Royal Mile. He loved children and specially enjoyed making toys for the young friends of his daughters; he amused them for hours with music and art and each year he gave them a ball, again to the disgruntled disapproval of the clergy. Grant in his *Old and New Edinburgh* relates the words of one of the young ladies, Mrs Murray of Henderland who, in 1840 approaching the age of one hundred years, recalled the days of her childhood,

> 'He (Allan Ramsay) was charming, he entered so heartily into the plays of the children. He, in particular, gained their hearts by making houses for their dolls. How pleasant it was to learn that our great pastoral poet was a man who, in his private capacity, loved to sweeten the daily life of his fellow creatures, and particularly the young.' [1]

Allan Ramsay died in 1758 and was buried in Greyfriars Churchyard. His son inherited Ramsay Lodge; a celebrated artist, he became portrait-painter to George III.

7. The Outlook Tower
The Geddes Heritage Trail -
Professor Patrick Geddes

The Patrick Geddes Trail in the Royal Mile starts at Castlehill where his Outlook Tower was built on the base of the mansion of Ramsay of Dalhousie. The trail is indicated through the Royal Mile with a series of plaques on which his face appears in bas-relief. Geddes gifted the Witches' Fountain on the Castle Esplanade in 1912 to commemorate the hundreds of poor old women who were burned at the stake between 1492 and 1722.

Who then, was Patrick Geddes? He was a true polymath of unbounded enthusiasm for his multi-faceted ideas. He is credited as the father of town-planning and did everything he could to restore and to revitalise the Royal Mile. In his efforts to convince anyone who would listen, he tried to persuade ordinary people, academics and others of influence to become interested in the world's geology and botany - he was before his time in the field of conservation.

He was born in 1854 in Ballater, forty miles inland from Aberdeen, and he was schooled in Perth where his first job was in a bank. Soon after entering the bank he left for London where he studied under the famous biologist T. H. Huxley at University College, London. His academic career was somewhat mercurial: he studied in Brittany and at the Sorbonne in Paris and he lasted a week in the Department of Botany at Edinburgh. But Huxley had undoubtedly broadened his mind and taught him to question established views - after all, Huxley himself had dismissed the notion of evolution until Darwin published his *Origin of Species* in 1859.

After seven years in London he grew tired of the bland assumption that London had some exclusive claim to all intellectual and original thought. He spent a short time in Mexico and returned to Scotland in 1880 determined to reawaken its 'Golden Age' which was considered to have ended with the death of Sir Walter Scott in 1832.

He became an active member of the Edinburgh Social Union which was mainly concerned with the state of the Royal Mile, its decaying properties and its deprived inhabitants. He set an example by moving from fashionable Princes Street to take up residence at James Court in the Lawnmarket while he built Ramsay Garden around Allan Ramsay's 'Goose-pie House' which he had purchased for his wife Norah soon after his marriage in 1886.

He saved the 17th century Russell House, at the foot of the Canongate, from demolition. He refurbished slum houses to create dwellings for over two-hundred teachers and students in the Royal Mile and he converted Maria Theresa Short's Camera Obscura Observatory into the **Outlook Tower**. The original building was the 17th century residence of the Ramsays of Dalhousie - the 'Laird o' Cockpen' (immortalised by Lady Nairne). Geddes extended its scope by adding a planetarium below the

The Camera Obscura and Tolbooth Church

camera, the Scotland Room, the Edinburgh Room and surveys of the vegetation and geology of Britain, Europe and the World Room with its geological globe and its vegetation globe. He was at pains to explain man's relationship with the environment - his was an early explanation of conservation.

In 1883, after several lectureships and lost promotion at Edinburgh, he was appointed Professor of Botany at University College, Dundee, one of the departments of the University of St Andrews, a post he held until 1920. He used the theory of evolution as his basis for ethics, history and sociology and he wrote, with Sir J.A.Thomson, *The Evolution of Sex* in 1889. Thomson, who was Professor of Natural History at the University of Aberdeen, said of him:

> "Professor Geddes is the most educative person I have ever heard or seen. His cerebral variability must be extraordinary. *Vivendo Discimus*, he is always saying; silently I mean, for he does not preach. Do something, don't write it, is his example. Be a citizen first, a scholar if time permits....Perhaps the biggest thing that Professor Geddes has done is what few people at present understand: he has thought out a notation. Our whole system is an intricate network of inter-relations. If we are to understand anything - a flower, a bird, a social phenomenon, a scientific theory, a religion - we must know its linkages. Most people see one aspect. A few see three aspects. But Geddes sees all that the wit of man can think of." [35]

His motto *Vivendo Discimus* (we learn by living together) was engraved in stone above the doorway of his summer school (a students' residence) in Riddles Court in the Lawnmarket.

In India, Geddes made about fifty town reports. He castigated those who tried to impose Western patterns and he argued with the sanitary authorities in Madras and with the callous, contemptuous city bureaucrats of Delhi. In 1916 he tried to persuade the authorities of Dacca not to spend £250,000 on absurd sewage schemes but to spend only one third of it to regenerate the town. He believed in the use of human manure and in his report on Lucknow he wrote: 'now, since a large proportion of the community do not and will not use latrines, but insist on communing with nature after the manner of the ancients, how much healthier to have their daily contributions absorbed by the cultivated land.'

He had strong opinions on town planning and, whilst not always entirely practical, he gave new impetus to this largely ignored subject.

He published his *City Development, Cities as Applied Sociology* and *Cities in Evolution* thereby influencing future planning. However, theories as expounded in his *An Analysis of Economics* were considered to be naive in that he tended to emphasise resources and to ignore the effect of finance in the development and creation of resources.

Shortly after his 77th birthday he wrote to his wife, Norah:

> 'Now advise me. As you may know, my old friend Lord Pentland sounded me twenty years ago or so as to acceptance of a Knighthood - but I declined on grounds of lifelong policy and views of life. But now Ramsay MacDonald repeats this for Xmas or the New Year honours. Should I accept?'

He did accept and received his knighthood on 25th February 1930 from George V, but he was to live less than two years to enjoy it. He died on 17th April 1932. Amelia Defries in her *The Interpreter Geddes* described the scene - 'His funeral was his final pageant. His uncoffined corpse was cremated in Marseilles, his beard and hair instantly flared alight and for an evanescent moment his outworn body became pure flame.' His death created a void in the Scottish educational scene. A character, an educator and above all, a dedicated enthusiast had gone.

David Hume

The Statue of DAVID HUME
by Alexander Stoddart

The statue of *David Hume* (1711-1776) was commissioned in 1993 by the Saltire Society, 9 Fountain Close, Edinburgh at the suggestion of its membership who were acutely aware of the absence of any commemoration in the Royal Mile to this famous and learned historian and philosopher of the 'Golden Age' (1760-90) - the sceptic of sceptics who was sceptical of scepticism itself.

The 8-foot statue was sculpted by Edinburgh born Alexander Stoddart and was sited on its 6-foot plinth outside the High Court of the Justiciary in the Lawnmarket in time for the opening of the Commonwealth Heads of Government Conference held in Edinburgh in October 1997.

The Saltire Society which exists to encourage Scottish arts and design in housing, civil engineering, and planning promoted a national appeal which gained excellent support mainly from Scots with additional support from American Philosophical Societies, the Scottish Arts Council, Lothian and Edinburgh Enterprise Ltd., and the Bank of Scotland plc.

Alexander Stoddart, born in 1959 and trained at the Glasgow School of Art, won the Saltire Society's competition in 1993 to execute the seated figure of Hume in classical drapery *al' antica* and his sculptural analogies in the empty stone tablet held by Hume - the apogee of his scepticism, even the ten commandments have been argued away; the dog heads at each end of the scroll on which Hume is leaning - the barking dogs of Diogenes' contemporary establishment; the hybrid Helio-Medussa - the sunburst of enlightenment with the rays of the sun intertwining with the snakes of Medussa's head; the satire of Hume's shining toe - representing Hume as the diety of humanists whose toe has been polished by touching and foot-kissing admirers. This meaningful, magnificent sculpture is a debt repaid at last.

8. James Court - David Hume in the Royal Mile

James Court (formerly Brownhill Court, Fairden's Court, Fountainhall Court) is named after James Brownhill the wright who built the court in 1723-7. He demolished the original close to make an open court in much the same way as Robert Milne had done at Milne's Court thirty years before.

Those who could afford this gracious living were prosperous burgesses and included learned men such as philosopher David Hume, Dr Hugh Blair, the Professor of Rhetoric and Belles Lettres of the University of Edinburgh and James Boswell the biographer of Dr Johnson of *Dictionary* fame. Johnson was one of Boswell's guests in 1773 which was not an agreeable arrangement as far as Mrs Boswell was concerned; she considered him an inconsiderate boor.

David Hume was, in his day, the greatest philosopher and historian in Europe. He was one of the leading lights of the 'Golden Age' (1760-1790). He was not a reclusive inhabitant of an 'ivory tower' but a gregarious man. He loved company, revelled in discussion, enjoyed a good argument and was a member of several clubs in Edinburgh.

His association with the Royal Mile was firstly his house at Riddles Court the corbelled door of which is dated 1726. He inherited this house at the age of nine on the death of his father. He came from Ninewells in Berwickshire to live there in June 1751 and it was here that he started the first of six volumes of his masterpiece, *The History of England*. Returning from France in 1766 he moved to Jack's Land (now demolished), opposite St John's Street in the Canongate and then, after a spell in Paris, he took up residence in James Court, having rented out his house in Riddle's Court.

He was born in Edinburgh on 26th April 1711. His family was a branch of the Earl of Home (or Hume) on his father's side. His mother was the daughter of Sir David Falconer, President of the College of Justice. His childhood in Berwickshire was one of strict Calvinism and at an early stage of his life he was, to use his own words, 'seized with a passion for literature', a passion he never lost. At age eleven he was sent to the University of Edinburgh for studies in law but his preference was for philosophy which led him secretly to Cicero and Virgil instead of Voet and Vinnius.

David Hume was not one of those whose family could afford to send him on the 'grand tour' of Europe complete with tutor. In 1734 lack of money forced him to find a job in Bristol but he gave this up as soon as he had sufficient money to take him to Reims where his aim was to improve his knowledge of literature. In Anjou he wrote his famous *Treatise of Human Nature* and after three agreeable years in France he returned to London to publish his work - it was not successful. Undeterred, he had it printed in Edinburgh and followed it with the first part of his *Essays Moral, Political and Literary* - this was an immediate success. Reading it today, it is still modern, still relevant. One can quote endlessly from his *Essays*, for example:

It is evident that every man loves himself better than any other person, he is naturally impelled to extend his acquisitions as much as possible; and nothing can restrain him in this propensity but reflection and experience, by which he learns the pernicious effects of that licence, and the total dissolution of society which must ensue from it.

A thought that today's conservationists would heartily agree.

At the invitation of the Marquess of Annandale he became his tutor but he could stand it for no longer than a year. His next appointment was aide-de-camp to General St Clair in his travels to France, Vienna and Turin. Hume lived frugally during these two years and saved £1000. He rewrote his *Treatise* renaming it *Enquiry of Human Understanding*;

this version was only slightly more successful. In 1749, while living with his brother, he wrote the second part of his *Essays*. Meantime, his Edinburgh bookseller found that his previous publications were being widely discussed and new editions were demanded. Of course the discussion brought both agreement and dissent but Hume resolutely refused to reply to his critics and kept himself clear of literary squabbles - he was much too busy.

In 1751 he moved back to Edinburgh to take up residence at Riddles Court where he started work on his *History of England*. Within a year his *Political Discourses* was published with immediate success. This puzzled him as he always considered that his *Enquiry concerning the Principles of Morals* was a far superior piece of work.

He was appointed librarian to the Faculty of Advocates in 1752. This gave him access to a great library and led him to plan his writing of his *History of England* starting with the House of Stuart. This, the first of six volumes, when published, was reproached, even detested because he had shown sympathy for the fate of Charles I and the Earl of Stratford - how dare he imply criticism of the House of Hanover! The book sank into oblivion. It was the first of its kind; no one before had undertaken such a task. However, he retired from the library in disgust when he was censured for the purchase of 'objectionable' French works without permission. He never forgave Lord Hailes, a curator of the library, who was the instigator of the complaint against him.

His next publication, in London, was his *Natural History of Religion*. It too was criticised especially by Dr Hurd, but Hume dismissed him saying, "he has all the illiberal petulance, arrogance and scurrility, which distinguish the Warburtonian School." (William Warburton (1698-1779) was Bishop of Gloucester who considered himself to be the leader of Christian apologetics and literary scholarship.) Hume's scepticism had attacked their idea of God (their anthropomorphism) and he asserted that 'no testimony for any kind of miracle has ever amounted to a probability, much less a proof.'

In 1756 he ignored public opinion and published the second volume of his *History of England* which dealt with the period from the death of Charles I to the revolution. It was deemed acceptable by the Whigs but Hume, ignoring their opinions, published his *History of the House of Tudor*. The outburst of anger against it equalled that against his first volume, but this was the raving of political self interest. By 1762 he had completed all six volumes - a mammoth task, an unrivalled masterpiece written whilst in residence at Jack's Close in the Canongate. In 1762 he bought his flat in James Court, a residence he was to long for while abroad.

In 1763, after a second invitation from the Earl of Hertford, Hume accepted the post of Secretary to the Embassy in Paris. After two years he became Chargé d'Affaire until the arrival of the Duke of Richmond. He left Paris in 1766 and returned to Edinburgh in a considerably improved financial state. He had intended to have a sabbatical for philosophical thought but in 1767 he was appointed an Under-Secretary of State in London. Two years later and much wealthier, he again returned to Edinburgh to take up residence at James Court. His next Edinburgh address was St Andrew Square which had just been built preceding James Craig's New Town plan.

Hume was now in great demand, his reputation was established; he was one of the leaders of the 'literati'. Edinburgh abounded with clubs and societies whose members discussed, debated and analysed in microscopic detail every aspect of philosophy and science. Edinburgh was the centre of intellectual stimulation in Europe for what came to be called the 'Scottish Enlightenment'. Hume was one of at least fifty geniuses to whom the King's Chemist, Mr Amyatt, referred when he lived in Edinburgh: "Here I stand at what is called the 'Cross of Edinburgh', and can, in a few minutes, take fifty men of genius and learning by the hand." 33. But David Hume was rebuked and ostracised by the Church for his religious scepticism and he was out-voted on two occasions in his elections for a professorship of the university. The famed Dr Johnson, during his visit to Scotland in 1773, refused to meet Hume and others were afraid to be seen in his company fearing the disapproval of the Church.

Hume's contemporaries included such as: Adam Smith (1723-90, the father of economics). Joseph Black (1728-99, the chemist who evolved the theory of latent heat), James Hutton (1726-97, father of geology), William Robertson (1721-93, founder of historiography), James Burnett, Lord Monboddo (1714-99, judge and anthropologist), Henry Home, Lord Kames (1696-1782, judge and philosopher), William Cullen (1710-90, teacher of clinical medicine), the Adam brothers, Robert (1728-92) and James (1730-94), (architects of the king's works) and many others of great distinction.

It was at St Andrew Square that Hume enjoyed the company of many old acquaintances, friends and distinguished visitors. One in the latter category was Benjamin Franklin with whom he discussed and agreed with the American position relating to American Independence. In a letter to his friend, Adam Smith, we gain a glimpse of their jovial but challenging relationship:

> "I want to know what you have been doing, and propose
> to exact a rigorous account of the method in which you

> have employed yourself during your Retreat. I am positive you are wrong in many of your speculations especially where you have the misfortune to differ from me - I expect to find a letter from you containing a bold acceptance of this defiance."

Hume and Smith were members of the Poker Club in Edinburgh. It was founded in 1762 with the original aim of reviving the Scottish Militia which was disbanded after the '45 Rising, but it developed into a forum for the *literati*.

In retirement he spent much of his time revising the *History* and he wrote his *Dialogues Concerning Natural Religion* but he did not live to hear the renewed outrage against him when the General Assembly of the Church of Scotland tried to have him expelled for his misunderstood scepticism and irreligion.

He became ill in 1775 and wrote *My Own Life* on which much of this short account is based. It was intended that it should be prefixed to the next edition of his works. As he wrote of himself,

> "that were I to name the period of my life which I should most choose to pass over again, I might be tempted to point to this latter period. I possess the same ardour as ever in study and the same gaiety in company. I consider, besides, that a man of sixty-five, by dying, cuts off only a few years of infirmities; and though I see many symptoms of my literary reputations breaking out at last with additional lustre, I knew that I could have but a few years to enjoy it."

The great man died on Sunday 25th August 1776 after a long illness during which he was attended at his house in St David Street by his old friend Dr Joseph Black. He was buried in the Old Calton Burying Ground which is entered from Waterloo Place. His monument, designed by Robert Adam in 1777, was the subject of a witticism by Robert Louis Stevenson:

> *Within this circular idea,*
> *called vulgarly a tomb,*
> *The impressions and Ideas rest*
> *That constituted Hume.*

9. Riddle's Court -
Bailie John Macmorran,
Major Thomas Weir,
Sir John Clerk, David Hume,
Sir Patrick Geddes

Riddle's Court (formerly Macmorran's Court, Royston's Court, Shaw's Court) was built about 1590 by the richest man in Edinburgh, **Bailie John Macmorran**, who had prospered from his humble beginning as one of Regent Morton's servants to become the richest merchant of Edinburgh and Burgh Treasurer. Regent Morton, was beheaded in the Grassmarket by the 'Maiden' (Edinburgh's guillotine) in 1581 for his part in the murder of Mary Queen of Scots' talented secretary, Rizzio.

In Macmorran's time Riddle's Court extended down to the Cowgate and the buildings on the south side of Lawnmarket were split apart when Victoria Street and Victoria Terrace were built as part of the 1827 Improvement Act scheme.

Riddle's Court has seen several changes from Macmorran's original L-shaped, three-storey blocks but much of it survives. However, the court was named after George Riddell, a wright (joiner) who rebuilt it in 1726 having purchased it for 10,000 merks (about £555) from Sir James Mackenzie of Royston when the Close was known as Royston's Close. The turret staircase is one of its notable features and several ceilings are of particular interest; the whole courtyard was restored in 1965.

Some of the occupants provide a few quite fantastic stories:

Bailie Macmorran, a very wealthy burgess, lived in the inner courtyard on the south and west of the court. On 15th September 1595 the pupils of the High School had barricaded themselves in the school - they were 'on strike' for extra holidays which had been refused. The boys had armed themselves with swords and pistols. They taunted any who approached with threats of instant death. They vied with each other in their insults and threats.

Macmorran, taking charge of the City Officers, ordered a battering ram to one of the entrances. The boys became more excited and one of them, William Sinclair, son of the Chancellor of Caithness, fired his pistol. His intention was probably to scare off the intruders, but tragedy struck. Macmorran was shot through the head and killed. The boys were stunned; this was not meant. Their protest ended immediately and the outraged Macmorran family demanded retribution but the culprits were the sons of 'gentlemen'. The Macmorran family received death threats if any boy was harmed. Lord Sinclair used his influence with James VI who interceded with the magistrates to allow his son to go free. No action was taken against any of the other culprits; their youth and their gentility saved them at a time when the petty offences of ordinary people were punished with brutal sadism and death.

The late Bailie Macmorran's house was the venue of a banquet given in honour of James VI, his Queen, Anne of Denmark, and her brother, the Duke of Holstein in 1598.

Major Thomas Weir provides by far the most strange and grizzly story of Riddle's Court. He lived in the house south-west of the courtyard in 1650, which was the year he commanded the City Guard at the execution of the Marquis of Montrose (whose effigy is in the Chepman Aisle of St Giles.) Thomas Weir of Kirktown was believed to have been tutored by his mother in the art of sorcery. Outwardly he was a man of religion, a devotee of a strict sect of Covenanters, and his house was a meeting-place for the 'Holy Sisters' who referred to him as 'Angelical Thomas'. He never married and his sister Grizell shared the house. But behind their facade of holiness lurked a pact with the devil. There, they practised their wizardry and evil deeds and, nearing the end of his life, he was driven to the point of insanity by thoughts of his hideous past and he confessed his sins. They were so unbelievably evil that the Lord Provost, Sir Andrew Ramsay, incredulous at first, refused to arrest them.

Weir's black staff became a symbol of his dreaded magic, Previously he had depended on it during his false prayers and at night he could be seen, adorned in his voluminous black cloak, almost floating through the streets. Such was the terror they generated, brother and sister were arrested and imprisoned at the Old Tolbooth.

At their trial on 9th April 1670 they were sentenced to be hanged and burned. To the last he refused to pray for pardon and was heard to say, "I have lived as a beast and must die like a beast."

It was said that at his burning on 12th April 1670 at Gallowlee on the site of Greenside Church his black staff was seen twisting and writhing and took as long as his body to be consumed by the flames.

His sister too was totally mad and would not believe that her brother was dead until she was told that his staff had been reduced to ashes. She flew into a rage and cursing and profaning she confirmed that her mother was a witch and she a sorceress. She was executed and burned at the Grassmarket with ten other old women accused of witchcraft.

The house at Riddle's Court remained unoccupied for over one hundred years, being thought to be haunted and observed to be lit up on several occasions during the night. The house was demolished as part of the 1827 Improvements Act.

Sir John Clerk of Penicuik (1676-1755), the antiquary, Baron of the Exchequer and supporter of the Union of the English and Scottish Parliaments in 1707, lived at Riddle's Court. He was one of the Commissioners to approve the 'Equivalent' of £398,085 as compensation for increased taxation and for losses in the Darien Scheme. He, in spite of his great intellect and learning, was completely besotted by the lovely Miss Susanna Kennedy, but she married the recently widowed Earl of Eglinton, almost thirty years her senior.

David Hume (1711-1771) *qv* (ref. 8. James Court), Europe's greatest philosopher and historian, lived in the house with the corbelled doorway dated 1726 at Riddle's Court and in 1751 he wrote the early part of his six-volume *History of England* in this, his first Edinburgh home. The University of Edinburgh's Hume Tower in George Square commemorates him.

Professor Sir Patrick Geddes (1854-1932) *qv* (ref. 7. The Outlook Tower) opened his students' residence at Riddle's Court in 1887. It was he who had the motto, *Vivendo Discimus* (we live and learn together), inscribed above the arched door. Described as the father of town planning, he bought the Camera Obscura and Allan Ramsay's 'Goosepie' house and extended it to form Ramsay Garden in 1892 as a Town-and-Gown hall of residence and home for his family. He did his utmost to encourage revival of the Old Town; the Geddes Trails in the Royal Mile commemorate this dedicated enthusiast.

Opposite: Ramsay Garden

10. Brodie's Close - Deacon Brodie

Brodie's Close in Lawnmarket (formerly Baker's Close, Cullen's Close, Little's Close) might hardly have deserved a mention but for the nefarious behaviour of William Brodie, the only son of Francis Brodie, a highly skilled and successful wright (joiner). He was a well-respected Deacon of the Incorporation of Wrights, a Master-craftsman, a Cabinet-maker, a Mason of the Lodge of Kilwinning, Canongate and a Town Councillor. Brodie's Close was his home and business premises.

The Closes in those days (the 1770's) extended down from Lawnmarket to the Cowgate. Brodie's living quarters over-looked the Lawn-market and his business, the timber yard, workshops and space for livestock, extended to the Cow-gate. (Victoria Street did not exist then; it was built between 1837 and 1852 after George IV Bridge was completed in 1836).

Francis Brodie had built up his business with contracts from the banks, courts, private houses, jewellers and the Town Council. By eighteenth century standards he was a well-respected, well-off member of the Edinburgh bourgeoisie. His son, William, on the other hand, was a playboy who, although a highly skilled wright, 'cocked-a-snoot' at the Edinburgh establishment. He preferred the company of raucous, heavy drinking gamblers in the taverns and gambling dens of loaded dice and fighting cocks.

The story, some fact, some fiction, therefore is about the infamous son, **William Brodie**, and starts about the time of his father's death. Even on his deathbed Francis Brodie berated his son for his negligence of their fine business. He was anxious that William should use his skill to execute more original work and should set about gaining orders for the fine houses of the New Town. William detested the continual criticism and the stifling family love. He knew that he would inherit the lucrative family business and he charmed his father, his sister Jean, the councillors, bailies, bankers, lawyers - in fact all his customers; but his father saw through him. William, who had never had to strive for

Opposite: John Knox Statue, St Giles Cathedral

anything, gave not a fig for his inheritance. On the night of his father's death Willliam was too busy gambling and drinking to bother. He felt free at last, but he gave a magnificent performance of a grieving son when he left the inn earlier than usual.

William Brodie had two families, each unknown to the other. He was generous to his five illegitimate children and to his mistresses, Ann Grant and Jean Watt. He gambled heavily and his expenses were high. His spinster sister Jean continuously pleaded with him to attend to the business. She worried and fretted about the possible loss of their social position; after all her brother was Deacon of Wrights and a member of the Canongate Kilwinning Masonic Lodge. He socialised occasionally with the judiciary and with such celebrities as Robert Burns and Sir Henry Raeburn, the famous portrait painter.

He had to have money and quickly. It was so simple - by merely taking wax impressions of the keys of the premises to which he had legitimate access through his profession - he made the keys and robbed the premises in the darkness of night to re-emerge next morning as a pleasant, plausible man-about-town. It seemed to thrill him; he loved the excitement. The adrenalin secretion quickened his pulse and the thrill of robbery became addictive to him. No sooner had he robbed one jeweller than he planned the next - a goldsmith, then the Royal Exchange.

During one of his gambling sessions Brodie was introduced to Englishman George Smith who was out of work and unable to return to England for 'legal' reasons. Smith was a skilled locksmith and he readily teamed up with Brodie. Together they continued their nefarious activities, Smith being useful not only for making keys and picking locks but as a lookout and a fence for the stolen jewellery - they had the impudence to steal the university's mace of solid silver.

Again, during a card game in John Clark's tavern, Brodie was persuaded, reluctantly at first, to take another partner. He was a shifty

eyed, self-effacing, obsequious character called Ainslie whose local knowledge could be helpful and the arrangement would increase the weight of stolen goods to be transported after each robbery - but greed tempted Brodie further when they were joined by yet another partner in crime, the foppish John Brown who used the alias Humphrey Moore to evade the English Courts.

The Town Council had become alarmed at the audacity and frequency of the thefts. A large and tempting reward for information leading to the arrest of the felons was advertised. There was now some suspicion that the perpetrators were not of the usual criminal fraternity; this was the work of someone of some standing in the community. But Brodie became more daring, almost foolhardy, such was his confidence in himself. He was however more than a little concerned when the rewards included a further incentive - that of a pardon for all previous criminal offences. Brown was a wanted man and could be tempted. Brodie became suspicious. He decided to have one last robbery - a really big one which would enable him to get rid of his business and quit Edinburgh forever. He planned it meticulously; the date, 5th March 1788; the place, the Excise Office in Chessels Court; the pickings were rich. The four men equipped themselves with rope to tie the watchmen, masks, a whistle, a spur detached from its buckle to mislead the magistrates into believing that horsemen were involved, picklocks, a chisel, a duplicate key, a lantern and pistols.

Brodie having fortified himself with an ample quantity of wine was an hour late at the rendezvous. Smith, Ainslie and Brown were furiously angry but they hurried to Chessel's Court. Brodie opened the outer door with ease; it took some time to force the door to the cashier's room and whilst the others worked on it Brodie found a chair in a quiet corner and fell sound asleep. They gained entry and started work on the desks; they found only £16; they were incensed with anger at Brodie. At that moment they were disturbed by Mr Bonar, the Deputy-Solicitor of Excise who had returned to collect some papers and imagined the noise he heard was caused by junior clerks who often worked late.

Ainslie, the lookout, was almost paralysed with fear. He blew his whistle as a warning to the others. Brodie woke with a start and fled for dear life. Smith and Brown heard Mr Bonar muttering as he left and they joined Ainslie in the yard. They left together cursing Brodie for his cowardice.

Their break-in was a total fiasco. The post-mortem brought recriminations and accusations; Brodie and Brown almost came to blows. Brown threatened to collect his reward and proceeded to do just that. The Procurator Fiscal listened avidly. Brodie was mortified when he heard that Smith and Ainslie had been arrested. He fled to Amsterdam and a reward of £200 (about £12,000 today) was posted for his capture.

He might have escaped justice had he not entrusted a letter to a traveller on his way home to Edinburgh. The traveller, on arriving home, recognised the description of the wanted man and opened the letter. This was the end for Brodie. He was arrested and extradited. The merciless Lord Braxfield, Scotland's hanging Judge with the vitriolic, razor sharp tongue was on the Bench. The Dean of Faculty defended him very ably but when Brodie's letter to Jean Watt was produced in Court, his guilt was finally established. He was sentenced to hang on 1st October 1788.

A final mystery ensued. Two of his fellow Deacons visited him in the Tolbooth prison and explained how he could cheat the scaffold (ironically, it was designed by Brodie himself). His coat would be provided with a harness through which the hangman (who had been suitably bribed) would pass his rope. A silver tube inserted in his throat, hopefully, would prevent constriction. Arrangements were made to transport his body immediately after the hanging so that he could be quickly resuscitated.

Did the coffin which was ceremoniously carried to the cemetery on that October day of 1788 contain his body or a load of rocks? There was a rumour circulating in Edinburgh that William Brodie had been seen in Paris!

11. Lady Stair's Close and House (formerly Lady Gray's Close and House)

The Close was known as Lady Gray's Close before it became **Lady Stair's Close**. The 17th century house, originally called Lady Gray's House, was saved from destruction by Professor Patrick Geddes who convinced the 5th Earl of Rosebery to purchase the house from the City. The house was originally built for a relative of Lord Rosebery, Sir William Gray of Pittendrum, in 1622. His initials with those of his wife, Geida Smith, 'WG:GS' are sculpted over the doorway with the words: *'Fear the Lord and depart from evil'*, a crest and the year 1622. Its north, west and south wings had been demolished and Lord Rosebery generously agreed to its restoration which was carried out by George S. Aitken in 1897. Lord Rosebery then gifted it, in its newly restored condition, to the City of Edinburgh. It is now a museum of interesting memorabilia of three of Scotland's great literary figures: Robert Burns (1756-96), Sir Walter Scott (1771-1832) and Robert Louis Stevenson (1850-94).

The name Lady Stair's Close and House take their names from Elizabeth, the 1st Countess of Stair who owned it from 1719. She died in 1731 and her son, the 2nd Earl of Stair, married Eleanor the widow of the 1st Viscount Primrose.

It is often mistakenly assumed that the house and Close were named after Eleanor rather than her mother-in-law probably because of the exciting stories told about her. She was a most strikingly beautiful woman. Many a male head turned around when she appeared in her sedan chair carried by her black servants. Her first marriage, to James, Viscount Primrose, was a disaster. He was a cruel, mean man who treated her very badly. She left him when he attacked her with murderous intention and she escaped him by jumping, half dressed, from a window of their house in the High Street.

He fled abroad and then unfolded an incredible occurrence: Lady Primrose, during a visit to a fortune-teller and while gazing into a mirror, saw a vision of her husband as a bridegroom and, just at the point of the actual marriage vows, she saw her brother, sword drawn, attacking her husband. The vision vanished as suddenly as it appeared. She recorded the details and her brother, on his return from Rotterdam, confirmed every detail adding that Lord Primrose had not been killed. However, he died a few years later in 1706 and her Ladyship swore that she would never marry again.

It was not long after her widowhood that Lord Stair, the hero of the Battle of Oudenarde on 11th July 1708 (a decisive battle of the Spanish Succession War), married her in secret. He had long admired her and had proposed marriage several times but she always rejected him. Undeterred, he bribed one of her servants to allow him to enter her house where he remained hidden overnight. Next morning he appeared partly dressed at her window overlooking the busy High Street. She had been well and truly compromised and, to avoid a scandal, she agreed to marry him. After all, he was the 2nd Earl of Stair, a man of high reputation having been aide-de-camp to the Duke of Marlborough in 1703 and was a colonel of the Scots Greys. He was truly devoted to her.

They were blissfully happy until one evening when he had been drinking heavily with friends he returned home, an argument ensued and he struck her while drunk. Next day he was so appalled by what he had done, he swore never to touch wine again unless it was administered to him by her hand; a promise he kept until his death in 1747.

As an elderly lady she answered an insult of Lord Dundonald, who had spread a rumour that she had referred to the Douglas twins as illegitimate. This was an attempt to nullify their claim to the Dukedom. Dundonald had challenged anyone to deny it, but he had reckoned without the determination of Lady Stair. In high dudgeon she ordered her servant to take her in her familiar sedan chair to Holyrood where the Duke and Duchess were in residence. She confronted them saying, "the Earl Dundonald is a damned villain." She repeated it twice more, each utterance louder than the last and with her stick she thumped the floor to emphasise her annoyance. She returned to her house in the Lawnmarket rarely to be seen again. The 'Douglas Cause' dragged on through the courts for twenty years and the surviving Douglas twin succeeded to his title but long after Lady Stair's death which occurred in 1759.

12. George IV Bridge

As a compliment to the reigning monarch, George IV, the Town Council of Edinburgh decided to name the new bridge over the Cowgate after him in 1827. The bridge provided a link via Forrest Road to the prestigious George Square.

George IV Bridge was built between 1827 and 1836 and was designed by Thomas Hamilton who had already designed the Royal High School in Regent Road, the King's Bridge over King's Stables Road and the Western Approach Scheme via Johnson Terrace. It was George IV's visit to Edinburgh in 1822, the first since that of Charles II in 1651, which prompted the Town Council to name this bridge after him.

The visit was a momentous event and was orchestrated in the most luxurious fashion by Sir Walter Scott. But then nothing less than extravagance would have been appropriate for this ostentatious monarch whose lifestyle had already accrued debts totalling £650,000 (almost £100 million today) in gambling, drinking, womanising and in patronising the arts. The tragedy of his life was that of a waste of great natural intelligence and talent especially in 'Regency' architecture and design.

George IV was born on 12th August 1762, the eldest of nine sons in a family of fifteen children. His upbringing, until he reached the age of nineteen years, was very strict. He rebelled and grew to detest his father who in turn could hardly stand the sight of his son. He annoyed and purposely aggravated his father through his gambling, his love affairs and his drunkenness. To compound his offensive behaviour he, secretly and without his father's permission, married a Roman Catholic lady, Mrs Fitzherbert, in 1785. The marriage was invalid under the Royal Marriages Act but he denied it in any case. Again to spite his father, Prince George chose the political association of the Whigs and of those statesmen whom his father detested - Fox, Burke and Sheridan. Even the Prime Minister, William Pitt, sided with the Prince against George III whose 'madness' reached maniacal proportions in November 1788; at dinner he attacked his son and tried to smash his head against a wall.

Pitt's Cabinet proposed a Regency Bill. The Prince was almost desperate to reign - in the taverns of London he boasted to his friends of what he would do when he became Regent, but his father foiled his ambitions when he made a remarkable recovery in February 1789.

The Prince had to wait another twelve years before becoming Regent. During this time his debts mounted to a colossal sum and Parliament agreed to pay them off provided that he settle down and marry. He agreed to marry Princess Caroline, daughter of the Duke of Brunswick. The Prince drank himself into a stupor for the marriage ceremony in 1795.

She was not at all bad-looking but perfumed rather than washed. The match was a disaster; they loathed each other from the start. On his wedding night he was disgustingly drunk and fell asleep with his head in the fireplace. Never-the-less the marriage was consummated and a daughter, Charlotte, was born in 1796. His wife left him soon after the birth and returned, in 1820, to claim her title when he became king. She was never recognised as Queen and, to her consternation and embarrassment, she was refused entry to Westminster Hall at the Coronation. He tried to divorce her by accusing her of adultery while he lived a life of licentiousness. He forced the introduction of a Bill through Parliament which would deprive her of the title, Queen, and declare the marriage 'forever wholly dissolved, annulled and made void'. Suspect evidence was produced to show her infidelity but the ensuing uproar caused the Bill to be dropped. A London mob threatened to riot in support of her, shouting "no Queen, no King", and George cleared out for safety's sake; at one point he was threatened with assassination. However, she died on 7th August 1821.

The year after his accession he visited Ireland and Hanover. His charisma and flamboyance delighted everyone and his visit to Scotland astonished the populace. Sir Walter Scott had written a pamphlet encouraging the nobility, the Council and anyone of substance to wear traditional dress; this started the cult of the tartan and the king paraded himself in the kilt complete with pink stockings; even the most thrawn of Scots were impressed but many laughed.

During his Regency and reign totalling eighteen years with the Tories, his Prime Ministers were Spencer Percival (1809), Earl of Liverpool (1812-1825), George Canning (1827), Viscount Goderich (1827) and the Duke of Wellington (1828). With the latter he strongly opposed the Reform Bill but he could not be trusted politically and was described in *The Times* as 'a hard-drinking, swearing man who at all times would prefer a girl and a bottle to politics and a sermon'. However, when he was sober his wit was positively brilliant and his conversation sparkled.

Towards the end of his life he lived in a world of fantasy. He imagined that he had played a key role in winning the Battle of Waterloo but no-one was quite sure whether or not he was teasing the ageing Duke of Wellington who had become quite exasperated with his monarch's crazy upside down world. Towards the end of his life George IV lived almost as a recluse at Windsor and died aged sixty-eight years on 26th June 1830. To his credit, his influence on architecture, furniture and sartorial elegance was quite splendid but lavishly expensive. He died a sorry figure.

Tour Walk 2 - High Street:

13. 5th Duke of Buccleuch Statue
    Heart of Midlothian
    - [Tolbooth Prison,]
    [Luckenbooths],
    [The Krames]

14. St Giles Cathedral
    Parliament House

15. Charles II Equestrian Statue

16. Byre's Close
    - Adam Bothwell,
    Bishop of Orkney,
    Advocate's Close

17. Writers' Court and
    Warriston's Close
    - Sir Archibald Johnston,
    Lord Warriston
    Craig's Close

18. City Chambers - Plaque,
    Mary Queen of Scots
    Mary King's Close,
    Mercat Cross,
    Old Post Office Close

19. Old Fishmarket Close
    - George Heriot
    Borthwick's Close,
    Old Assembly Close

20. Anchor Close
    - George Drummond

21. Covenant Close
    - Lord Braxfield

22. North Foulis Close
    - Plaque to James Gillespie

23. 219 High Street
    - Dr Elsie Maud Inglis
    Old Stamp Office Close
    Bell's Wynd,
    Tron Church
    Fleshmarket Close

24. Cockburn Street
    - Lord Cockburn

25. Blair Street, Hunter Square
    - James Hunter Blair

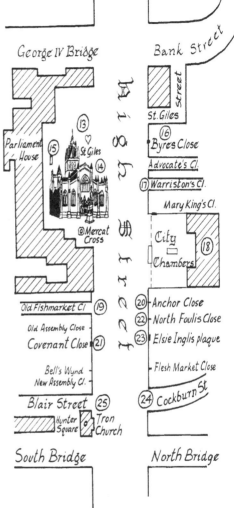

Tour Walk 2 - Summary

High Street

At the junction of George IV Bridge, Bank Street and the High Street, the brass studs embedded in the roadway mark the spot where the gallows were erected, in 1864, for the last public hanging in Edinburgh. A previous victim was the notorious Irishman, William Burke (1792-1829) who, with his accomplice, William Hare, committed 17 murders and sold the corpses for £7 10s. each to the anatomist Dr Robert Knox who ran the School of Anatomy between 1826 and 1840. Hare, the evil leader and Irish Nationalist, turned King's evidence and was allowed to go free but he died in misery, a blind beggar in London.

13. Statue of the 5th Duke of Buccleuch, by J.Edgar Boem in 1887 and its hexagonal base by Rowand Anderson, stands outside the west entrance of St Giles Cathedral. The 5th Duke, Walter Francis Scott (1805-1884) built and personally paid for Granton pier and breakwater in 1835. He entertained two monarchs, George IV and Queen Victoria, at Dalkeith House and he held many high appointments.

The *Heart of Midlothian*, near the Buccleuch statue, is embedded in the roadway in granite blocks and marks the position of the entrance to the Old Tolbooth Prison which stood there from 1561 until 1817 when a new prison was built at the Calton Hill. The Tolbooth jail, a high turretted edifice with iron gates, was the venue for the Scots Parliament, a Town Hall, the Chambers of the Privy Council, a College of Justice and, after 1640, a jail for debtors and criminals - "a living grave".

The Luckenbooths (locked booths), in the middle of the High Street also removed in 1817, were nearby where George Heriot ('Jinglin' Geordie') *qv* (19. Old Fishmarket Close) had his stall and where Allan Ramsay *qv* (6. Ramsay Garden) had his bookshop and set up the first lending library nearby. The narrow passage between the Luckenbooths and St Giles High Kirk was a veritable "Arabian Nights bazaar" and known as the Krames (or Creams) crammed with an array of toys and tinsel - a child's delight.

14. St Giles Cathedral is named after the patron saint of cripples, beggars and lepers and was built on the site of an ancient church thought to date from 854 AD. The central pillars of St Giles date from 1120 but the enlarged church was consecrated by the Bishop of St Andrews in

1243. The church was burned down in 1385 by the English king Richard II, but it was soon restored and enlarged by Robert III (1390-1406). Its Collegiate status was given in 1467 by the Pope. The stonework at the east door dates from 1400 as does the Albany Aisle. The Preston Aisle dates from 1455 and the tower and crown spire were added in 1495. After the Reformation in 1560 John Knox was the first Protestant minister but in 1637 Charles I imposed Episcopacy and made St Giles a Bishopric and a Cathedral. The new Prayer Book brought shouts of anger from many in the congregation one of whom, Jenny Geddes, threw her stool at the dean who had dared to read from it.

From about 1630 until 1817 St Giles was almost surrounded by small wooden stalls called luckenbooths. By Charles I's Royal Charter of 1633 St Giles became a Cathedral for the next six years. The astonishingly beautiful Thistle Chapel, by Sir Robert Stoddart Lorimer, was added in 1909-11. The chapel, originally intended for Holyrood Abbey, contains the exquisitely carved stalls and coloured Coats of Arms of the sixteen Knights of The Most Ancient and the Most Noble Order of the Thistle. It was dedicated in 1943 as a memorial to King George V.

Parliament House, built in 1632-39 and refaced by Robert Reid (1775-1856), was the venue for the Scottish Parliament until the Union with England's Parliament in 1707. The buildings now accommodate the High Court, the Court of Session, the Advocates' Library, the Solicitors' Library and the Signet Library. Several old luckenbooths, including that of George Heriot, were demolished about 1809 when the extension of the Advocates' Library was built.

15. The **equestrian statue of Charles II**, in the middle of Parliament Square, is thought to have been imported from Holland. It was given to Edinburgh in 1685 by the Surveyor of the King's Works, James Smith. It is made of lead and depicts the King as Caesar. Charles II came to Scotland for his crowning at Scone Palace on 1st January 1651. The statue was removed to the Calton Jail for safe-keeping after the great fire of 1824; it was returned to its present site in 1835.

16. In **Byre's Close** (formerly Lauder's Close and Malcolme's Close), almost opposite the Heart of Midlothian, was the mansion of **Adam Bothwell** (1530-93), the Bishop of Orkney and Commendator of Holyrood who, on 15th May 1567, performed the marriage ceremony of Mary Queen of Scots and the Earl of Bothwell at Holyrood. The Bishop refused them Catholic rites and after Queen Mary was made a Prisoner of State in the castle of Loch Leven he performed the crowning ceremony of her son as James VI at Stirling. His sister was the mother of Lord John Napier, the inventor of logarithms.

The Close takes its name from a later resident, John Byres, a rich 17th century merchant, a bailie, City Treasurer and Lord Provost who bought the estate of Coates where St Mary's Cathedral stands in Palmerston Place; he died in 1629.

Advocate's Close (formerly Home's Close and Provost Stewart's Close), opposite St Giles, takes its name from the fact that this was the residence of Scotland's first Lord Advocate, Sir James Stewart (1635-1713) of Goodtrees who was appointed in 1692. Another previous name of this Close was **Cant's Close** after Harry Cant, a Burgess, whose 'great tenement' was built here from 1475 to 1485. His nephew, Alexander Cant extended the property east and west but he was beaten to death by his wife and mother-in-law in 1535. The year '1590' is engraved in stone above the entrance and signifies the completion of refurbishment by a new owner, Clement Cor. Inside there is a fine stair tower and two doorways with inscriptions: 'SPES ALTERA VITAE 1590' and initials 'CC HB', meaning - Another Hope of Life, and Clement Cor and his wife Helen Bellenden. The other door has the inscription: '1590 CC BLESSIT BE GOD OF AL HIS GIFTS'. In 1654 the Close was renamed **Home's Close** until Lord Provost Sir James Stewart of Coltness bought the property and it became **Stewart's Close**. When the property was inherited by his son, Sir James Stewart of Goodtrees, the Lord Advocate from 1692 to 1713 the Close became known by its present name - Advocate's Close.

17. [Writers' Court], leading to [Warriston's Close], now part of the City Chambers, was the manse of John Knox when he was minister at St Giles between 1560 and 1566. His first wife, Marjory Bowes, died during the first year of his residency here.

Writers' Court accommodated the writers to the signet (lawyers) and their library in 1699. Here the 'Mirror Club' met at Cleriheugh's tavern, the 'Star and Garter', of which Henry MacKenzie (author of the *Man of Feeling*) was an illustrious member.

Warriston's Close (formerly Bruce's Close) takes its name from the jurist Lord Warriston who was one of the main authors of the National Covenant which can be seen in St Giles Cathedral. The Close takes its name from the mansion of Sir Archibald Johnston, Lord Warriston, who was a judge and a powerful champion of the Covenanters cause. In **[Craig's Close]**, (formerly Alexander Dennistoun's Close and Birnie's Close) a 1610 edition of the Bible was printed by Andrew Hart. William Creech (1745-1815), the publisher of the works of many of the 'literati' of Edinburgh and of the poems of Robert Burns, lived here. The Close was the first premises of Archibald Constable who published Sir Walter Scott's works. The Close was also the first office of the *The Scotsman* newspaper in 1816.

18. The City Chambers, almost opposite St Giles, has a three-sided courtyard designed by John Adam (1721-92) with modifications by John Fergus. He added the fluted Corinthian pilasters in the centre and in doing so he had to reduce the third storey windows in the frieze. The initiative of Lord Provost George Drummond (1687-1766) *qv* (20. Anchor Close), it was built as the Royal Exchange in 1753-61 and the statue of Alexander and Bucephalus by John Steell, which was cast in 1886, was installed in the courtyard in 1916 having been brought from St Andrew Square. Edinburgh's Cenotaph in the courtyard near the street commemorates the dead of World War 1914-18.

The Mary Queen of Scots Plaque, on the west wall of the courtyard of City Chambers, commemorates the fact that Mary Queen of Scots spent her last night here, in the house of Sir Simon Preston, before being imprisoned in Lochleven Castle in 1567.

Near this plaque is the entrance to the underground **Mary King's Close** (formerly Alexander King's Close and Touris Close) which was sealed off during the plague of Edinburgh in 1645. Much of the Close is still intact and in its original state. Shops and houses can be seen and some ghostly figures have been experienced over the years in this 'Street of Sorrows'. Its walls were so thick and well constructed they formed the foundations for building the City Chambers above. Mary King was thought to be the daughter of Alexander King, owner of the property and Advocate to Mary Queen of Scots.

The **Mercat Cross** stands opposite the City Chambers on the east side of St Giles. An earlier position of a previous Mercat Cross is marked by the stone cobbles just opposite Fishmarket Close. It was from this cross that kings were proclaimed, deaths of national importance were announced, law-breaking nobles were 'put to the horn' and executions were performed. Archibald Johnston, Lord Warriston *qv* (17) with other Covenanters made their vociferous objections to the Episcopacy of Charles II at the Mercat Cross and it was here that Warriston was put to death for his Covenanting beliefs.

The cross was demolished in 1756 but Prime Minister William Ewart Gladstone (1809-98) *qv* (46) saved it from destruction and restored it in 1885. Royal Proclamations are still made from its platform.

Old Post Office Close (formerly Jacob Barron's Close, Little's Close and Old Post House Close) was Edinburgh's first Post Office in 1713 from which the City's only postman made his deliveries. The Close was demolished in 1932 for the building of offices for the City Chambers.

19. Old Fishmarket Close (formerly Gourlay's Close, Humph's Close, Suittie's Close and Swift's Close) takes its name from the 18th century fish market where fish were thrown into the street and sold by women and boys. In 1586 this Close was the residence of **George Heriot**, Jeweller to the King (James VI), who left a fortune for the building of George Heriot's School. He is the Heriot of Heriot-Watt University at Riccarton. A later resident was novelist, journalist and spy, Daniel Defoe (1660-1731); he spied for the English Government during the negotiations for the Union of Parliaments of 1707.

Borthwick's Close (formerly Lord Durie's Close) was named after David Borthwick of Lochill, an advocate who defended the Earl of Bothwell after the murder of Lord Darnley. The trial was a judicial farce; Bothwell, who was found guiltless, was not even present at court. Borthwick was appointed a King's Advocate and a Lord of Session in 1573. He was Lord Advocate of Scotland in the reign of James VI. He detested his son and said of him, "I give him to the devil that gets a fool, and makes not a fool of him." This became known as 'David Borthwick's Testament'. Lord John Napier of Merchiston, the inventor of logarithms, lived here about 1580.

Old Assembly Close (formerly Barnes' Close, Gillespie's Close and Little's Close), takes its name from the 'Assembly', a dancing group who used the rooms in 1710 and purchased them in 1720. The new Assembly Rooms in Bell's Wynd opened in 1756 and finally, with the advent of the New Town, the Assembly Rooms, by John Henderson, in George Street were opened in 1787. The Music Hall was added in 1843.

16th century residents of this Close included brothers William and Clement Little. The former was Provost of Edinburgh and the latter gifted his library of 300 religious books to found the library of the University of Edinburgh.

20. Anchor Close (formerly Fordyce Close, Foular's Close and Fullar's Close) was the site of the town house of **George Drummond** (1687-1766), six times Lord Provost of Edinburgh and the inspiration and prime mover of the New Town. He died in 1766 and never saw his dream to fruition. He played a major part in the development of the University, then known as the 'Tounis College', and the existence of the Royal Infirmary is due to his tireless determination.

The offices of the printer William Smellie were in Anchor Close. He printed the first edition of the *Encyclopaedia Britannica* in 1768 and the Edinburgh edition of the poems of Robert Burns in 1787. The Close was the venue for the 'Crochallan Fencibles', one of many clubs of Old Edinburgh, to which William Smellie introduced Burns as a 'man of original character and talent'.

21. Covenant Close is named from the "National Covenant" against the imposition of the Liturgy by Charles I. This Covenant was signed by nobles and thousands of others at Greyfriars Church. A copy of it lay in a room in this Close so that anyone could sign it - they were the Covenanters, many of whom would suffer persecution and death.

The Close was an early residence of the feared Scottish Judge, **Robert Macqueen, Lord Braxfield** (1722-99), characterised as 'The Weir of Hermiston' by Robert Louis Stevenson and described by some as 'Scotland's Hanging Judge' during the Pitt-Dundas 'reign of terror' following the French Revolution in 1789.

22. North Foulis Close (formerly Fowler's Close and Fowlis Close), at Gordon's Frattoria Italian Restaurant, was named from an owner, John Foulis of Colinton, who was an apothecary in the city, but the shop was the snuff shop of **John Gillespie** whose brother, **James Gillespie** (1717-97), is commemorated by means of a wall-plaque. It is a reminder of the rich manufacturer of snuff whose mills were in the village of Colinton. He left sufficient money for a school in his name - Gillespie's High School.

23. No. 219 High Street - Elsie Inglis plaque - was the address of a hospital for the City's poor mothers and their children founded by Dr Elsie Inglis a heroine of the Great War in France, Serbia and Russia. The wall-plaque above commemorates this dedicated doctor who died aged 53 on her return from the front line in 1917.

Old Stamp Office Close (formerly Fortune's Close, Newbank Close Old Bank Close, Old Ship Close and Ship Tavern Close) was the Government Stamp Office until 1821 when it was transferred to Waterloo Place.

The third and extremely attractive, six-foot tall wife, Susanna, of Archibald, 9th Earl of Eglinton, and her seven stunningly beautiful daughters lived in the Close and caused many a male head to turn when they emerged from the Close in a procession of gilded sedan chairs.

Flora MacDonald, who helped Prince Charles Edward to escape after his defeat at Culloden in 1746, attended boarding-school here. The Royal Bank used the Close from 1727 to 1753.

From 1754 to 1787 the elegant Fortune's Tavern in this Close was a venue for receptions of the Lord High Commissioner of the General Assembly of the Church of Scotland, the 2nd Earl of Hopetoun.

Bell's Wynd was named after a brewer in 1529, John Bell after whom it became the residence of **George Crichton, the Bishop of Dunkeld** from 1527 to 1543. He was James V's Lord Keeper of the Privy Seal and on his elevation to the bishopric he presented a lectern cast in brass to Holyrood Abbey. It was stolen in 1544 when Edinburgh was sacked by the Earl of Hertford. The lectern, inscribed: 'Georgius Creichtoun, Episcopus Dunkenensis', was found by a grave digger in 1750 at St Stephen's Church, St Albans in Hertfordshire.

A room in the first floor of this Wynd is said to be haunted by the ghost of an unfaithful wife who was murdered by her outraged husband. The house had lain empty for over twenty years and a locksmith named George Gourlay, who lived with his wife above the haunted room, decided to explore it. His wife, who had lived as a servant in the house below, always refused to talk about it. Using the tools of his trade he entered the mysterious room to be confronted by the ghost which slipped silently passed him but worse was to come - there, on the bed before him, lay the skeleton of the murdered wife.

Tron Church takes its name from the existence of a 'tron' or weigh beam on this site. The church was built as 'Christ's Kirk at the Tron' in 1637-47 by John Mylne junior for the overflow congregation of St Giles who had been pushed out when Charles I's Episcopacy was established. The Tron Church's wooden spire was burned down in the great fire of 1824 and the stone spire was built in 1828. The Church is now the **Old Town Information Centre** in the centre of which is evidence of an early cobbled street which ran downhill to the Cowgate. It was called **Marlin's Wynd** after a French mason, Walter Marlion, who is said to have been the first to pave the High Street in 1532.

Fleshmarket Close (formerly Old Greenmarket Close and Provost's Close) was named from the 18th century fleshmarket which led to a slaughter house at the side of the Nor' Loch.

It was previously known as 'Provost's Close' and was the 17th century residence of David Aitkenhead, four times Lord Provost of Edinburgh

Opposite: The Tron Church, High Street

during a period when it was a crime for ladies to wear a plaid or to cover their faces; three Acts were passed by the Council in 1631, 1633 and 1636 forbidding the 'barbarous habit' under a penalty of £5.

The close was an early residence of **Henry Dundas** (1742-1811) *qv*(28) who was born at Bishop's Close. Fleshmarket Close was also the venue for the Marrow-bone club which held its political meetings in Cameron's Tavern.

24. Cockburn Street was cut through the Closes of the High Street in 1856 to give access to the Waverley Station. It is named after the Scottish judge **Henry Cockburn** who fought to preserve much of old Edinburgh (he saved John Knox's House from demolition). His *Memorials of His Time* give a vivid portrait of the Scottish intelligensia of his day.

25. Blair Street and **Hunter Square** are named after **Sir James Hunter-Blair** who was Lord Provost of Edinburgh in 1784. He was MP for the City between 1781 and 1784. Whereas George Drummond is deservedly credited with the North Bridge and the New Town so Hunter-Blair deserves the credit for the South Bridge, the new buildings of South Bridge and for the rebuilding of the University.

Opposite: Moubray House, adjacent to John Knox House, High Street

13. Statue of the 5th Duke of Buccleuch

This magnificent statue outside St Giles west entrance, by J. Edgar Boehm in 1887, depicts the 5th Duke of Buccleuch resplendent in the robes of the Most Noble Order of the Garter of which he was senior Knight. The hexagonal base, by Rowand Anderson, is impressive with its six bucks each having the Coat of Arms of the families allied by marriage to the Duke. The relief panel displays six events in Buccleuch history and the figures symbolise fortitude, liberality, temperance, prudence, charity and truth.

His full title is Walter Francis Montagu-Douglas-Scott, Duke of Buccleuch, Duke of Queensberry and Earl of Doncaster. Nineteenth century Edinburgh was proud to have such a man of great eminence in its midst; he held high political office, he built and paid for the breakwater and pier at Granton and he entertained Royalty at Dalkeith House where he was born on 25th November 1805. Aged thirteen years, he succeeded his elder brother who had died of measles on 11th March 1818. His father, the 3rd Duke, died of consumption, aged forty-seven, in Lisbon.

The 5th Duke was educated at Eton and St John's College, Cambridge where he gained his MA degree in 1827. A memorable event of his youth was the visit of George IV to Scotland in 1822. The young Duke was sixteen years of age when he entertained the king for fourteen days at Dalkeith House. This was the first visit of a monarch to Scotland since that of Charles II in 1651. Twenty years after George IV's visit he was to entertain Queen Victoria and the Prince Consort, again at Dalkeith House.

He was Lord Lieutenant of Midlothian from 1828 and of Roxburgh from 1841 where he owned Bowhill. In 1835 he, as owner of Caroline Park at Granton, conceived the idea that a second great port was necessary for Edinburgh. He paid over £500,000 (over £35 million today) for the construction of a pier and breakwater which was opened in 1838. Four years later Queen Victoria landed at the Duke's private pier to be received by the Duke himself and the Prime minister, Sir Robert Peel. The growth of Granton was mainly due to this investment and from 1852 many ships were built and ship repairs were carried out and the Duke with Sir John Gladstone initiated a ferry service between Granton and Burntisland. The Duke did not confine his interests to trade and commerce, he followed a family tradition with a keen interest in agriculture and, following in his father's footsteps, he became President of the Highland Agricultural Society (1831-35).

In politics he was a Conservative and in Peel's ministry he was appointed Lord Privy Seal in February 1842 until his appointment as Lord President of the Council from January to July 1846 when Peel was defeated on an Irish Protection of Life Bill and retired.

On 13th August 1829 he married Charlotte Anne, third and youngest daughter of the 2nd Marquis of Bath.

His titles and honours were numerous:

Lord Lieutenant of Midlothian (1828)

Knight of the Most Ancient and Most Noble Order of the Thistle (1830-1835)

Fellow of the Royal Society (1833)

Honorary Doctor of Civil Law of Oxford University (1834)

Knight of the Most Noble Order of the Garter (1835)

Captain General of the Royal Bodyguard of Archers (1838-death)

Lord Lieutenant of Roxburgh (1841)

Privy Councillor (1842)

High Steward of Westminster (1842)

Honorary Doctor of Laws, Cambridge University (1842)

Militia ADC to Queen Victoria (1857)

President of the Society of Antiquaries (1862-73)

Honorary Doctor of Laws, Edinburgh University (1874)

President of the British Association (1867)

Chancellor of the University of Glasgow (1878)

On 16th April 1884 he died, aged seventy-eight, at peaceful Bowhill in the County of Selkirk and he was buried at St Mary's Chapel at Dalkeith.

14. St Giles Cathedral (High Kirk)

The crown spire of St Giles is unmistakable in the silhouette of the Royal Mile. Its tower is late medieval, the church itself being founded about 1120, although there was a church on this site during the 9th century (854 AD).

The four huge pillars which support the tower and the pillars of the choir were part of the Norman church built by Alexander I (r.1107-1124). It was during the reign of Haddington born Alexander II, in 1243, that St Giles, as patron saint of Edinburgh, was given its name by the Bishop of St Andrews.

St Giles was rebuilt about 1360, its central tower being added about 1370. However, Richard II's army burned it down in 1385 during the sacking of Edinburgh. The stone structure survived, and by 1395 the transepts and a chapel were built. The five bays of the nave, the choir, the inner transepts are 12th century. The choir, completed about 1419, was remodelled and raised and two east bays were added to it by 1467, when St Giles received its Collegiate status. The church was now allowed to train its own priests and received freedom from the jurisdiction of St Andrews. It was around the year 1495 that the central tower was raised and the crown spire added.

Edinburgh's Guild of Craftsmen provided their chapel and spent lavishly furnishing it, presumably to reserve their places in heaven. As a Catholic Church St Giles was attacked by the Reformers; priceless hangings were burned and carvings and sculptures were destroyed in the Protestant belief that these were idolatrous. However, Catholic services were resumed when Mary of Guise (Queen Regent and mother of Mary Queen of Scots), with help from the French, drove out the Reformers. It was because of this that the Reformers decided to replace the figure of St Giles with the thistle in the Scottish banner.

Mary of Guise died suddenly in 1560, the French left and the Reformers took over again and desecrated the churchyard which was grossly overcrowded and closed about 1566. John Knox, as their leader, became the parish minister of St Giles for twelve years. He was buried in the churchyard in 1572. Episcopacy was revived under Charles I and II and finally, from 1688, Presbyterianism became the national religion.

After the Reformation St Giles accommodated three congregations which were separated from each other by partitions: the High, the Old and the Tolbooth Churches. Charles I ordered the removal of the partitions and made St Giles a cathedral in 1633. The partitions were replaced about 1660 and in 1689 the New Church added a fourth partition. In 1829-33 the nave was heightened. The aisles on both the north and south sides added to the width of the cathedral. The full splendour of the church remained hidden until Lord Provost William Chambers, the well-known publisher, financed its complete restoration in 1872. Sadly Chambers died only two days before its opening service in 1883.

St Giles is sometimes described as the 'Church of Reconciliation' and several pairs of old adversaries have been brought together under its roof:

(i) the brass plaques to Jenny Geddes and Dean Hannah. When, on 23rd July 1637 he read, for the first and last time, from 'Laud's Liturgy' - Charles I's Service Book - Jenny was said to have been so incensed with anger she threw her stool at him.

(ii) The effigies of the Marquis of Montrose and the Duke of Argyll; they were bitter enemies, the former, disillusioned with the Covenanter cause, joined the Royalists and defeated the Duke of Argyll's forces many times. Their executions, ten years apart, took place outside St Giles.

(iii) John Knox severed his friendship with the Earl of Moray when the nobles of Scotland refused to ratify the Treaty of Edinburgh (1560) much to the delight of Mary Queen of Scots.

(iv) Dr Elsie Maud Inglis, the Great War heroine of France, Serbia and Russia, who disagreed with Dr Jex-Blake's peremptory dismissal of two sisters from Leith Hospital in 1887.

Plan of St Giles Cathedral

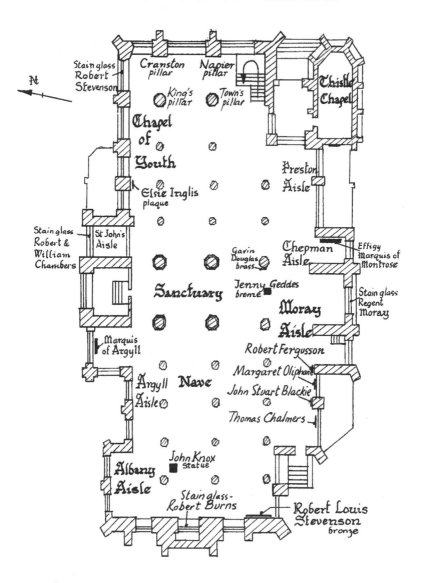

N

Stain glass Robert Stevenson

Cranston pillar

Napier pillar

King's pillar

Town's pillar

Thistle Chapel

Chapel of Youth

Preston Aisle

Elsie Inglis plaque

Stain glass Robert & William Chambers

St John's Aisle

Gavin Douglas brass

Chepman Aisle

Effigy Marquis of Montrose

Jenny Geddes brass

Sanctuary

Moray Aisle

Stain glass Regent Moray

Marquis of Argyll

Robert Fergusson

Margaret Oliphant

John Stuart Blackie

Thomas Chalmers

Argyll Aisle

Nave

John Knox Statue

Albany Aisle

Stain glass Robert Burns

Robert Louis Stevenson bronze

St Giles embodies much of the history of Scotland as will be seen from this brief tour of a few memorials. Starting from the west entrance going clockwise:

- **Royal Scots (Edinburgh Light Infantry Militia) Memorial**, South Africa, 1900-02.
- **Royal Scots Greys**, Camel Corps Sudan Campaign, Battle of Abu Klea, Memorial Celtic cross, 1885.
- **Queen's Own Cameron Highlanders** LXXIX, South African War 1900-02.
- The **Albany Aisle**, added in 1401-10, has two bays divided by a cloistered pillar with the Arms of the Duke of Albany (brother of Robert III (r.1390 -1406)) and Archibald, 4th Earl of Douglas. They provided this Aisle hoping for forgiveness for starving the Duke of Rothesay to death in 1402. He was heir to the throne and Albany became Regent on the death of Robert III whose son, James I, had been kidnapped at sea by the English. Douglas with Albany held supreme power, being in no hurry to raise the £40,000 ransom for James's release. When James I returned in 1415 he wiped out the Albany line and Douglas died in France having fled there. In 1951 the Albany Aisle was transformed into a War Memorial containing twelve memorials of the Sudan Campaign 1885, South African War 1900-02, the Great War 1914-18. The Aisle was re-dedicated to those killed during the 1939-45 War.
- The **Argyll Aisle** is the chapel of Archibald Campbell, Marquis of Argyll and bears the inscription:

> 'Beheaded near this cathedral AD1661. Leader in Council and in the field for the Reformed religion. *"I set the crown on the King's head. He hastens me to a better crown than his own."*'

Argyll had been no match against the clever Marquis of Montrose and had signed a treaty with Cromwell against the Royalists. However, after Charles I was put to death in 1649 Argyll then regarded Charles II as lawful king. After Montrose was captured and executed as a traitor to the Covenant, Charles II reluctantly accepted the Covenant in Scotland and was crowned by the Marquis of Argyll in 1651 at Scone. Cromwell died in 1658 and Charles reigned from 1660. Argyll was tried for his previous conduct and found guilty of treason. He was sentenced to death in 1661.

The brass in the Argyll Aisle is inscribed:

> *In memory of Sir James Dalrymple Bart., 1st Viscount Stair, Lord Glenluce and Stranraer in the peerage of Scotland. PC. Lord President of the Court of Session a distinguished lawyer and author of the Institutes of the Law of Scotland. Born 1619, died November 23rd 1695. Buried in this Church.*

72

He resigned his office when James VII (II of England), during the 'Killing Time', demanded the conversion of all Scots to Catholicism and required all holders of public office, including Sir James, to take the 'Test' - an oath which Sir James agreed insofar as it did not contradict itself. For making this provision he was imprisoned for treason. He escaped from the Castle dressed as a page. After King James was deposed Sir James, as Secretary of State, was the most powerful man in Scotland and he convinced the King, William of Orange, to sign the 'Letter of Fire and Sword' to massacre the MacDonalds in Glencoe having withheld the knowledge that they had already signed the oath of allegiance, albeit a few days late.

- **Sir Gordon Haddo plaque** - commemorates Royalist Sir John Gordon's defence of his Castle of Kelly against the Covenanters. He was imprisoned in 'Haddo's Hole' which was part of St Giles before his execution on 19th June 1644. This priest's room, demolished c. 1790, was a prison for Covenanters.

- **Statue of John Knox** by J Pittendrigh MacGillivray, 1905, commemorates the leader of the Reformation in Scotland. He was born in 1505 near Haddington and educated at Haddington and the University of Glasgow for the priesthood. Disenchanted and disgusted with the cruelty and corruption of the Catholic Church he surrendered his Orders in 1544. Cardinal Beaton ordered his assassination, he was captured and enslaved aboard a French galley and was released on the plea of Edward VI, but he had to flee the vindictiveness of 'Bloody' Mary.

Later he was put on trial by Mary Queen of Scots. He translated the Geneva Bible and was minister of St Giles for twelve years between 1560 and 1572. He led Scotland into the Reformed Church. He died in 1572 and was described by Regent Morton during a tearful eulogium, "Here lies one who never feared the face of man."

- **St John's Aisle** is part of the Chapel of Youth and the stained glass is a memorial to the brothers, Robert and William Chambers of publishing fame. The chapel is a memorial to 'William Chambers of Glenmoriston LLD' who, when Lord Provost (1865-68), donated £30,000 from his own funds for the restoration and transformation of St Giles by removing the dividing walls and renewing the roof and floor. After twelve years of work Chambers died only two days before the opening service.

- **The Chapel of Youth** contains commemorative plaques to Sophia Jex-Blake the first woman doctor in Scotland and to Sir William Smith, founder of the Boys' Brigade in 1883 for the "promotion of habits of obedience, reverence, discipline, self-respect, and all that tends towards a true Christian manliness."

- The **Elsie Maud Inglis Memorial**, 1917, is a stone tablet commemorating this heroic surgeon of the 1914-18 War who dedicated her life to the poor mothers of Edinburgh and died of exhaustion on her way home from the front in France in 1917.

- The **Scottish Nurses 1914-18 Memorial** is a stone tablet to the heroic nurses who gave their lives for the men they nursed during the war.

- The **94th (City of Edinburgh) H.A.A. Regiment Memorial** commemorates those of that regiment who died during the 1939-45 War.

- **Robert Stevenson FRSE, FGS, Stained Glass**. Engineer to the Northern Lighthouse Board. Born at Glasgow 1772, died at Edinburgh 1850. He erected most of the lighthouses on the Scottish coast the most hazardous being that of the Bell Rock. Stevenson College in west Edinburgh is named after him. His grandson was the celebrated Scottish novelist Robert Louis Stevenson whose life-size bronze is in the South Aisle.

- The **King's Pillar** is a memorial to James II (r.1437-1460) who had ordered the extension of the choir of St Giles but he was killed when one of his own cannons burst during his attack on Roxburgh Castle. His Queen, with the support of the people of Edinburgh, continued his work and she specially commissioned the King's Pillar which bears the shields of his most faithful followers.

- The **Cranston Pillar** commemorates Lord Provost Sir Robert Cranston KCVO, CB, CBE who was a Brigadier-General in the Volunteer Movement and Lord Provost from 1903 to 1906. He started the Cranston Hotels in Edinburgh and London.

- The **Napier Pillar**, with the Arms of the Napiers of Merchiston, commemorates this illustrious family. Alexander Napier was Provost in 1438, his son Alexander was James II's Comptroller of Scotland, Vice Admiral, Ambassador to England and Provost 1469-71. Sir

Alexander Napier was killed with James IV at Flodden in 1513. John Napier was Provost in 1484 and his son founded an altar to St Salvator in St Giles in 1493. Sir Archibald Napier was killed at the Battle of Pinkie in 1547 and his son, Lord John Napier (1550-1617), was the famous mathematician and inventor of logarithms who is commemorated in Napier University which is named after him.

- The **Town's Pillar** has the shields of John Halkerston (designer of the east extension of the church), Bishop Kennedy of St Andrews, the Castle of Edinburgh Coat of Arms and Sir William Preston of Gorton (see Preston Aisle).

- The **Thistle Chapel** was built in 1909-11 for The Most Ancient and Most Noble Order of the Thistle which was instituted in 1687 and revived by Queen Anne in 1703 (some authorities give its foundation as 787). Its famous motto is *nemo me impune lacessit (*no-one provokes me with impunity). Knighthood of the Order is restricted to sixteen distinguished Scotsmen plus selected members of Royal families. The 11th Earl of Leven left the sum of £40,000 to restore Holyrood Abbey as a Chapel for the Order but its walls were too weak. The present ornate construction, designed by Sir Robert Stodart Lorimer, is a stone sculpted two-bay antichapel with stone carved thistles, roses and shamrocks on the bosses of the arched stone ceiling. The chapel itself consists of exquisitely carved knights' stalls each with steepled canopies and their coats of arms. The largest is the Sovereign's stall in the canopy of which are the figures of Saints Margaret, Columba and Kentigern with the Royal Coat of Arms of Scotland on its desk front but on each side there is a tiny carving of a fox and a rabbit.

- The **Preston Aisle** took thirty-two years to build by the Town Council and was completed in 1455, Sir William Preston of Gourton having presented an arm bone of St Giles to the Church in 1450. His commemorative brass was provided by the Town Council. The Royal Pew with its stalls for the Queen and the Duke of Edinburgh may be occupied by the Lord Lyon, King of Arms and the Lord High Commissioner representing the Queen. In 1643 the Solemn League and Covenant was signed in this Aisle in defiance against Charles I's imposition of the Service Book. The stone on the east wall commemorates the architect of the Thistle Chapel, **Sir Robert S. Lorimer**.

- The **Chepman Aisle**, built in 1507 and consecrated in 1513, opens out of the west bay of the Preston Aisle and was founded by Walter Chepman, the first Scottish printer. He was a clerk at Holyrood and introduced the printed word to Scotland being encouraged by James IV of Scotland and Margaret Tudor of England. Chepman also endowed the alter to St John honouring James IV only one month before he was killed at the Battle of Flodden on Scotland's darkest day, 9th September 1513. Chepman died in 1538.

- The **effigy of James Graham, 1st Marquis of Montrose**, in the **Chepman Aisle**, commemorates Scotland's finest soldier who became disaffected with the Covenanter's cause to become a Royalist in support of Charles I against Oliver Cromwell. Montrose was eventually captured after many brilliant victories. He was hanged outside St Giles on 21st May 1650 before a saddened crowd of onlookers much affected by his dignity and calmness. His remains were collected together in 1662 and buried in St Giles. His effigy was placed in its present position in 1888. His greatest rival, the Marquis of Argyll, was executed eleven years afterwards, in 1661, as a traitor to the king (ref. Argyll Aisle).

- The **John Craig brass** is affixed to the pillar opposite the Chepman Aisle. John Craig was a distinguished and brave co-adjutor of John Knox. He was born in 1512, educated at St Andrews, entered the Order of Dominican Friars and became disgusted at the bigotry of the clergy. He left Scotland travelling to England, France and Italy. At Bologna, on the recommendation of Cardinal Pole, he was admitted among the Dominicans. However, after reading Calvin's *Institutions* he became a convert to the Reformation. He was arrested for heresy and taken to Rome to be burned at the stake. He escaped and undertook the dangerous journey in disguise through Europe returning to Scotland to become Assistant minister to John Knox, and minister to the King's Household. He died in his 89th year in Edinburgh in 1600.

- The **Moray Aisle** has a stained glass to Regent Moray, 'The Good Regent', who brought a period of relative peace in Scotland after the troubled times of Mary Queen of Scots. He was murdered by a power-seeking Hamilton in 1570. John Knox, preaching his funeral sermon at St Giles, was said to have reduced 3000 people to tears for the loss of 'such a good and Godly governor.'

- The **Cutty Stool** by Marlyn Smith, 1992 is dedicated to Jenny Geddes 1637 by Scotswomen. A much lighter version was said to have been thrown at the dean, James Hannay DD, when he dared to read from Charles I's Service Book ('Laud's Liturgy'). The floor plaque reads:

> *Constant oral tradition affirms that near this spot a brave*
> *Scotch woman Janet Geddes on 23rd July 1637 struck*
> *the first blow in the great struggle for freedom of*
> *conscience which after a conflict of half a century ended*
> *in the establishment of civil and religious liberty.*

- **Plaque to James Hannay DD** *Dean of this Cathedral 1634-1639. He was the first and last to read the Service Book in this church.*

- The **Wauchope Memorial Window**, adjacent to the Moray Aisle, commemorates Major-General Andrew Gilbert Wauchope of Niddrie Marischal who was killed at Magersfontein during the Boer War of 1899-1902.

- The **Robert Fergusson bronze** is a memorial to the young poet (1751-1774) so admired by Robert Burns that he erected a touching gravestone to his memory in the Canongate burial ground.

- The **Margaret O. W. Oliphant (1828-97) brass** commemorates the Scottish novelist born at Wallyford. She was widowed with three children and earned her livelihood in writing about Scottish character and life.

- The **John Stuart Blackie stone** (1809-95) commemorates the Professor of Greek of the University of Edinburgh (1852-82) who raised the money for the Chair of Celtic Studies and who spoke against the 'harsh, inhuman and impolitic' Highland Clearances.

- The **Thomas Chalmers stone** commemorates the Scottish minister who led the 'Disruption' of 1843 when 470 churchmen left the General Assembly of the Church of Scotland to form the Free Church. Their protest was against patronage in the church.

- The **Robert Louis Stevenson bronze** (1850-94) by the Dublin born American sculptor, Augustus Saint Gaudens, on the west wall commemorates the Scottish novelist who died in Samoa. The original showed a cigarette in his right hand but it was substituted for a pen as more suitable for the church. The inscription is Stevenson's own Requiem:

> *Under the wide and starry sky, Dig the grave and let me*
> *lie. Glad did I live and gladly die, And I laid me down*
> *with a will. This be the verse you grave for me: Here he*
> *lies where he longed to be; Home is the sailor, home*
> *from the sea, And the hunter home from the hill.*

- The **Royal Scots Boer War Memorial** depicts in bronze, soldiers attacking a kopje, by W. Birnie Rhind in 1903.

- The **Robert Burns stained glass** in the Great West Window above the west entrance is a tribute to Scotland's great poet (1759-96). It was commissioned in 1984 from Iceland's Leifur Breidfjord and depicts: nature - *Love the cloudless summer sun, Nature Gay adorning*, the brotherhood of man - *That man to man the world o'er Shall brithers be for a' that*, and the supremacy of love - *My love is like a red, red rose, that's newly sprung in June.*

St Giles - brief biography
The church was dedicated to St Giles by Bishop Kennedy in 1243 because Edinburgh was part of the diocese of the Bishop of St Andrews.

The Reformers, in protest against the Catholic Queen Regent, Mary of Guise, took the statue of St Giles from the High Church in 1558 and threw it into the Nor Loch, now Princes Street Gardens.

St Giles the man was a Greek born in Athens in 640 AD. He was of royal lineage and, having been orphaned as a boy, he decided to become an Anchorite monk. After some time in Arles, between Nimes and Marseilles, he chose to live in solitude - a cave-life of prayer and meditation. His only companion was a tame hind which lived with him. He survived on its milk with roots and herbs.

After several years he was discovered by huntsmen of the king of the Visigoths, Flavius Wamba, when one of their arrows aimed at the hind struck St Giles who had protected the animal with his body. The King so admired the bravery and kindness of the hermit he ordered his doctor to tend his wound and gave him a grant of land on which he built a Monastery and remained as its Abbot until his death on 1st September, AD 723. St Giles became King Wamba's spiritual adviser and the monastery he founded in Provence was called Saint-Gilles. As an old man he travelled to Rome to offer his monastery to the Pope and after its acceptance he received the customary Papal privileges and protection.

His shrine in Provence was an important pilgrimage for the Crusaders who helped to spread his cult throughout Europe; in addition, it was believed that to be formally blessed through St Giles was so effective that full confession was no longer necessary. St Giles is the patron saint of cripples, lepers and nursing mothers.

In England 162 ancient churches were dedicated to him - the most famous in Britain being St Giles at Edinburgh and St Giles, Cripplegate, London. The arms of the City of Edinburgh consist of a castle surmounted by an anchor and a cross with a female figure on one side and a hind on the other; the hind is that of St Giles.

15. Charles II Statue - Parliament Square

The six-ton lead equestrian statue of Charles II, in the middle of Parliament Square, is the oldest of its kind in Britain. It depicts him as a Caesarian Roman Emperor. It was delivered to Edinburgh in the year of his death, 1685, from Holland by James Smith, the King's Surveyor of Works. Robert Louis Stevenson described it as: 'a bandy-legged and garlanded Charles second made of lead, bestrides a tun-bellied charger.'

When it was decided to paint it white to protect it from the rays of the sun, James Boswell, the Scottish man-of-letters, penned a short poem about it:

> The milk-white steed is well enough,
> But why thus daub the man all over,
> And to the swarthy Stewart give
> The cream complexion of Hanover?

After the great fire of 1824 the statue was taken to Calton Jail for safe-keeping and returned to its present position in 1835.

When the news of his father's execution, on 30th January 1649, was received, young Charles was in Holland. The death warrant of Charles I had been signed by 59 men including Oliver Cromwell. All Scotland was horrified. Rather than be ruled by Oliver Cromwell and his dreaded

Independents, the Scots chose to proclaim Charles II as king of Great Britain and Ireland. This proclamation was read at the Market Cross of Edinburgh on 5th February 1649 and Commissioners were sent to Holland with the message that Charles would be crowned King of Scotland if he accepted the National Covenant of 1638. His father had refused to do so and the eighteen year-old Charles, having fewer scruples about religion, sent the Marquis of Montrose to try to win the crown without the necessity of signing. Montrose was eventually captured and put to death by the Covenanters who hated him for going against them during the reign of Charles 1. Young Charles, therefore, had no option but to accept the Covenant and the Marquis of Argyll, a staunch Presbyterian and sworn enemy of Montrose, crowned him at Scone; an event entered into without enthusiasm from either side. Cromwell now marched on Edinburgh to face the army of David Leslie and King Charles was removed to Dunfermline for his safety.

Charles II was born on 29th May 1630 at St James's Palace. He was nine years old when he was created Prince of Wales, twelve years old when he fought alongside his father at the Battle of Edgehill at the start of the Civil War, at fourteen he was nominal Commander-in-Chief over the west of England, at fifteen he was chased over England by the Parliamentarians and at eighteen he commanded those warships whose crews had joined the Royalist cause. He fled to Holland where he learned of his father's execution in 1649. After being crowned at Scone he raised an army but marched into defeat at Worcester in 1651 and with a price of £1000 on his head he fled the country in a coal brig from Shoreham to Normandy.

After an absence of nine years and the death of Oliver Cromwell, General George Monck organised his return and welcome back to a war-torn and impoverished England. On 14th May 1660 Charles was proclaimed King of three kingdoms at Edinburgh and he was crowned on 23rd April 1661. A year later he married Princess Catherine of Braganza, daughter of John IV of Portugal. This brought commercial advantages, Bombay and Tangier and a dowry of £300,000, but the marriage was childless.

Charles II was a clever manipulator of men. His reign was punctuated with threats, broken promises, secret treaties and religious and political intrigue, but never-the-less he was known as the 'Merrie Monarch' who enjoyed his ease and considered that God would not deny a man a little pleasure. He treated his eight mistresses with great generosity, Nell Gwynne being the most favoured.

According to Pepys's diaries his greatest interests were his laboratories and his dockyards. Sir Isaac Newton the scientist and mathematician,

Robert Boyle the chemist and Edmond Halley the astronomer were all patronised; the observatory at Greenwich was built, the Nautical Almanac was produced and Christopher Wren built his fifty London churches.

The laws of equity and Shaftesbury's Habeas Corpus Act of 1679 ensured the liberty of all men. He restored prosperity, having inherited a huge debt, and it was said by Sir Josiah Child, who had made £200,000 as a navy victualler and a director of the East India Company: 'there were more men to be found on the Exchange worth £10,000 than in 1651 had been worth £1000'. There was a general rise in the standard of living and the security of England was assured by the greatest navy in the world; the English flag was flown by over 300,000 tons of merchant shipping.

By contrast his brother, the Duke of York who became James II, was an arrogant, self-righteous, religious bigot and Charles, even though he was aware of the dread and fear with which Catholic James was held, refused to legitimise his natural son, the Duke of Monmouth, as his heir to the throne and he refused to agree to the Exclusion Bill by pressurising the House of Lords. When the King's advisers, the Cabal (an acronym of Clifford, Arlington, Buckingham, Ashley and Lauderdale), tried again in 1680, he simply dissolved Parliament.

Charles manipulated sympathy on his own behalf when the Rye House Plot, to assassinate him with his brother, was discovered. The Whig leaders fled abroad and Shaftesbury died in Holland. Others involved included 'The Patriot', Andrew Fletcher who, with Robert Fergusson, escaped to the Continent, the latter having been concealed by a friend in the Old Tolbooth of Edinburgh.

Having dispensed with his implacable opposition Charles II spent the last few years of his life in relative calm; his control of the army and navy held the country from any threat of another civil war, but he had charm and a sense of humour which endeared him to his people. He embraced the Catholic faith just before he died of apoplexy on 6th February 1685.

16. Byres' Close -
Adam Bothwell, Bishop of Orkney

Byres' Close is the first Close on the north side of the High Street after the Sheriff Court. Earlier names were Lauder's Close and Malcolme's Close but the name Byres is that of a wealthy merchant, **John Byres of Coates** (1569-1629), who became a Bailie, City Treasurer and Lord Provost of Edinburgh during the reign of James VI. He bought the Coates estate in 1610 and his son Sir John Byres built East Coates House (1615) now occupied by St Mary's Music School adjacent to St Mary's Cathedral in Palmerston Place.

The tenements are 17th century, but the Close led to a four-storey, narrow house which was rebuilt for **Sir William Dick of Braid** (c.1630) who was sufficiently rich to lend £6000 to James VI. His huge financial support of the Covenanters while provost of the City, his later support of the Royalist cause and the fines levied on him by the Parliamentary Party led to his abject poverty. He was imprisoned for petty debt and died in his lodgings at Westminster in 1655 having gone to London in the hope of recovering money he lent on Government security.

An earlier resident was **Adam Bothwell, Bishop of Orkney**, Commendator of Holyrood House and uncle of Lord John Napier the illustrious inventor of logarithms. Adam Bothwell was one of many important figures during the tumultuous five-year reign of Mary Queen of Scots. He officiated at her third marriage to James Hepburn, Earl of Bothwell in 1567 and he conducted the ceremony in Protestant form. After her arrest and abdication on 24th July 1567, he crowned and anointed her son five days later, the one-year old James.

Adam Bothwell was born c1527, the second son of Francis Bothwell, a Lord of Session. His mother, Janet Richardson, was a co-heiress of Patrick Richardson of Meldrumsheugh, a Burgess of Edinburgh. Little is known of his boyhood or education but he was well-versed in canon and civil law. His first official mention appears in October 1559 when he was given the See of Orkney in succession to Robert Reid who had died on his return from the marriage of the sixteen-year-old Mary Queen of Scots to the Dauphin of France in 1558.

Bothwell had little interest in his new diocese or in the church itself. However, a few years afterwards, he gave up his Catholic faith to become a lukewarm supporter of the Reformed movement, but he returned to Catholicism when he was elected by the new Chapter of Orkney and his Bishopric was confirmed by Mary Queen of Scots on

8th October 1562, she having returned to Scotland on the death of her husband, the Dauphin of France.

He was appointed an extraordinary Lord of Session on 14th January 1563, claiming to have been 'required by the Queen to accept the office.' He was a Commissioner for revising John Knox's *Book of Discipline* and at the General Assembly of 1564, his dual appointment as Bishop of Orkney and Lord of Session was questioned. His appointment as an ordinary Lord of Session was made on 13th November 1565 and he had hardly bothered to visit his diocese in Orkney, preferring instead to attend to his legal duties.

His place in Scotland's history would probably have gone unnoticed but for the next momentous event - the third marriage of Mary Queen of Scots. Her second husband, the overbearing Lord Darnley, had been murdered in February 1567 and her next husband, the Earl of Bothwell, was the prime suspect. After a sham trial, in which he was found guiltless, and a quick divorce, their marriage banns were unwillingly announced by the assistant minister of St Giles, John Craig. Adam Bothwell, as Bishop of Orkney, performed the marriage ceremony in the Council Chamber of Holyroodhouse on 15th May 1567. The Earl of Bothwell was said to have repented his former offensive life and to have joined the Reformed religion. The marriage ceremony was performed in Protestant form, although some sources claim that it was performed under Catholic rites and followed by a Protestant ceremony, it being thought highly improbable that Mary would 'acquiesce in a Protestant marriage.'

Adam Bothwell was now charged on four counts by the General Assembly for: (i) failing to visit the churches of Orkney, (ii) simultaneously holding the appointment of a Lord of Session, (iii) befriending and giving charity to a Papist, Francis Bothwell, and (iv) performing the marriage of Queen Mary and the Earl of Bothwell, a divorced adulterer. Adam Bothwell appeared before the General Assembly of the Church of Scotland and excused himself from residing in Orkney for reasons of climate and poor health and he denied knowing that Francis Bothwell was Catholic. However, he was deprived of 'all function in the ministry' for solemnising the Royal marriage. A few months later he was restored to the ministry but his diocese of Orkney was not renewed. This did not displease him and he exchanged the See of Orkney with Robert Stuart, Queen Mary's brother, for the Abbacy of Holyrood, but he still retained the title Bishop of Orkney to which he added the title Abbot of Holyroodhouse.

At Carberry Hill Queen Mary and Bothwell had to submit to the confederate lords. Her husband was allowed to escape and she was brought back to Edinburgh amid jeers and shouts of "burn the whore".

After her inprisonment at Lochleven Castle she had no alternative but to abdicate. Five days later, on 29th July, Adam Bothwell crowned and anointed the one-year old baby of Mary Queen of Scots, James VI. This was a revolution almost unheard of in annals of Scottish history; such an event had not taken place for almost five hundred years (when Edgar displaced Donald Bane in 1097). Adam Bothwell was the only one suitably qualified to perform the ceremony; he had been consecrated in 1559 and in spite of his sympathies for the Reformed Church he was prepared to give unction. The Bishop of St Andrews was the first choice but he was on the side of Mary Queen of Scots.

There followed a succession of Regents - Earl of Moray, assassinated in 1570; Earl of Lennox, killed in 1571; Earl of Mar who died after a year in office (Adam Bothwell was present at his election in September 1571) and James Douglas, Earl of Morton. Adam Bothwell protested against Morton's extreme measures in calling for help from the English to attack Edinburgh Castle, Mary's last stronghold. For his objection Bothwell was imprisoned in 1578 in Stirling Castle. Soon afterwards he was released and became one of the council of twelve members of the provisional government which was quickly overthrown.

Bothwell had neglected his ministry and was questioned again by representatives of the General Assembly. He pleaded age and poor health but his excuse was doubted and the Edinburgh Presbytery was requested 'to try his ability.' Further action against him was overtaken with the alarm and fear of Catholic, pro-Mary foreign agents in Scotland.

James VI was now fourteen years old and, having never known his parents, he had given his affection to his father's cousin, Esme Stewart, a Frenchman who opposed Regent Morton and was the cause of his arrest and execution. A pro-Mary and pro-Catholic movement was feared and in the panic James VI was seized by the Protestant 'Ruthven Raiders'. When James escaped in June 1583 the power of the General Assembly was severely diminished. Bothwell was now appointed as one of the 'lords of the articles' at the Parliament in May 1584. He was given the baronies of Whitekirk and Brighouse and retired in comfort. He died on 23rd August 1593 and was buried at Holyrood. His eldest son John became a Lord of Session and Commendator of Holyrood, being created Baron Holyroodhouse in 1607.

17. Writers' Court and Warriston's Close - Sir Archibald Johnston, Lord Warriston

Writers' Court and **Warriston's Close** are part of the west section of the City Chambers. Writers' Court was named from 1699 when the Writers to H.M. Signet purchased several flats in the Court for their library. An earlier occupant of a house in Warriston's Close was John Knox *qv* whose first wife, Marjory Bowes, died there in 1560.

Warriston's Close (formerly Bruce's Close) takes its name from the mansion of **Sir Archibald Johnston, Lord Warriston** who was a judge and a powerful champion of the Covenanters' cause - as Clerk of the General Assembly he wrote the denunciation of the king's conduct and with the Rev. Alexander Henderson he wrote the National Covenant of 1638 (a revival of the confession of 1591). After the Restoration in 1660 Charles II singled him out for punishment. He had accepted high office under Cromwell and was hanged at the Market Cross of Edinburgh in 1663.

He was born about 1610 in Edinburgh. His father was James Warriston, a prosperous merchant, and his mother was Elizabeth Craig, a daughter of the famous feudal lawyer Sir Thomas Craig of Riccarton who owned the property when it was named Craig's Close.

Archibald Johnston's education was influenced by Robert Baillie who became Principal of Glasgow University. He was admitted to the Faculty of Advocates in 1633 and later gave advice to the committee which opposed Charles I's imposition of Episcopacy in the Scottish Church.

Johnston became an influential figure and read the protestation against the Royal proclamations of 1638 at the Market Cross. His additions to the Confession of 1591 with those of the Moderator of the Church of Scotland, Rev. Alexander Henderson, got rid of bishops, the Five Articles of Perth and the Liturgy - in fact they replaced Episcopacy with Presbyterianism - the National Covenant was born and Charles I dismissed it as illegal. Archbishop Spottiswood *qv* (ref. Carrubber's Close), who had so persuasively convinced the Assembly to accept the Articles, now fled to England.

Johnston was elected Clerk of the General Assembly at Glasgow in 1638 and he wrote the denunciation of the king's conduct. He was now appointed Procurator of the Kirk in control of all of its publications.

Charles I's army came face to face with the Covenanting army at Berwick and Johnston with Henderson accompanied the Scottish commissioners to negotiate the 'Pacification of Berwick' which averted the 'First Bishops' War' for the time being. Johnston wrote to Archbishop Loudon in London to explore which members of the English nobility might be sympathetic to an invasion of England.

In 1640 he helped the Scottish Commissioners of Estates in their negotiation of the Treaty of Ripon which brought about the end of the Second Bishops' War and the Scottish Parliament formally praised Johnston for his work.

The king granted a number of concessions one of which was the appointment of Johnston as a Lord of Session and he took the title of Lord Warriston from his estate 'Warynston' near Currie. He was given a pension of £200 per year and made a commissioner to negotiate a permanent settlement of the kingdom.

In 1642 Charles I's Parliament had rebelled against him, Civil War broke out but the English Parliament agreed the *Solemn League and Covenant* (1643) to gain Scottish support. In 1648 the King's party of the Scottish Parliament formed its 'Engagement' in support of the king and Johnston strongly opposed them. The 'Engagers' were beaten at Preston and Cromwell marched on Edinburgh where he met with the Duke of Argyll and David Leslie, the commander of the Covenanter army. They agreed the exclusion of the Engagers from Parliament and Johnston took his seat as Commissioner for Argyllshire.

Leslie made the mistake of marching his Covenanting army into England while the Marquis of Montrose, on the King's side, won several consecutive victories in Scotland. After the king's defeat at Naseby (1645) the English Parliament refused to pay the Scots' expenses. The Scots withdrew to Newark and finding the king in their camp they took him to Newcastle. During his talks Charles could not accept the Covenant but appointed Johnston King's Advocate (Lord Advocate) and the Estates voted him £3000 to recompense his expenses and time.

The English Parliament threatened war against the Covenanters unless Charles was handed over. This was agreed with the provision that no harm should befall him. Expenses were paid and the Scots returned home to tackle Montrose. All of Scotland was stunned when news arrived of the king's execution on 30th January 1649.

A reluctant Johnston was present when Charles II was proclaimed king in Edinburgh. In March 1649 Johnston was appointed Lord Clerk Register giving him custody of Scottish records. After the Battle of Dunbar on 3rd September 1650, when Cromwell defeated Leslie's army, Johnston had several meetings with Cromwell but he was unable to ally himself to his cause. Equally, he could not support the king having recently lectured him on moral laxity. He joined the Independents while Cromwell ruled Scotland for nine years, General Monck having subdued the Lowlands and the Highlands.

In 1652 the fearless Johnston composed and signed his protest against the subordination of the kirk to the state under English rule. He had become greatly frustrated and was described; 'Lord Warriston is angry at everything but himself, and at that too sometimes.' However he accepted his old office of Lord Clerk Register in 1657 and was a Commissioner in Cromwell's House of Peers. Cromwell died in 1658, Monck returned to London and in 1660 Charles II was restored to the throne.

Now the price of Johnston's Covenanting past and his acceptance of high office under Cromwell had to be paid. Charles II singled him out for punishment and a judgement of death and forfeiture of his lands was issued against him for high treason. Johnston escaped to Hamburg and then to Rouen where he was arrested with the compliance of the French government. He was brought back to London and imprisoned in the Tower. His wife pleaded to be allowed to travel with him to Scotland and he was held for trial in the Old Tolbooth almost opposite his mansion in Warriston's Close.

He had been badly treated and his mental state was such that he did not even recognise his own children. His first hearing was cancelled and in Parliament a plea was made for compassion but the Earl of Lauderdale, the power behind the throne in Scotland, demanded that he must be tried without delay. He was hanged on 23rd July 1663 and his head was fixed high on the Netherbow Port.

18. Mary Queen of Scots - Plaque at City Chambers, Mary King's Close

The bronze plaque on the west wall of the courtyard of the City Chambers is a reminder of the fall of Mary, Queen of Scots; it was 'erected by the Lord Provost, Magistrates and Council of Edinburgh. March 1894' and reads:

M 1567 R

On this site stood the lodgings of Sir Simon Preston of Craigmillar, Provost of the City of Edinburgh 1566-7; in which lodging Mary Queen of Scotland after her surrender to the Confederate Lords at Carberry Hill, spent her last night in Edinburgh 15th June 1567. On the following evening she was conveyed to Holyrood and thereafter to Lochleven Castle as a State prisoner.

The youthful, beautiful Mary, Queen of Scots could not have landed at Leith at a worse time. She had a foretaste of trouble to come even before she set foot on Scottish soil. Her ships, on the journey from France, had been chased in the North Sea by ships of Queen Elizabeth's fleet. It was 19th August 1561. She walked into a turmoil of trouble between the crown and the kirk and between Catholics and zealous Reformers. She was a mere eighteen years of age when she was confronted with the dialectic of the greatest orator in Scotland, John Knox. It was no wonder that occasionally she would break down in tears before the onslaught of his harsh criticism.

Her short reign, it lasted less than six years, was punctuated with peaceful religious contemplation at one end of her spectrum of emotion to jealous rage at the other. So much has been written about her reign, she has become almost a cult figure.

She was born at Linlithgow Palace on 8th December 1542. Her father, James V, had suffered a humiliating defeat at the Battle of Solway Moss only two weeks before her birth and to exacerbate his depression the baby was a girl. His two sons had died in 1541 and, his depression was so deep, he died when Mary was six days old with the words, "It came with a lass, it will pass with a lass." He was, of course, referring to the House of Stuart which did, as he predicted, end with Queen Anne in 1714.

Soon after James's death, Henry VIII negotiated the 'Treaty of Greenwich' under which his six year-old son, Prince Edward, would marry the infant Queen. Henry was furious when Cardinal Beaton convinced the Scottish Parliament to repudiate the treaty. Henry's ambitions of domination over Scotland had been thwarted and he sent an army, under the Earl of Hertford, to burn and pillage everything in his path - this was the 'rough wooing.'

Cardinal Beaton was murdered in 1546, a conspiracy which certainly pleased King Henry. The French helped to eject the English from Scotland but on condition that young Mary be sent to France for upbringing and eventually to marry the heir to their throne. Her betrothal to the son of the Earl of Arran was broken after the defeat of the Scots at the Battle of Pinkie (10th September 1547), near Musselburgh and, at six years of age, she was sent to France.

Mary spent the next ten years being educated at the French court of Henry II and Catherine de Medici. She became an accomplished musician and writer of prose and poetry. She spoke four languages and conversed with charm and kindness. When she reached the age of twelve, Arran was persuaded, with the reward of the Duchy of Châtelherault, to resign his Regency in Scotland and he was replaced by Mary of Guise, young Mary's mother.

On 24th April 1558 Mary was married to the Dauphin at the Cathedral of Notre Dame. She had signed a secret deed in which her sovereignty of Scotland and her right to succession of the English throne would transfer to the French if she died childless. Had this become known, rebellion could well have erupted in Scotland. Her father-in-law died in 1559 and her husband became Francis II; she was now Queen of France.

In May 1559, John Knox arrived back in Scotland from Geneva, Mary of Guise tackled the Protestant ministers head on and, with French troops, she attacked Reformers without mercy. The French were besieged at Leith and the sudden death of Mary of Guise ended the French presence. There was now some doubt about whether or not young Mary would return to Scotland. After all, she was Queen of France, and Scotland was not an attractive prospect. However, her situation changed suddenly on the death, in December 1560, of her husband. Her status was reduced to that of a dowager Queen and she left France in August 1561.

Her ships evaded English vessels in the fog and she was received at Leith by her illegitimate brother, Lord James Stewart, and Secretary of State, William Maitland of Lethington.

The young Earl of Arran was so desperate to marry her, his obsession drove him to a mental breakdown. Lord James Stewart and Secretary Maitland became her mentors and advised tolerance and conciliation towards Protestants. She wanted to practise her religion in peace leaving the Reformers to their own devices, but of course, she would have preferred another alliance with France and, as for saying mass at Holyrood, John Knox could never agree.

In 1562 she travelled north for a short holiday but the Earl of Huntly rebelled against her. Mary displayed surprising determination and bravery in a comely twenty-year-old. Huntly was quickly defeated at Corrichie, near Aberdeen, and was killed in the fight. She gave his estates to James Stuart and created him Earl of Moray.

Her marriage, in 1565, to her odious cousin, Lord Darnley, was an unmitigated disaster. He was overbearing, conceited and jealous to the point of paranoia, so much so, that he plotted the heinous murder of his wife's talented secretary, Rizzio. This took place at Holyrood and but for the quick thinking of the Countess of Argyll, Mary, six months pregnant, would probably have been a victim. Darnley had been promised kingship and was second in line, after Mary, to the throne of England. Mary had refused him the kingdom of Scotland. He was desperate for power.

The Protestant Lords had been so disgusted with Mary's choice of husband that the Earl of Moray and Châtelherault rebelled. Mary personally led her troops to suppress the rebels and Moray fled to England. After the murder of Rizzio she split her enemies by offering terms to Moray and becoming reconciled with Darnley. She gave birth to Prince James on 19th June 1566 in Edinburgh Castle and his Catholic baptism aggravated the Protestants. By the end of the year it was clear that Mary and Darnley were estranged and she was attracted by the dashing Earl of Bothwell.

The mystery of Darnley's death in February 1567 centred around the question: how much did she know? There was talk of divorce, she seems certain to have been aware of schemes for his elimination, she restored the Archbishop of St Andrews - perhaps to facilitate the divorce of Bothwell from his recently wedded wife, she pardoned Rizzio's murderers who were known to be seeking revenge on Darnley for his abandonment of them. On the other hand she was pregnant again and another reconciliation with Darnley was essential. He was ill and she brought him back from Glasgow to nurse him at Kirk 'o Field. She visited him almost daily and often spent the night in a ground floor room beneath his. On the night of his murder she was expected there. Did the murderers hope to eliminate Mary too? Or, did Darnley himself hope to end Mary's life so that his future claim to the throne would appeal to the Pope; recently, his devotions had been more than usual.

These and many other questions remain unanswered, but it is a fact that someone had placed a huge amount of gunpowder under Kirk o'

Field. It demolished the building. The mystery deepens. Darnley did not die in the blast; he had been smothered. Bothwell was blamed and put on trial. It was a sham: in his absence he was found guiltless.

Bothwell now divorced his wife, Jean Gordon, sister of the late Earl of Huntly. He abducted Mary in April 1567; she was thought to have been a willing victim. He took her to his castle at Dunbar where he supposedly ravaged her. She wrote: "he took my body and made it his own although my heart was not yet won." Mary now created him Duke of Orkney and on 15th May they were married by Adam Bothwell, Bishop of Orkney and Commendator of Holyrood.

There was public outrage over her blatant disregard of her husband's death and her suspected compliance with Bothwell but she had come perilously close to a mental breakdown and increasingly she depended on Bothwell for support in ruling her divided country.

The Confederate Lords confronted the couple at Carberry. Bothwell fled the country and Mary was taken to Edinburgh to be jeered to shouts of, "burn the whore."

An old and trusted friend who, in better times, had happily given over his castle at Craigmillar to her to use as a retreat, observed her piteous state and offered her refuge in his house which was situated in the centre of the present courtyard of the City Chambers in the High Street (the plaque above commemorates this). This was Sir Simon Preston, the Lord Provost. Next day she was taken to Holyrood and then to Lochleven Castle where she was forced to abdicate in favour of her one year-old son. In the trauma of these events she miscarried twins.

This deposition of a monarch was unheard of in the history of Scotland; it was all the more strange as only a minority were in favour of it. At the coronation of her son only five earls and eight lords were present. The strength of her cause became evident after her escape from Loch Leven when nine earls, nine bishops, twelve commendators and eighteen lords came to her side and with an army of 6000 she faced Regent Moray on 13th May 1568 at Langside. She was defeated by a superior general and fled to England.

Elizabeth I had her placed in various prisons for the next twenty years. As one plot followed another she was a perpetual aggravation to Elizabeth and when the Spanish plot to free Mary was discovered on the arrest of a Spanish agent she was moved to a safer prison at Chartley. There her correspondence was intercepted and the arrest of her priest and a page boy confirmed a plot to assassinate Queen Elizabeth. George Buchanan, tutor to James VI, had tampered with the 'Casket Letters' having stolen twelve of Mary's sonnets and other papers. In 1571 he cleverly selected parts of them and merged them with other incriminating material. This was presented as evidence of her complicity with Bothwell to murder her husband. The evidence against her (discredited by modern historians) seemed conclusive and she was found guilty by a special commission in September 1586. Elizabeth could not bring herself to sign the death warrant until 1st February 1587. One week later she was beheaded at Fotheringay Castle. She died in prayer and with the dignity of a martyr.

Mary King's Close

Mary King's Close (formerly Alexander King's Close and Touris Close) is thought to be named after the daughter of Alexander King, owner of the property and Advocate to Mary Queen of Scots. The Close was sealed off during the plague of Edinburgh in 1645. Many of its inhabitants had died and the Close was considered to be cursed. The refuse from the windows of the fourteen storeys above accumulated on the pathways below. The stench was unbearable; it was a haven for vermin and the spread of disease was inevitable but the cause, obvious today, was unknown then.

In 1685 there was an acute problem of overcrowding in the High Street and the City Council agreed to appoint a 'Foul Clenger' to clear out the corpses and to clean out the refuse. Some of the refugees from the Close were rehoused in Advocate's Close; among them was the remarkable engraver, Andrew Bell, who engraved the banknotes of the Royal Bank of Scotland as well as the illustrations for the first edition of the *Encyclopaedia Britannica.*

The flats of Mary King's Close were offered for rent but only one man and his wife, Mr and Mrs Thomas Coltheart, took up residence. Their maid fled in fear of her life when she claimed to have heard mysterious noises and to have seen a ghost.

The Colthearts were made of stern stuff. They remained in spite of the appearance of several ghostly apparitions. On one occasion, whilst in bed and reading their Bibles a bearded head stared at them. During the weeks that followed they reported other phantoms such as the head of a child, a human arm and several domestic animals. On the day of Thomas Coltheart's death his ghost appeared to a friend in Penicuik who rushed in to Edinburgh and was shocked to find that his friend was indeed dead.

Much of the Close is still intact and in its original state. Shops and houses can be inspected but some ghostly figures have been experienced over the years in this 'Street of Sorrows.'

Its walls were so thick and well constructed they formed the foundations for building the Royal Exchange now City Chambers above. During World War II rooms in Mary King's Close were opened up for the safe storage of Council records in case of bombing. Today tours of the Close are organised and there have been reports of 'cold spots'. One visitor reported the appearance of a poorly dressed young girl accompanied by a dog. Many visitors have complained that whilst underground their cameras have inexplicably failed to operate.

19. Old Fishmarket Close - George Heriot

Old Fishmarket Close (formerly Gourlay's Close, Humph's Close and Swift's Close) was named from an 18th century fishmarket and was known locally as 'stinking ravine'. Before its fishmarket days the close was the residence of the King's Jeweller, George Heriot in the year 1590 (his landlord was his brother-in-law, Simon Marjoribanks).

George Heriot became exceedingly rich during the reign of James VI of Scotland (I of England) to whom he was appointed for life as the King's Jeweller. Heriot's house was a short walk to his booth (or shop) - one of the Luckenbooths around St Giles where he started his business as a goldsmith in 1586.

He married Christian, daughter of Simon Marjoribanks senior, on 14th January 1586 and, for a wedding present his father, George Heriot senior (1540-1610), who was one of the Heriots of Trabroun in East Lothian, set him up in business with the "necessaries to ane buith" plus 1500 merks (£80, about £80,000 today). His seven by seven foot square booth was fully equipped with bellows, crucibles and tools for the art of goldsmithing.

His father was a prosperous goldsmith and had given his eldest son, from an early age, a thorough training in the art of making exquisite jewellery. Young George was an apt pupil and it was without hesitation that his father had given him this generous gift of the shop in the busiest part of town. His artistry was soon in demand and he was admitted a member of the Incorporation of Edinburgh Goldsmiths on 28th May 1588.

Born on 15th June 1563, George Heriot was one of that fortunate and rare breed of men who combined skilful excellence, business acumen and a pleasing, generous personality. His jewellery and his polite eloquence caught the eye and the ear of James VI and his Queen, Anne of Denmark. She had very expensive taste and George Heriot received many orders from her and many more through her Royal patronage. She delighted in his workmanship; the Royal jewels were the envy of the court.

In July 1597 Heriot was appointed Goldsmith for life to Queen Anne and such was the trust placed upon him (he had become exceedingly useful to James VI) that his appointment as Jeweller to the King was announced from the Mercat Cross in April 1601. His future was assured; 'Jinglin Geordie' had arrived (this nick-name was given to him by Sir Walter Scott in his *Fortunes of Nigel*.)

In the ten years before the Union of the Crowns in 1603, it was estimated that Queen Anne bought £50,000 worth of jewellery (about £50 million today). George Heriot became very rich, so rich that he became the money-lender who virtually financed the Court. He lent money to the King and Queen who allowed him to pawn their jewellery deposited as security. On one occasion he held the title deeds of the Chapel Royal of Stirling as collateral security on loans to the King and Queen. Inevitably, he was caught up in many of King James's intrigues and he performed many confidential services for his monarch. He was discreet and his style was not in the least demanding. Such was the King's confidence in Heriot as a trusted friend, he allotted him an apartment at Holyrood and appointed him to membership of a syndicate commissioned to issue a new Scottish currency.

In his *Traditions of Edinburgh*, Chambers relates a wonderful story of Heriot's visit to the Royal apartments at Holyrood where he found the king sitting by a pleasant fire of sweet smelling wood. Heriot remarked upon it and suggested to His Majesty that he could show him an even more pleasing fire at his shop. The King promised to visit him and, on his arrival at Heriot's tiny shop in the High Street, he found an ordinary fire. "Is this then your fire?" asked the king. "Wait a little till I get my fuel." Heriot produced a bond for £2000 (about £2 million today) from his desk which was part of the King's debt. He placed it upon the fire and asked, "Now, whether is your Majesty's fire or mine most expensive?" The king conceded with a gracious grin.

When James VI left Edinburgh in the spring of 1603, succeeding Elizabeth I to become James I of England, Heriot followed him to London shortly afterwards. He set up home and business at Cornhill near the New Exchange on the site of what was to become the Adelphi Theatre. Within a month of his arrival at Court he was one of three men to be appointed Jewellers to the King. For the next five years he amassed a great fortune. He had become a banker as well as a goldsmith.

Heriot's wife died in 1608 and about a year later he returned to Scotland to marry Alison, the eldest daughter of James Primrose, Clerk to the Privy Council in Scotland (his grandson became 1st Earl of Rosebery). The happy couple returned to London and Heriot found himself so busy he was unable to keep pace with the demand for his services. He explained his difficulty to the King who immediately ordered an official notice to all local authorities directing them to assist 'His Majesty's Jeweller' in 'taking up of such workmen as he shall necessarily use for the furthering of the service.'

Heriot was heartbroken when his wife died in 1613. He was now fifty years of age and such was his grief, he never remarried, preferring to live alone and absorb himself in work. Realising that his vast fortune would be inherited solely by his niece, who lived in Genoa, Italy, he decided to make his intentions known. Accordingly he executed a 'disposition and assignation' dated 3rd September 1613, leaving the bulk of his wealth for 'the education of children of decayed burgesses and freemen of Edinburgh.' In addition he made provision for his two illegitimate daughters and other relatives.

About this time, Queen Anne owed George Heriot £18,000 and in 1620 he was granted three years imposition on sugar as compensation for his financial assistance to the Royal family. In one of her letters to Heriot, Queen Anne asked him, "to send me two hundrethe pundis vithe all expidition" for a visit to her son in Stirling.

George Heriot died on 12 February 1624 and was buried in London at St Martin's in the Fields. In his last will and testament, dated 10th December 1623-4, he left most of his huge fortune "for and towards the founding and erecting of an Hospital within the said Towne of Edonburgh in perpetuitie ..... to bee ymployed for the maintetenance reliefe bringing upp and educacon of so manie poore fatherlesse boyes freemens sonnes of that towne of Edonburgh." The sum of £23,625 was available to build the charity school, George Heriot's School in Laurieston Place, a Scots Renaissance design. The architect is unknown but the style bears a strong resemblance to the work of Inigo Jones (1573-1652). The first builder was the King's Master Mason, William Wallace who died in 1631. His assistants, William Ayton and John Watt, continued the work until 1639 when money became scarce. Cromwell requisitioned the building as a hospital after the Battle of Dunbar in 1650 until 1658. The first thirty boys took up residence in 1659. Additional money from his estate was invested in land, the feu income from which paid for an extension to the Watt Mechanics Institute which became the Heriot-Watt College in Chambers Street, now Heriot-Watt University at Riccarton.

20. Anchor Close -
Lord Provost George Drummond

Anchor Close (formerly Fordyce Close, Foular's Close and Fuller's Close) dates back to 1521 being named from the Anchor Tavern which was frequented by the Lord High Commissioner. The Close was the venue for the Crochallan Fencibles, one of several famous Edinburgh clubs, to which Scotland's national bard, Robert Burns, was introduced, in 1787, by his printer, William Smellie. He printed the first edition of the *Encyclopaedia Britannica* in three volumes in this Close.

In Anchor Close stood the town house of Lord Provost **George Drummond**. If any man deserves a special place in the hearts of the citizens of Edinburgh it is this man. He probably achieved more than any other Lord Provost before or since in the development of Edinburgh during the 18th century. Despite extreme oscillations in his wealth he became Lord Provost six times and it is difficult to place his achievements in order of merit. Putting the welfare of the people first, he almost single-handedly raised the money to build the Royal Infirmary of Edinburgh, he was instrumental in the creation of the medical faculty of the University and it was his dream to see the extension of Edinburgh - the New Town - to alleviate the disease and over-crowding of the Old Town.

Born at Newton Castle, Blairgowrie on 27th June 1687, his father, John Drummond, was factor of the Drummond of Blair estates and young George often accompanied him on business trips to Edinburgh. He was interested in his father's work and soon displayed talents in accountancy and the economics of business. His father eventually set up business in Edinburgh and became a burgess. George attended the High School from 1699 to 1704.

He was twenty years old when the Union of the Scottish and English Parliaments (1707) took place. He was very much aware of the bitter arguments for and against it and was soon in the thick of Edinburgh politics. He was a strong supporter of the Union and openly displayed his animosity towards the Jacobites. Edinburgh had lost much of its status and national independence. The Church of Scotland felt threatened with a return to Episcopacy and had preached against it, but Drummond, a passionate Presbyterian, fought for an independent Church of Scotland.

Still in his teens he helped to calculate the 'national accounts' and in so doing he gained the respect of Sir John Clerk of Penicuik, a Commissioner who had been appointed to negotiate the Union. The so-called 'Equivalent' was agreed at £400,000 which was eventually paid to those who had lost money in the disastrous Darien Expedition. The opponents of the Union regarded this as nothing more than a bribe. Drummond's work was rewarded with his appointment as Accountant General of the Board of Excise with a salary of £80 per year.

The political storm and civil unrest which persisted after the Union gave the Jacobites the opportunity for their first rising in 1715. In spite of some public opinion against him, George Drummond raised a private army and joined the Duke of Argyll at Sherrifmuir to defeat the Earl of Mar. Drummond, elated by the victory, brought news of it back to Edinburgh. This was good news to the Whig establishment and Drummond was rewarded with a high and lucrative appointment as a Commissioner of Customs, confirming his efficiency as Accountant General.

He was elected to the Town Council on 25th September 1717 and two weeks later he was given the title 'Old Treasurer'. Within two months he was made 'Bailie of Butter and Cheese' and appointed to membership of several committees. When he was elected Treasurer some members of the Council felt that Drummond was becoming too powerful but their opposition collapsed. In 1725 he was elected Lord Provost for the first time. One of his first acts was to establish a fund to build a hospital for the sick poor. It reached £2000 by the end of his term of office. His last duty as Provost was to proclaim George II's succession to the throne - 14th June 1727.

The University of Edinburgh owes its Faculty of Medicine to Drummond. The University's Professor of Anatomy, Alexander Munro, had petitioned for a medical school and a public hospital and Drummond, captivated by the Professor's enthusiasm, convinced the Town Council to create four additional Professorships of Medicine.

Drummond had a clear vision of Edinburgh as the leading centre of excellence in medical science. By December 1728 Drummond, with the able assistance of his Quaker sister May, had raised money sufficient for its interest to finance the rent of a house in Robertson's Close at the foot of the Canongate. The first patients were treated there in August 1729. Such was its success that the Managers (of which Drummond was one) decided to apply for a Royal Charter. The title 'Royal Infirmary of Edinburgh' was granted in 1736.

Having completed the negotiations for the amalgamation of the Infirmary and the Surgeons' Hospital, Drummond now set about the purchase of land for a new building. The site was purchased from the Governors of George Watson's Hospital and the present buildings in Laurieston Place were erected to a design of William Adam. Building started in 1738, but funds would allow only the completion of the eastern section and Drummond was invited to lay its foundation stone. More money was needed to complete the building and Drummond's energetic fund-raising enabled the start of the western section in 1740 which was completed eight years later.

By now Drummond had married three times. His first wife, whom he married aged twenty, was Mary Campbell and they had five children, but three of them died in infancy. She died in 1715 and three years later he married Catherine Campbell who bore him nine children, but one died. She died in 1727 and for the next eleven years he brought up his large family with the help of his sister. He was a strict father and insisted on daily worship but he worried about the lack of maternal influence. About this time he had lost a large sum in a business venture and his financial affairs threatened ruin. In 1739 he married a rich widow, Hannah Parsons, and the Drummond family moved from Liberton to the 16th century Colinton Castle (now part of Merchiston Castle School).

As Commissioner for the Customs and Lord Provost, Drummond's connections were undoubtedly beneficial to the world of banking and he became one of the first directors of the Royal Bank of Scotland which had received its charter in 1727. When hereditary jurisdictions were abolished he obtained compensation for the bank amounting to £152,000 (over £24 million today). Drummond's report was the cause of the bank's competitor, (The Bank of Scotland) in having its notes refused by the Lords of the Treasury. As a representative on the Convention of Royal Burghs he was involved with the allotment of Burghal Taxation. He became President of the Convention on each occasion he was Lord Provost.

To Drummond the 1745 Rising was a threat to the Church of Scotland as well as a severe impediment to his plans for the City. He hated Jacobites and equally the Jacobites detested him. Drummond was a Hanoverian first and last and it was unthinkable to have a Stuart on the throne again. His patronage included the powerful 2nd Duke of Argyll and his brother Lord Islay (who succeeded him as the 3rd Duke in 1743) and it was through Drummond that his tentacles reached into the Convention of Royal Burghs, the Town Council, the General Assembly and many other committees.

Drummond had neglected his job as Commissioner and his financial state was again precarious. His sons, John, George and Alexander had got themselves into debt and absorbed most of his wife's money. In 1742 his wife died and he lost himself in work. He was elected Lord Provost again in 1746 and he promptly offered the Duke of Cumberland ('the butcher' of Culloden) the Freedom of the City. The defeated Highlanders never forgave him for that.

Drummond was acutely aware that the overcrowding and lack of proper sanitation in the City was the cause of disease and death. Edinburgh was stifled, an obnoxious smell pervaded the place, trade was affected; the trades and professions lived almost side by side. There was no space for expansion and Drummond was determined to provide handsome houses for the gentry.

The idea of extending the City to the north was not new, the Duke of York, the Earl of Mar and Lord Minto had, in their time, suggested spanning the chasms to the north and south. The Convention of Royal Burghs gave historical, geographical and economic reasons for the creation of the 'New Town' in a remarkable document of 1752; its author was probably Lord Minto, but it was the energetic Drummond who provided the formula for progress - money. Again he was successful. His subscription attracted men of property. He laid the foundation stone of the new Royal Exchange (now the City Chambers) to be followed in 1763 by his laying the foundation stone of the first North Bridge - at last, this was the access to his dream shortly to become a reality in spite of the fact that he had been refused an extension to the City's Royalty. The bridge was opened to traffic in 1772 but not without a fatal setback three years before; the south side had collapsed killing five people.

The Town Council now advertised a competition for the design of the New Town. A young and relatively unknown architect won. His name was James Craig. He was given the Freedom of the City and a gold medal. Drummond was delighted, at last his dream would come to fruition, but he had been ill for some months and only two months after the announcement he died on 4th December 1766. He never saw his beloved New Town but the credit was his.

Drummond may have had his critics, even enemies, but if the attendance at his funeral was a reflection of the high esteem and great respect in which he was held, this was proof of it. There were Town Councillors, Magistrates, Professors, Lords of Session, Commissioners of Customs and Excise and the streets were lined with thousands of mourning admirers. He was buried at the Canongate Churchyard in the Royal Mile.

21. Covenant Close -
Robert Macqueen, Lord Braxfield

Covenant Close, almost midway between St Giles Church and the **Tron Church**, takes its name from the fact that a copy of the 'National Covenant' of 1638 lay in a room in this Close and was signed here by nobles and as many people as possible. It included the "Negative Confession" against Catholicism and against Charles I's insistence on the Liturgy. The original Covenant had been drawn up at Greyfriars Church and signed by nobles and thousands of others who became the Covenanters during the Bishops' Wars (1639-41).

This Close was the residence of a judge who was characterised as the 'Weir of Hermiston' by Robert Louis Stevenson - **Robert Macqueen, Lord Braxfield**, who has been described as Scotland's 'hanging judge' during a time of repression of reformers (of Parliament) and any who were sympathetic to the cause of the French Revolution of 1789.

This Scottish judge has his place in history primarily because of his harsh tongue and his stiff sentences during the 'reign of terror' in the Pitt-Dundas era. There were understandable fears of riot and revolution in 1789 when the French peasants had revolted and in Scotland there was growing sympathy for their cause. £1400 was raised in Glasgow for the French cause and the effigy of Henry Dundas was burned in Edinburgh; there was an atmosphere of reform.

Lord Braxfield and Henry Dundas were friends of long standing It was not therefore surprising that Braxfield should come to his aid in the suppression of the *Friends of the People* and any who supported reform, and in this aim he used the courts to great effect. Braxfield was heard to say, "Bring me the prisoners, and I will find you the law."

He was, to use the words of Lord Cockburn in his *Memorials*: 'strong built and dark, with rough eyebrows, powerful eyes, threatening lips, and a low growling voice, he was like a formidable blacksmith.' 5

Robert Macqueen, Lord Braxfield, the eldest son of John Macqueen of Braxfield in Lanarkshire, was born on 4th May 1722. His father was a lawyer and his grandfather was gardener to the Earl of Selkirk. Young Robert was educated at Lanark Grammar School and sent to Edinburgh University to study Civil Law 'where his honesty and good nature made him a general favourite.'

Robert Macqueen met Henry Dundas (later 1st Viscount Melville) quite by chance at Bonnytown. Dundas was immediately taken with Macqueen's forthright honesty; their friendship grew and Dundas advised him to come to Edinburgh to take up the practice of law rather than become a lawyer in the anonymity of the countryside. Advice from Dundas was not to be ignored; this was an invitation to succeed. Macqueen grasped the opportunity and found that his rough country manners and speech lent emphasis to his unexpected intelligence and competence. He was apprenticed to a writer to the signet and was admitted to the bar on 14th February 1744.

After the Rising of 1745 and the defeat of Prince Charles Edward at Culloden in 1746, the Jacobite lords lost their titles and estates. Dundas appointed Macqueen as one of his deputes and, as counsel for the crown, he settled many feudal questions which arose out of the forfeitures of 1745. He became the foremost feudal lawyer in the country; his practice grew with his reputation and became the largest in Scotland.

In 1776 he was elevated as an ordinary lord of session, assuming the title, Lord Braxfield, a name which was to become feared and reviled during the 'reign of terror' at the start of the French Revolution in 1789. He was appointed a Lord of the Justiciary on 1st March 1780 and was promoted Lord-Justice Clerk on 15th January 1788. His competent judgements were beyond question. His strength lay in his clarity but, conscious of his superior position, he bullied those who dared to argue, especially those who failed to match his coarseness.

An example of his autocracy took place at Perth: in the middle of a trial, the accused, who was clearly guilty, stopped Braxfield in his giving judgement and threw a loaf of bread at him. It just missed his lordship, and without any further inquiry Braxfield ordered his release. But Braxfield's behaviour during the sedition trials of 1793/4 condemned him as a criminal judge. He presided over the case against those who were to be commemorated in the Martyrs' Monument, the obelisk at the Old Calton Burying Ground, off Waterloo Place. The blatantly obvious injustice during the trial of Thomas Muir, Thomas Fyshe

Palmer, William Skirving, Maurice Margarot and Joseph Gerrald became an international outrage. Muir, a young advocate, defended himself, proving his innocence beyond doubt, Margarot in his speech vilified Braxfield as contemptible. Gerrald, in explanation of their aims for nothing more than reform, pointed out: "that Christianity was an innovation and that all great men had been reformers, even our Saviour himself." Braxfield leaned over the bench and, with an evil grin, he said,

"Muckle he made o' that, he was hanget!"

They were all given stiff sentences of transportation to Botany Bay. Afterwards a jury member was heard to say,

"we were all mad that day."

Lord Cockburn in *Memorials of His Time*, summed him up with: 'It is impossible to condemn Braxfield's conduct as a criminal judge too gravely, or too severely. It was a disgrace to the age.' It has to be borne in mind that Lord Cockburn (1779-1854) never met Braxfield and Cockburn's strong Whig views were diametrically opposed to those of Braxfield.

These trials were criticised in Parliament and abroad and Dundas, in a letter to Braxfield, informed him of representations he had received; the legality of the sentences had been questioned but Braxfield replied simply that the court considered the sentences legal and urged that the Royal mercy should not be extended to the condemned men. This was the last trial over which he presided; in effect he was sacked.

Robert Macqueen, Lord Braxfield, died at his home in George Square on 30th May 1799, aged seventy-seven. He was buried at Lanark.

22. North Foulis Close -
James Gillespie's Plaque

This Close (formerly Foulis Close, Fowler's Close and Fowlis Close) takes its name from the Foulis family of Colinton. They were Lords of Colinton, Senators of the College of Justice - James in 1532 and John in 1541. Alexander Foulis was knighted in 1634 and his son, Sir James, was taken prisoner by Cromwell's army. After the Restoration he was raised to the Bench as Lord Colinton. His son, also a judge, was a member of the last Scottish Parliament in 1707 and was firmly against the Union. The Close however, is thought to take its name from a less illustrious member of the family, one John Foulis, an apothecary who owned the property.

The wall-plaque at No.231 High Street, commemorating **James Gillespie**, marks the site of his brother's snuff shop at Geddes Close and North Foulis Close. John Gillespie's shop, at street level, sold the produce from his brother's snuff mill at Colinton.

Above the shop was the abode of the famed caricaturist, John Kay(1742-1826), whose fearless satirical caricatures and sketches delighted some but irked others - his subjects included the Edinburgh Town Guard, passers-by and events of his day. His sketches, of which there were over 900, give a unique record of 19th century Edinburgh.

James Gillespie was born in 1726 at Roslin where his parents brought him up in strict observance of the Solemn League and Covenant for Reformation (1643). As young men James and John left the countryside of Roslin to set up as tobacconists in Edinburgh. They were a pair of 'canny Scots' who between them had a very profitable business arrangement. In 1759 they purchased the snuff mills in Colinton and James managed the manufacturing side of the business while John looked after the retailing in his shop in the High Street. They had cut out the middle-man. They never married, they lived frugally and they worked conscientiously and therefore most profitably.

James amassed a tidy fortune which enabled him to acquire the estate of Spylaw by 1768 and within five years he had purchased Bonaly and Fernielaw. But still money flowed into his coffers. In 1776 he lent £500 (about £65,000 today) on security of property in Leith and a few years later he advanced £1000 (about £130,000 today) on a bond over the Woodhall estate. He built Spylaw House in 1773 on the site of the original 1650 house.

He rarely travelled into Edinburgh and lived alone except for his servants and, to obtain news of the town, he paid regular social visits to his workers in their cottages in Spylaw Street. He was a genial soul, self-effacing, not a deep thinker but he was good to his workers and often forgot (on purpose) to collect their rents. He loved to hear the latest gossip, for example he would hear of Allan Ramsay, the poet, who had opened his theatre and had to close it again when Edinburgh's guardians of public morality, the magistrates, strongly disapproved. There was, of course, the siege by Prince Charles Edward Stewart in 1745, this was a subject for great debate. Lord Provost George Drummond was pressing to extend the City and to build a New Town but most exciting of all was the series of mysteriously cunning burglaries - this was food for much speculation. There was a great stir to find that the culprit was a respected and high-living deacon - one William Brodie. These events and many more were given an airing.

James Gillespie permitted himself one rather ostentatious luxury; he bought a coach but rarely used it. It was bright yellow and adorned with his coat-of-arms. Lord Erskine, the witty Lord Advocate, facetiously suggested a motto for it:

'Wha wad hae thocht it,
That noses could hae bocht it!'

The 'laird of Colinton' became very rich indeed, not only from making snuff in his factory at Spylaw Park but from his shrewd investments in the tobacco industry of America during the War of Independence.

His brother died in 1795 and, for company, James befriended a young man who was helpful to him in his later years. He intended to make him his heir but during an argument he had been offended and he altered his Will in 1796, bequeathing his estates plus £2000 to build a hospital 'for the maintenance of old men and women.' A further £2,700 was bequeathed to found a school for children of the poor in his name, James Gillespie's School - but for the insolence of a young man this school might never have existed. The Governors of the hospital leased the lands of Bonaly to the Town Council for a water supply but in 1869 they dispensed with the hospital and gave pensions to 167 female and 42 male pensioners. The benefits to the school were increased and by 1887 the enrolment was 1450 children - today it is 1180

James Gillespie died on 8th April 1797 and was buried beside his brother in Colinton Churchyard where a pedimented mausoleum stands over their graves. James had obtained permission to have it built three years before his death. Inside the Church there is a mural monument to their memory.

23. No. 219 High Street -
The Hospice, Dr Elsie Inglis

At No. 219 High Street there was 'The Hospice', a surgery and gynaecological centre which was opened in 1895 by **Dr Elsie Maud Inglis** at a time of scarce facilities for poor women and their babies and for training midwives.

The story of Elsie Inglis is an inspiring one of dedicated and selfless heroism. That she qualified as a doctor was in itself a feat of great determination and extremely hard work. Women were still discouraged from entering this male dominated profession. Only a few years before, students of the Faculty of Medicine at Edinburgh had rioted to prevent women from attending classes at Surgeons' Hall.

Elsie's tutor, Dr Sophia Jex-Blake, was the first woman doctor in Scotland and she had had to go to Berne in Switzerland to qualify. It was not until 1916 that the School of Medicine of the University of Edinburgh eventually allowed women to enrol.

Elsie Inglis was born on 16th August 1864 in India where her father, John Forbes Inglis, was a senior administrator in the Indian Civil Service. She was the seventh of a family of nine children and when her father retired, in 1876, he took his family to Tasmania where Elsie received two years of her early education.

On their return home they settled at No.10 Bruntsfield Place and Elsie, with her sister Eva, was sent to the Young Ladies' Institution at No. 23 Charlotte Square. Her father had chosen this school for its emphasis on academic excellence rather than the usual emphasis on social graces. After further schooling in France, Elsie returned to Edinburgh about the same time as Dr Sophia Jex-Blake founded the Edinburgh School of Medicine for Women at High School Yards - the first in Scotland (the Act of Parliament which removed all barriers against women entering medicine had been passed in 1873).

With her father's strong encouragement Elsie Inglis decided upon a medical career, but tragedy struck the family: her mother, Harriet (nee Thompson) died suddenly in 1885 and Elsie took over the running of the household for the next five years.

Dr Jex-Blake, a formidable lady, ran a highly disciplined regime, no doubt with good reason; she knew that women would not have an easy passage in their chosen career. Elsie Inglis, on the other hand, was mild-mannered and of a sympathetic nature; she was extremely upset when two sisters were sacked for a seemingly trivial reason. But Elsie Inglis was not to be put off her chosen profession; in 1887, with the two sisters, she started a rival medical college for women at No.30 Chambers Street. She studied clinical medicine at the Universities of Glasgow and Edinburgh where she gained the degrees: Bachelor of Medicine M.B. and Master of Surgery C.M.

In London she lectured in gynaecology and was responsible for the women's hall of residence which she opened in 1898. She became the first resident surgeon of the New Hospital for Women and worked with another great pioneer, Dr Elizabeth Garrett Anderson (1836-1917), the first woman to qualify as a doctor in Britain, after whom a London hospital was named.

After a short spell practising midwifery in Dublin she returned to Edinburgh. Her father had taken ill and his death in 1894 was a dreadful blow to her; she loved her father dearly and respected him greatly. Towards the end of her own life she was heard to say, "If I have been able to do anything, I owe it all to my father."

She set up in practice with Dr Jessie McGregor at No.9 Atholl Place. Her next address in Edinburgh was No.8 Walker Street where she took in many convalescent patients without charge, so inadequate were the facilities for the poor.

Her deep concern for the plight of the poor led her to make an appeal for funds to open a Nursing Home at No 11 George Square. This was extended to 'The Hospice' in the High Street and was staffed entirely by women. This gynaecology unit was also a teaching hospice which trained midwives and nurses. In addition to her work in the High Street she practised at the dispensary in Morrison Street where she was held in great respect and admiration by the local community.

She was one of three surgeons of Bruntsfield Hospital, then called the Edinburgh Hospital and Dispensary for Women and Sick Children, (founded by Dr Jex-Blake) and she supported its amalgamation with her Hospice in the High Street in 1910. She was responsible for the Women's Residence - Muir Hall in George Square - for women medical students.

At the outbreak of war in 1914 Dr Elsie Inglis offered her services, with those of the Scottish Women's Hospitals, to the War Office in London. She was told bluntly, "to go home and sit still!" However, the Red Cross and the French Army readily accepted her offer of much needed help and the first mobile unit arrived in France in November 1914.

Already there were over 50,000 British casualties at the Marne, a defensive action to stop the German 'race to the sea.' Medical facilities were almost non-existent. She was confronted with an impossible situation of human carnage. This was a baptism of fire and her team worked to exhaustion to save life and to give relief and comfort to thousands of dying men.

In 1915 Dr Inglis replaced Dr Eleanor Soltau in Serbia who had contracted diphtheria. Conditions on the Serbian front were horrific. She worked night and day at the operating table helping Serbian doctors and taking over when they dropped from exhaustion. Her energy and stamina were born of outrage at such awful waste of young lives. Young men, many in their teens, were dying from amputations, frostbite, typhus and typhoid fever. Most of the injured had lain untended for weeks on end. Three members of her team died of typhoid.

The Germans, Austrians and Bulgarians invaded again and her Scottish Women's Hospital was forced to evacuate south to Krusevac.

She established an unequalled reputation for dedicated hard work and such was her influence she was permitted to set up three military hospitals. She refused to leave her patients when the battle line overran her and she was captured by the Austro-Hungarian Army. After repatriation she refused to give up; she rejoined the Serbs to be given a warm welcome back.

Her 300-bed hospital was set up near the battle front. Scottish women, oblivious of the danger to their lives, collected the wounded from the firing line and transported them back to the operating table of Dr Elsie Inglis; the flow was endless.

The strain of months of overwork affected her health and she was advised to leave again and again. Eventually the Serb fighting came to an end and only then did she accept repatriation. She was awarded the Order of the White Eagle. This was the highest honour awarded by the Yugoslav government and never before awarded to a woman. She was decorated by the French for valour and awarded the St George Medal for bravery by the Russians. Her voluntary corps had to be withdrawn after the Russian Revolution in 1917.

She returned home by ship arriving at Newcastle. She was completely worn out and had hoped, after rest, to return home to Edinburgh. But it was not to be, she was so weak that she died within a few weeks of her arrival at Newcastle, on 26th November 1917. She was fifty-three years of age. Her body was brought back to Edinburgh to be buried with full military honours at Dean Cemetery. Her coffin was draped with the flags of the allies and her funeral service at St Giles was attended by members of the Royal families of Britain and Serbia.

A stone tablet at the north choir aisle of St Giles Church commemorates this heroine of the Great War of 1914-18. The tablet is inscribed:

> *To the beloved and honoured memory of ELSIE MAUD INGLIS surgeon, philanthropist, founder in 1914 of the Scottish Women's Hospitals for service with the allies in France, Serbia and Russia. Born 1864, died on active service 1917. Mors Janva Vitae.*

Another commemoration which would have pleased her greatly was the 'Elsie Inglis Memorial Hospital' in Spring Gardens which was built from the Elsie Inglis Memorial Fund of 1918 but it was closed in October 1992.

24. Cockburn Street

Cockburn Street runs from the High Street in a curve downhill to Market Street. It was designed by Peddie and Kinnear and built between 1859 and 1864 to provide access to the railway. The Railway Station Access Company bought the High Street Closes in the vicinity and partly demolished them to cut the new street through to Market Street.

Cockburn Street is named after **Henry Thomas Cockburn** (1779-1854), the famous Scottish Whig Judge, who is probably known today from the work of the Cockburn Society which bears his name and is dedicated to the preservation and restoration of old buildings in Edinburgh.

Cockburn's *Memorials of His Time* first published in 1856 is a remarkable insight of the lives and times in Edinburgh. It was written between 1821 and 1830 but covers a much wider period. Its opening words are: *I was born on 26th October 1779. This event took place, I suspect, in one of the many flats of the lofty range of dwelling-houses which then formed the east side of Parliament Square.*

His father was a baron of the Exchequer and of his mother he wrote: *My mother was the best woman I have ever known. If I were to survive her for a thousand years, I should still have a deep and grateful recollection of her kindness, her piety, her devotion to her family, and her earnest, gentle, and Christian anxiety for their happiness in this life and in the life to come.*

Henry Cockburn was educated at the High School, then situated at the foot of Infirmary Street, in 1787, and at the University of Edinburgh in 1793 where he studied law to become an advocate at the age of twenty-one. Of the High School he wrote, *six hours a day were spent on Latin....Out of the whole four years of my attendance there were probably not ten days in which I was not flogged, at least once. Yet I never entered the class, nor left it, without feeling perfectly qualified, both in ability and preparation, for its whole business.*

As a boy he was aware of the political trials in which Thomas Muir, the young advocate, was sentenced to fourteen years transportation for sedition and a year later, in 1794, the hanging of Robert Watt in another political trial; this was the era of the infamous Lord Braxfield (ref. 21. Covenanters Close), Scotland's 'hanging judge' who, with Henry Dundas (ref. 28. Bishops Close), suppressed the reformers accused of sedition. Braxfield suffered Cockburn's description of him in his *'Memorials*:

But the giant of the Bench was Braxfield. His very name makes people start yet. Strong built and dark; with rough eyebrows, powerful eyes, threatening lips and a growling voice, he was like a formidable blacksmith. [5]

As a student Cockburn watched the funeral procession of Lord President Dundas (1787) and the laying of the foundation stone of the University by Lord Napier of Merchiston (1789). As a member of the Speculative Society (Edinburgh abounded with clubs formed by the *literati* in those years of the 'Scottish Enlightenment'), his associates included Walter Scott, Francis Jeffrey, Francis Horner, Henry Brougham and many other literary, philosophical, scientific and political friends.

Cockburn was called to the Bar in 1800 and was clearly destined for greatness; he was appointed Advocate Depute in 1807 by his uncle, Lord Melville, but he was dismissed four years later because of his outspoken sympathies with the Radicals, although he was a Whig.

His work in the courts grew with his success. In 1813 he moved to No. 14 Charlotte Square where he lived for the next five years. He had already bought (in 1811) the farm house at Bonaly from James Gillespie of Spylaw *qv*, the Colinton snuff maker (ref. 22 North Foulis Close). His friend and famous architect, W H Playfair designed the tower adjoining the farm house. He loved the countryside at Colinton at the foot of the Pentland Hills where he was affectionately known as 'Cocky Cockburn.' Thomas Carlyle, the 'Sage of Chelsea', described him as, "small, solid and genuine....a gentleman, I should say and perfectly in the Scotch type, perhaps the very last of the peculiar species."

Cockburn's defence of Robert Knox, the anatomist, who unquestioningly accepted corpses from the infamous Burke and Hare and who was accused (by Sir Walter Scott) "of trading deep in human flesh", gained Knox vindication but not without disgrace. So great was Cockburn's reputation, he was appointed Solicitor-General for Scotland in 1830, the same year as his friend, Francis Jeffrey, (ref. 39. Jeffrey Street) was appointed Lord Advocate.

A strong supporter of Parliamentary reform, Cockburn's was the main contribution to the drafting of the Scottish Reform Bill. In 1831 he was elected Lord Rector of Glasgow University and in 1834 he was elevated to the Bench as Lord Cockburn.

In his later years he wrote *Life of Jeffrey* in 1852, *Journal 1831-44* in two volumes published in 1874 and his partly autobiographical, *Memorials of his Time* in which he gives a highly descriptive and humorous picture of Edinburgh and the numerous 'intelligensia' of its 'Golden Age'. Lord Rosebery, commending it to the students of the University, suggested that it should be read 'at least once every year'. It was published posthumously in 1856.

Henry Cockburn died peacefully at Bonaly in 1854. His statue, by William Brodie in 1863 is in the north-east corner of Parliament Hall in Edinburgh. He was buried at Dean Cemetery in 'Judges Row' beside his old friend Francis Jeffrey who had died four years before.

Today the Cockburn Conservation Trust does excellent work in the preservation of Edinburgh buildings and streets. Cockburn was intensely interested in the preservation of medieval Edinburgh - he saved John Knox's house from destruction but he was saddened by the tree felling in Bellevue and Drumsheugh to give way to the building of the extended New Town.

25. Hunter Square, Blair Street - Sir James Hunter Blair

Hunter Square, surrounding the Tron Church, has hardly changed since it was built in 1786 and **Blair Street** runs from it downhill to the Cowgate.

These streets are named after **Sir James Hunter Blair**, Lord Provost of Edinburgh in 1784 whose own name was Hunter to which he added his wife's maiden name when she, Jane Blair, inherited her father's estates of Blair of Dunskey in Wigtownshire. Her father, John Blair, was printer to George III when the King's Printing Office was in Blair Street. His six sons pre-deceased him and his estates were inherited by his eldest daughter. James Hunter adopted the name and arms of Blair on his marriage to his heiress bride. The ancestry of the Hunters of Hunterston in Ayrshire can be traced back to 1100.

Whereas Drummond dragged Edinburgh out of the overcrowded and disease ridden Royal Mile with the development of the New Town as well as enabling the University to become the leading centre of excellence through its medical faculty and single-handedly raising the funds for the Royal Infirmary, James Hunter Blair deserves the credit for the development of the South Bridge Scheme and the rebuilding of the University. In addition, the bridge linking Princes Street to the east was his idea as far back as 1784 - the Regent Bridge in Waterloo Place was opened in 1817.

James Hunter, the second son of John Hunter was born on 21st February 1741 at the family seat of Hunterston in Ayrshire and he started his working life in 1756 as an apprentice in Coutt's Bank on the south side of Parliament Square. A contemporary was William Forbes, a clerk, who was to become Sir William Forbes.

The apprenticeship was a seven-year period of training and after the death of Thomas Coutts and the retiral of another of the Coutts family, Forbes and Hunter, who by now were partners in the bank, formed a new company - Forbes Hunter and Co.

In 1770 James Hunter married Jane Blair. Their marriage was happy; she had sixteen children and is described by Lord Cockburn in his *Memorials*:

> *Lady Blair's elegance and sprightliness would have graced and enlivened the best society; but her tastes and virtues were entirely domestic, and made her the most delightful of household dieties. Mild, affectionate, and cheerful, she attracted the love of all ages, and closed her many days without once knowing what selfishness or want of charity meant.*

Edinburgh, during Hunter Blair's time, was in the midst of its 'Golden Age'' It was a contradiction of opulence for privileged intellectuals on the one hand and the squalid poverty of the poor on the other; in the New Town there was stately elegance and in the Royal Mile the stench of over-crowding and an absence of drains was all too obvious. It was the Dundas era; Henry Dundas held political power and could promise Pitt the support of three-quarters of the Scottish members through nepotism and bribery.

In 1781 James Hunter Blair was elected the Member of Parliament for the City of Edinburgh until 1784, when Pitt the Younger became Prime Minister. He resigned his parliamentary seat to concentrate on his banking business, but at home in Edinburgh he soon became involved with the Town Council. As soon as he became Lord Provost in 1784 he ordered a study of the site over which the South Bridge would span the gorge over the Cowgate and thus give access to the south side of Edinburgh. The North Bridge had already been built and the New Town Development was proceeding apace. The foundation stone of the new South Bridge was laid on 1st August 1785 by Lord Haddo and it was opened for pedestrians on 19th November 1786 and for carriages in 1787, but as Drummond had died before he saw his dream New Town, Hunter Blair died before the completion of South Bridge and the Scheme to follow.

Hunter Blair's extremely hard work in promoting the South Bridge Scheme and his enthusiasm for the rebuilding of the University were rewarded with a Baronetcy from George III in 1786. The University Old Quad was Robert Adam's greatest public work (1789). Its interior was designed by W.H. Playfair in 1819-27. These schemes were unfinished on Hunter Blair's death at Harrogate in 1787. He was buried at Greyfriars Church.

He had met, admired and befriended Robert Burns when Burns visited Edinburgh in 1786. Saddened by the death of this good man Burns penned a short poem:

> *Oh! long shall they lament the stroke that tore*
> *A ready Prop from Merit; from the Poor*
> *A careful Guardian; from his weeping Family*
> *A loved and tender Father; from his Country*
> *A zealous Patriot - from the World a Friend.*

The Hunter Blair family today live at Blairquhan Castle in Ayrshire which encompassed 14,000 acres a few years ago. Sir James Hunter Blair purchased the old castle for his eldest son, Sir David Hunter Blair, who commissioned William Burn (1789-1870) the Edinburgh architect to rebuild and restore it.

Tour Walk 3 - High Street (continued)

26. Niddry Street
    - Wauchope of Niddry

27. Carrubber's Close
    - Bishop Spottiswood's
    House

28. Bishop's Close
    - Henry Dundas

29. Strichen's Close
    - Sir George Mackenzie

30. Blackfriars Street
    - Regent Morton's House

31. Paisley Close
    - Sir William Fettes

32. South Gray's Close
    - Henry Erskine

33. Hyndford Close
    - Professor Daniel
    Rutherford
      Moubray House

34. John Knox's House
    - John Knox
    Fountain Close

35. Tweeddale Court
    - 1st & 2nd Marquis
    of Tweeddale

36. World's End Close
    - Sir James Stanfield

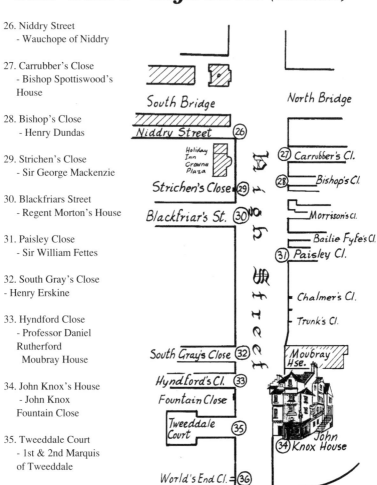

Tour Walk 3 - Summary

26. Niddry Street, at the corner of which is the Holiday Inn Crowne Plaza, takes its name from the **Wauchopes of Niddry** whose mansion was in the vicinity. In 1591 Archibald Wauchope, with others, unsuccessfully raided Holyrood in an attempt on the life of James VI. John Wauchope was knighted by Charles I in 1633 when he visited Edinburgh. Sir John was a zealous Covenanter who supported Argyll against Montrose during the Civil War of 1642-8.

27. Carrubber's Close is supposedly named after a rich merchant and magistrate, William Carroberos, in 1450.

This Close was the venue for Allan Ramsay's theatre, opened on 1st November 1736, but he was forced to close it down by disapproving magistrates and church authorities who considered that such activities were sinful and would inflame the minds of the ordinary people.

The mansion of **John Spottiswood, Archbishop of St Andrews** has the inscription '1578 rebuilt 1864' above its entrance in the close. 'The Mitre', a pleasant bar-restaurant, was part of his house and several para-normal events are thought to have been experienced in the vicinity of the bishop's chair which is said to be entombed under the cellar.

Sir James Young Simpson (of chloroform fame) had his dispensary in the Close in 1860.

28. Bishop's Close (formerly Alexander Lindsay's Close, Edward Nisbet's Close, James Nisbet's Close and Lindsay's Close) was built for Thomas Sydserf (1581-1663) who was Bishop of Brechin, then Galloway and finally of Orkney. At different times this was the residence of several bishops including the Bishop of Glasgow, the Bishop of Dunkeld, the Bishop of Orkney and the Archbishop of St Andrews, John Spottiswood.

Lord President Dundas was a later resident and his famous son, Henry Dundas, who became 1st Viscount Melville, was born here in 1742. **Henry Dundas, 1st Viscount Melville**, became the most powerful man in Scotland. Such was his influence, he could present three-quarters of the Scottish Parliamentary seats to William Pitt during the 'Pitt-Dundas' era. He was elevated to a viscountcy in 1802 and died in 1811.

29. Strichen's Close (formerly Rosehaugh's Close), took its name from a kindly old judge, **Alexander Fraser of Strichen**, **Lord Strichen**, who was elevated to the bench in 1730 and lived in this close for forty-five years. He died at Strichen in Aberdeenshire in 1775.

This was the address of an earlier judge who became Lord Advocate in 1677, **Sir George Mackenzie of Rosehaugh**; he founded the Advocates' Library in 1682. This highly intellectual jurist, whose *Institutions of the Law of Scotland* was a great contribution to clarification of criminal law, was given the nick-name 'Bluidy Mackenzie' for his prosecution of Covenanters.

An even earlier resident of Strichen's Close was **Walter Chepman**, the first printer in Scotland who, under the patronage of James IV, introduced the first printing press in Scotland in 1507. That year he dedicated the Chepman Aisle in St Giles to James IV.

30. Blackfriars Street takes its name from the Monastery of the Dominican Black Friars in the Cowgate which was founded in 1230 by Alexander II and destroyed by fire in 1528.

Dr Guthrie established a 'Ragged School' in 1847 in St Anne's School which is reached from Blackfriars Street.

Regent Morton's House is on the west side of Blackfriars Street. He was **James Douglas, 4th Earl of Morton** (c1525-81) who, in 1566, was involved in the murder of Rizzio, the secretary of Mary Queen of Scots. He joined the confederacy of nobles against her at Carberry Hill and at Langside in 1568. After the Regencies of Moray, Lennox and Mar he became Regent in 1572. He was beheaded by the 'Maiden' (Edinburgh's guillotine) in 1581 for his part in Darnley's murder at Holyrood.

31. Paisley Close (formerly East Bailie Fyfe's Close and Smith's Close) owned by Henry Paislie in 1711, is almost opposite Blackfriars Street and has a quotation engraved in stone above the entrance: *Heave Awa' Chaps I'm no Dead Yet.* These words were shouted by a young boy, Joseph McIver, who was trapped in the rubble of the 90-foot, five-storey, building which had suddenly collapsed in November 1861. The death toll of thirty-five people was one of the worst disasters of the Old Town.

William Fettes (1750-1836), twice Lord Provost, had his wine and tea merchant's business at Paisley Close. He left £166,000 for the establishment of Fettes College.

32. South Gray's Close (formerly Coyne-House Close, Coynie Close and Mint Close) was the home of John Gray, a burgess of Edinburgh in 1512. In 1574 it became Mint Close the Royal Mint being housed there.

This was the birthplace of the famous Erskine brothers: David Stewart Erskine (1742-1819) who became 11th Earl of Buchan and founded the Society of Antiquaries of Scotland, **Henry Erskine** (1746-1817) the popular jurist who was twice Lord Advocate (sadly his plaque at the entrance has disappeared; it was inscribed: 'No poor man wanted a friend while Harry Erskine lived') and Thomas Erskine (1750-1823) who became Lord Chancellor of England.

33. Hyndford's Close (formerly Charteris Close and Collington's Close) was named after the Earls of Hyndford the 3rd of whom was the Lieutenant-Colonel of the Scots Foot Guards, twice Commissioner to the General Assembly prior to 1740 and a Lord of Police in Scotland. He was the plenipotentiary-extraordinary at the Treaty of Breslau after Frederick the Great had invaded Silesia in 1741. Hyndford was created a Knight of the Thistle by George II. The earldom became extinct in 1817. The house was next occupied by **Dr Daniel Rutherford**, the discoverer of the distinction between nitrogen and carbon dioxide. He was professor of botany in 1786 at the University of Edinburgh and an uncle of Sir Walter Scott.

  Robert Burns was a frequent guest of the beautiful Duchess of Gordon when she lived in Hyndford Close. It is now the Museum of Childhood - a fascinating look into the past amusements of children.

Moubray House, adjacent to John Knox House, is probably the oldest house in the Royal Mile. It was built in 1477 for Robert Moubray and rebuilt in 1529 by Andrew Moubray, a wright (carpenter), but the present building is mainly of 17th century construction. Daniel Defoe, author of *Robinson Crusoe,* lived here in 1710 when he was editor of the *Edinburgh Courant.* Archibald Constable (1774-1827), the publisher of the *Scots Magazine* (1801), the *Edinburgh Review* (1802) and the works of Sir Walter Scott, had his bookshop at Moubray House. In 1910 its dilapidated condition threatened its demolition but it was saved by the Cockburn Society.

34. John Knox's House is a museum and shop in which the leader of the Reformation, **John Knox** (c1505-1572), supposedly lived in 1561. The house was never owned by John Knox; it was owned by James Mossman, jeweller to Mary Queen of Scots; he was executed for treason. John Knox, born near Haddington, was educated for the priesthood but he surrendered his Orders in 1544 and was mainly responsible for the establishment of the Reformed Church in Scotland.

Fountain Close (formerly Bassendean's Close, Colington's Close, David Stevenson's Close, Fullarton's Close, John Barton's Close and Moubray's Close) was named from the Public Well which was immediately opposite the Close. The well was moved across the street opposite Moubray House to ease the passage of carriages in 1813.

It was in Fountain Close that Thomas Bassandyne with Alexander Arbuthnot printed the first translation of the New Testament in 1574. This was the first publication by subscription and such were the difficulties, they had to plead before the Privy Council for a time extension of nine months and promised to refund the money to the Parishes if they failed to meet the time limit.

35. Tweeddale Court (formerly Alexander Young's Court, James Brown's Court and John Laing's Court) and **Tweeddale House** were built during the 16th century. The house was inherited in 1585 by Neil Laing, a Keeper of the Signet, who sold it to Sir William Bruce (1630-1710), the King's Surveyor who extended Holyrood Palace for Charles II. Bruce sold it to **John Hay, 2nd Earl of Tweeddale** in 1670. He was a Privy Councillor of Charles II and James II. He was appointed a Lord of the Treasury and Lord High Chancellor in 1689 under William III and was created 1st Marquis of Tweeddale in 1694.

36. World's End Close (formerly Stanfield's Close, Sweit's Close and Swift's Close) is the last close in the High Street. As far as the pre-1867 residents were concerned this was the end of their world. At that time the Canongate was outside the Edinburgh boundary. In 1690 this was the Edinburgh residence of **Sir James Stanfield** a colonel in Cromwell's Parliamentary army who ran a successful cloth manufactory in Haddington where he was strangled by his spendthrift son. The son was hanged in Edinburgh and his head was displayed on the East Port of Haddington

26. Niddry Street

Niddry Street which contained 'Niddrie's Wynd' was the site of the mansion of the **Wauchopes of Niddry** from whom the street takes its name.

A chapel in Niddry, in the district of Craigmillar in Edinburgh, was founded by Robert Wauchope of Niddry in 1389 who was a hereditary bailie of Midlothian to the Keith Marischal of Scotland from whom he obtained the lands of Niddry Marischal in Craigmillar.

Gilbert Wauchope was Depute Marischal in Parliament from 1527 to 1535 and he was a member of the Reformed Parliament in 1560.

John Wauchope, whose great-grandfather was Robert Wauchope above, was knighted when Charles I visited Edinburgh in 1633. He was the son of Francis Wauchope descended from the family of Wauchope of the Parish of Langholm, Dumfriesshire who owned land at Culter, Aberdeenshire. Sir John inherited the lands of Niddry Marischal in Craigmillar where a small part of Niddrie Marischal House can be seen in Niddrie Mains Drive. The lands were forfeited in 1587 after he and his son, the 'Wild Laird of Niddrie', Archibald Wauchope, took part in the murder of Lord Darnley, the husband of Mary Queen of Scots. His lands were temporarily restored to him but in December 1591 he took part in a raid at Holyrood against James VI; fifteen of the raiders including Wauchope had their lands forfeited.

At the start of the Civil War (1642-8) Scotland remained neutral. A petition was prepared by noblemen, burgesses and ministers to the Scottish Privy Council on which Sir John Wauchope's signature appears: "... praying that nothing should be enacted prejudicial to the work of the Reformation and the preservation of peace between the two kingdoms." Sir John Wauchope, who lived at his town mansion in Niddry Street, was a zealous Covenanter and supported the Duke of Argyll against the Marquis of Montrose.

Montrose was a brilliant general who swept through Scotland the victor of four quick battles, when he arrived at the Argyll stronghold of Inverlochy. His army consisted of tough Irishmen and Highlanders who inflicted a humiliating defeat over Argyll and Wauchope who were aboard ship during the fighting.

Sir John Wauchope died in January 1682 and was survived by two sons by his wife Anne who was the daughter of Sir Andrew Hamilton of Redhouse.

Sir John's eldest son, Andrew, married Margaret, daughter of Sir John Gilmour of Craigmillar, the President of the Court of Session. They had nine sons and ten daughters. The eldest survivor was William, the seventh son, who succeeded to the title, but only for five months; he died in June 1711. His only son, William, was killed in a duel in Padua in 1726, aged twenty. His brother, Andrew, succeeded to the title and married Helen, daughter of Sir Andrew Home. They had three sons and two daughters. The eldest, Captain Andrew Wauchope of Niddrie, succeeded to the title in 1776 and married a sister of East Lothian's great general, Sir David Baird of Newbyth. They had four daughters and five sons. Andrew, the eldest, was killed at the battle of the Pyrenees and was succeeded by his brother, William, a lieutenant-colonel who married Elizabeth, daughter of Robert Baird of Newbyth in 1812. Their son, Andrew Wauchope of Niddrie, was born in December 1818 and succeeded to the title in 1826. He married Frances Maria, daughter of Henry Lloyd of Lloydsborough in Tipperary. He had a distinguished military career as General Andrew Gilbert Wauchope, Colonel of the Black Watch who led the Highland Brigade at the Battle of Magersfontein during the South African War in which he was killed with 700 men of whom 200 were from the Black Watch. The Wauchope memorial window, by Ballantyne and Gardiner 1900 -01, is in St Giles Cathedral.

27. Carruber's Close - John Spottiswood, Archbishop of St. Andrews

Carrubber's Close on the north side of High Street is probably named after one William Carriberis whose house in the Close dated back to 1450.

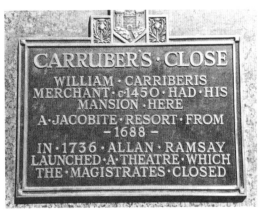

Adjacent is the 'The Mitre', a pleasant bar-restuarant which is part of the Bishop Spottiswood's House in the Close above the entrance to which is dated: '1578 rebuilt 1864.'

This Close was the venue for Allan Ramsay's first theatre which he opened on 1st November 1736, but he was forced to close it. The City Magistrates with pressure from the Church refused him a licence and Ramsay lost a considerable sum of money. Public performances of this kind were thought to inflame the minds of the ordinary citizens.

'The Mitre', a restaurant/bar, takes its name from the fact that **John Spottiswood** (1565-1639), Archbishop of St Andrews, lived here. His Bishop's chair is said to be sealed below the floor, a few feet inside the entrance. Does this account for a number of paranormal events said to have taken place?

John Spottiswood, the Archbishop of St Andrews and eminent Scottish historian, accompanied James VI to London in 1603 and helped the king in trying to unite the English and Scottish Churches. He was made a Privy Councillor to James VI and Lord Chancellor to Charles I whom he crowned at Holyrood in 1633. He tried to delay the introduction of 'Laud's Liturgy' and was at St Giles during the riot on 23rd July 1637 against its imposition. After the Covenant was signed in 1638 he fled to Newcastle and died an Episcopalian in London.

John Spottiswood was born in 1565 and educated at the University of Glasgow, gaining his MA degree in 1581. He became minister at Calder, succeeding his father at the age of eighteen and was known for his strict Presbyterian views when he refused to agree the king's annulment of the sentence against a Catholic, Patrick Adamson. In 1596 he was appointed a Commissioner to visit the south-western area of Scotland.

Spottiswood supported the king, James VI, when relations were under strain between king and kirk. In 1600 he supported the 'king's side' in the representation of the church by bishops in Parliament. In 1601 he accompanied the Duke of Lennox to France and remained there for two years.

When James VI acceded to the English throne in 1603, Spottiswood accompanied him to London. His powers of persuasion were now tested to the limit; he had the difficult and delicate task of coercing those against an assimilation of the English and Scottish Churches in accordance with the wishes of his king - he failed.

In May 1605, for his efforts, he was appointed to the Privy Council. In 1610 he was given the Archbishopric of Glasgow and he was Moderator of the General Assembly at which the Presbytery was abolished. That year he and two other bishops were consecrated to the Episcopal office by the Bishops of London, Ely and Bath. This was the express wish of the king but the Scottish Kirk was not impressed.

Matters worsened considerably when Spottiswood, in a sermon at St Giles, did his best to justify the release of Catholic George Gordon, 6th Earl of Huntly, by order of the king. Huntly had been summoned before the Court of High Commission to explain his adherence to Catholicism. He refused to take the confession of faith and was imprisoned in the Castle. He was sent to London and, after his release was ordered by the king, he was absolved by the Archbishop of Canterbury. This was regarded as an insult to the Church of Scotland and Spottiswood suffered strong criticism verging on defamation.

This good servant of the king was now made Archbishop of St Andrews and, during the king's visit in 1617 for the opening of Parliament, Spottiswood preached a sermon in praise of the king but he could not bring himself to support Regal authority over the Church and managed to mollify the king by his acceptance of some ceremonial reforms.

At the Assembly of 1618, held in Perth, Spottiswood took the Moderator's chair and he used all his considerable powers of persuasion to promulgate the Five Articles of Perth - communion must be taken kneeling, communion may be administered privately in cases of sickness, baptism may similarly be administered, children must be blessed by the Bishop and festival days should be revived. In a sermon he exhorted Councillors and Magistrates to set a good example by complying with these articles. He urged compulsion and he threatened the utmost penalties against any minister who refused to conform. But trouble was in store for Spottiswood when, at the conference of bishops of 23rd November 1619 at St Andrews, his insistence on their enforcement almost failed and, in April 1620, at the Diocesan Synod at St Andrews almost all bishops walked out when he proposed to censure those ministers who had failed to conform. At the point of ratification a huge peel of thunder so frightened them, it was thought to be the wrath of God.

James VI died in 1625 and Spottiswood, having officiated at the coronation of Charles I in 1633 at Holyrood, continued in Royal favour, so much so that Charles I commanded that he should, as Archbishop of St Andrews, have precedence over the Lord Chancellor of Scotland, Sir George Hay, who stoutly refused to allow it. However, Sir George died in January 1635 and the problem was solved by appointing Spottiswood Lord Chancellor.

The king's insistence on introducing the Liturgy in Scotland was clearly going to cause an uproar and Spottiswood tried to delay matters. However, Charles I insisted and Spottiswood, with zealous loyalty enforced the royal command. To make his own position easier he procured a Royal Warrant which commanded all churches to comply.

He was present at St Giles on 23rd July 1637 when Dean James Hannay read from the Service Book (Laud's Liturgy) for the first and last time. It was during this service that Jenny Geddes was reputed to have started the riot by throwing her stool at the Dean. Whether or not a stool was actually thrown is uncertain but it is true that a riot ensued and Spottiswood with the Dean and other dignitaries had to leave the church amidst a jeering crowd.

Spottiswood with other Privy Councillors signed a letter to the king indicating the overwhelming objections of the Scottish people to the Service Book. Spottiswood tried to obtain a change in policy but in the middle of his genuine efforts the National Covenant was signed (1st March 1638) and he raised his arms in despair, saying, "Now all that we have been doing these thirty years past is thrown down at once."

Spottiswood's life was now in danger and he left for Newcastle. On 4th December 1638 the General Assembly voted several defamatory charges against him for:

> *profaning the Sabbath, carding and dicing, riding*
> *through the country the whole day, tippling and drinking*

> *in taverns till midnight, falsifying the acts of the Aberdeen assembly, lying and slandering the old assembly and covenant in his wicked book, of adultery, incest, sacrilege and frequent simony.*

This was, of course, nothing more than partisan spite.

Spottiswood remained in Newcastle for almost a year and left for London in November 1639. A recurrence of the fever he had contracted in Newcastle killed him on 26th November. He was buried at Westminster with great pomp. His great work, published posthumously in 1655, was his *History of the Church and State of Scotland from the year of our Lord 203 to the end of the reign of King James VI in 1625.*

28. Bishop's Close -
Henry Dundas, 1st Viscount Melville

Passing by the North Bridge and Carrubber's Close, **Bishop's Close** (formerly Alexander Lindsay's Close, Edward Nisbet's Close and Lindsay's Close) on the left takes its name from Bishop's Land in which the first Bishop to reside there was Thomas Sydserf, Bishop of Brechin, then of Galloway and finally of Orkney. The Bishops of Glasgow and Dunkeld lived here at different times.

Thomas Sydserf (1581-1663) built Bishop's Land within the Close but he was very unpopular in Edinburgh through his friendship with William Laud the Archbishop of Canterbury. Archbishop Laud was the leader of the anti-Calvinist Arminians and the author of the new prayer-book, 'Laud's Liturgy', which caused an uproar when it was read by Dean Hannay at St Giles Cathedral in 1637.

From about 1705 members of the family of Nisbet of Dirleton lived at Bishop's Close (ref. 52. Nisbet of Dirleton's House in the Canongate). William Nisbet disponed the property to the Town Council in 1740.

A later resident was Lord President Robert Dundas whose son, **Henry Dundas**, was born here in 1742. Henry Dundas was to become the most powerful and influential man in all Scotland. His family background was ideally suited for his ascendancy to power. Nepotism was the order of the day; there was nothing remarkable in the use of family connections or a little bribery for advancement.

Henry Dundas had four generations of legal power at the highest level behind him: his elder half-brother was Lord Advocate and President of the Court of Session, his father, Sir Robert Dundas of Arniston, was Lord President of the Court of Session, his grandfather and great-grandfather were Lord Presidents.

Following a High School education Henry Dundas took his law degree at the University of Edinburgh and became an advocate at the age of twenty-one. He was elected MP for Midlothian in 1774 and a year later he was appointed Lord Advocate of Scotland.

For the twenty-three years between 1782 and 1805 Henry Dundas virtually 'managed' Scotland. Lord Cockburn in his *Memorials* describes him:

> *...an Edinburgh man, and well calculated by talent and manner to make despotism popular, was absolute dictator of Scotland, and of extinguishing opposition beyond what were ever exercised in modern times by one person in any portion of the empire, ...*

but Cockburn was a dedicated Whig and such an opinion was natural to him.

Henry Dundas was undoubtedly charismatic and behind his benign, smiling exterior were hidden many intrigues and secret ambitions. At that time there were forty-five Parliamentary seats in Scotland - 2662 voters for thirty County seats and fifteen seats from the old self-perpetuating Royal Burghs. In 1790, such was the influence of Dundas, he could guarantee to give thirty-four (three-quarters) of these Scottish seats to his Prime Minister, William Pitt. This was both jobbery and simony on a grand scale. It was simply a matter of manoeuvring well-established contacts through whom Dundas obtained these votes - a promise here, a favour there and a few appointments in high places, often in India. But he meant well, he used these same powers of persuasion and influence to have titles and lands restored to the Highland Chiefs who had suffered loss and other penalties after the Jacobite Rising of 1745; in this he succeeded with his Acts passed in 1782 and 1784. However, he did not support its results - the greed of the Whig landlords when most of them ruthlessly replaced their Highland tenants with the importation of sheep - 'The Clearances'- they were dispossessed and left to die or to emigrate.

Having successfully strengthened the British Navy in 1782 Dundas was removed from his post as Treasurer of the Navy by the Fox-North coalition. However, when Pitt became Prime Minister in 1784, Dundas regained his Navy Treasurership and was soon to hold several high offices: Secretary for War, First Lord of the Admiralty and President of the Board of Control for India.

In 1791 Dundas was appointed Home Secretary; then followed 'Pitt's reign of terror' 1793-94. The repression continued for another thirty years. Pitt was well supported by the Dundas family who in turn had the judicial support of the fearsome Lord Braxfield (ref.21 Covenant Close) - a faithful crown prosecutor and old friend of Dundas, described by those who suffered from his rough justice as the 'Judge Jeffreys of Scotland'. During the political trials of 1793-94, he sentenced many to long terms of deportation or to be hanged for sedition, sometimes on the flimsiest evidence. The brilliant young Advocate Thomas Muir was one of those unfortunates to be sentenced for sedition and even though the prosecution could not prove the charge, he was sentenced to fourteen years' transportation. The prosecutor was Robert Dundas, nephew of Henry Dundas. But such was the outcry, Braxfield was given no more prosecutions.

Henry Dundas had married into title and considerable wealth but in his busy and ambitious Parliamentary career he woefully neglected his young wife who, during his many absences from home, left him for a younger and more attentive man, Captain Faukener.

By 1796, opposition was growing against Dundas's unseemly and overt power. An Edinburgh mob had burned his effigy and the popular Henry Erskine, who led the opposition through what came to be called 'Dundas Despotism', had prepared a most damning document - a complete list of the family, the affiliations and the finances of the 2662 Shire voters in Scotland - three quarters of whom had been 'bought'. Erskine found himself deposed from his Deanship of the Faculty of Advocates in 1796. This was serious because no-one was held in greater esteem than the popular Henry Erskine *qv* (ref. 32. South Gray's Close). In 1801 Dundas resigned his Ministerial post with Prime Minister Pitt over the Irish problem. The following year Dundas was elevated to Viscount Melville and Baron of Dunira.

While serving as Secretary of War in 1805 he was accused of using Navy funds to purchase shares in the East India Company. As Treasurer of the Navy he had controlled the finances in his own way for over forty years without question. His paymaster, Alexander Trotter of Dreghorn, had made a tidy profit from their arrangements in which he habitually took cheques for 'storage' in his account in his cousin Coutt's bank. Dundas had allegedly borrowed money from this source. He was impeached of 'gross malversation and breach of duty'. His two-week trial in the House of Lords acquitted him. His friends, including Sir Walter Scott, were overjoyed and a public dinner was given in his honour by the Edinburgh Town Council on 27th June 1806. His only fault was described as carelessness rather than acquisitiveness but his career was over and he retired to his estate of Dunira near Comrie in Perthshire.

He died in May 1811 on the day before the funeral of his friend and neighbour, Lord President Robert Blair, whose sudden death undoubtedly affected him. One of his last acts was one of kindness. He wrote a letter to the Government pleading for some provision for Blair's family. The two great men lay dead next door to each other in their adjacent houses in George Square. Henry Dundas, 1st Viscount Melville was buried at Lasswade.

29. Strichen's Close, Blackfriars Street - 'Bloody Mackenzie'

Passing the Holiday Inn Crowne Plaza, **Strichen's Close** in Blackfriars Street takes its name from Lord Strichen (1699-1775), a judge of the Court of Session for forty-five years from 1730. He became owner of the old house at the end of Rosehaugh's Close on his marriage to a descendant of Sir George Mackenzie.

This was the residence of **Sir George Mackenzie** of Rosehaugh (in Ross-shire) who was Advocate to Charles II and James VII (II of England). Mackenzie bought the property in 1677 and the passageway led into Rosehaugh's Close, named from the Mackenzie estate near Fortrose in Ross-shire, but renamed Strichen's Close after 1730.

The Covenanters named him 'Bluidy Mackenzie' for his persecution of them. In this respect he was said to have excelled his predecessor, Sir John Nisbet of Dirleton (ref. 52.). It is interesting to note that Nisbet defended the Marquis of Montrose, who had forsaken the Covenanters to support his king, whereas Mackenzie defended the enemy of Montrose, the Marquis of Argyll; both were executed, Montrose in 1650 and Argyll in 1661.

George Mackenzie was born of the nobility; he was a son of the 2nd Earl of Seaforth and his birthplace was at Dundee in 1636. His education at the Universities of Aberdeen and St Andrews was completed at Bourges in France.

He was called to the bar in 1659 and his defence of the Marquis of Argyll, by one so young, was so ably conducted it brought his name into prominence in legal circles and to the attention of John Maitland, the Earl of Lauderdale, who became Royal Commissioner in 1668 for Charles II. This was the highest patronage possible in Scotland; Mackenzie's practice flourished and he was appointed Lord Advocate in 1677. He refused the appointment at first, because his friend, Sir John Nisbet, had been forced to resign over an offence of which Mackenzie was convinced that Nisbet was innocent.

This was a time of cruel persecution of Covenanters who were virtually hunted and shot on the spot unless they abandoned the 'Apologetical Declaration'. If they denied it they were spared for trial by Sir George Mackenzie. This was itself a fearful experience for them as they knew beforehand that the likely outcome would be the death sentence. His reputation for ruthlessness earned him the nickname, 'Bluidy

Mackenzie'. He became as feared as the merciless soldier, John Graham of Claverhouse ('Bluidy Clavers') who perpetrated the on-the-spot shootings of Covenanters.

These were merciless times on both sides and the Covenanters were not themselves innocent churchgoers who would hurt no-one. On the contrary, they were law-breakers who had commonly stoned ministers who had not signed the Covenant. After all, the Apologetical Declaration was a Covenanters' avowal to kill those who hunted them.

'Bluidy Mackenzie' he may have been, but his intellectual contribution to the law of Scotland was great. In 1682 he founded the Advocates' Library and was among the first to show that the evidence presented at the trials of witches was deeply suspect and generally served the greed of the accusers who could claim compensation from the wretched victims. In 1684 his *Institutions of the Law of Scotland* was a clear exposition of criminal law in Scotland and a concomitant to the publication of 1681 with the same title dealing with Civil Law by the strong Covenanter James Dalrymple, 1st Viscount Stair. These works laid down the fundamental differences between Scots law and English law. Mackenzie's other publications included works on heraldry and a novel, *Aretina*, thought to be a first in Scotland. His *Memoirs of the Affairs of Scotland during the reign of Charles II* was his contribution to history from the Government's viewpoint.

His service to James VII (II of England) as crown prosecutor was as dedicated as that to Charles II but when it became apparent that James's reign was to be usurped by the invitation to his son-in-law and daughter, William and Mary, to replace him, Mackenzie retired to Oxford.

He died in London on 8th May 1691 and was buried in Edinburgh. His Mausoleum in Greyfriars churchyard, by James Smith, was thought to be haunted by the ghosts of Covenanters. Chambers in his *Traditions of Edinburgh* relates the story of small boys who, for a dare, would, in days gone by, walk boldly towards the door of the mausoleum and nervously shout through the keyhole,

> *"Bloody Mackenzie, come out if you daur,*
> *Lift the sneck and draw the bar!"*

30. Blackfriars Street - Regent Morton's House

Blackfriars Street was named after the old Dominican monastery in the Cowgate - the Monastery of the Black Friars which was founded in 1230 by Alexander II (r.1214-49) and destroyed accidentally by fire in 1528. The first 'Hie Schule' of Edinburgh was built in 1567 (the year of the abdication of Mary Queen of Scots) in the garden of the monastery at High School Yards.

Regent Morton's House is a little way down Blackfriars Street on the west side. Inside the house is a framed fragment of a piece of stone, perhaps part of a lintel, which is inscribed with indecipherable initials and the year '1564'. The house is easily recognised from its obvious antiquity in comparison to its neighbours and it is clearly signed: 'The High Street Hostel', a well-used and welcoming stop-over for students and touring back-packers who may stay for a few days or longer at reduced rates.

The 16th century owner of the house was **Regent Morton, James Douglas, 4th Earl of Morton**, who lived during a tumultuous time in Scottish history - the era of Mary, Queen of Scots, the Reformation and the early reign of James VI during which Morton was Regent for the boy king.

The 4th Earl's part in all of this was remarkable: he was a co-conspirator in the murder of Mary's secretary, Rizzio, he fought at Langside against the Queen's army, he was elected Regent in 1572, he supported Elizabeth I and he discovered the 'Casket Letters' which incriminated Mary in the murder of her husband. Morton, accused of complicity in the murder, met his end in 1581 by courtesy of the 'Maiden' - Edinburgh's guillotine.

James Douglas was born about 1525, the younger son of Sir George Douglas of Pittendriech. His father, a supporter of George Wishart (the Scottish Reformer who was burned at St Andrews), had to flee to England in 1528 and young James Douglas was left to his own devices at the expense of his education.

He inherited the lands of Pittendriech and became 4th Earl of Morton in 1553 through his marriage to Elizabeth Douglas, daughter of the 3rd Earl of Morton. Through his father's influence, his sympathies lay with the Reformers and he helped to draw up the first Covenant in 1557, but his absence was noticeable when Mary of Guise, Queen Regent, attacked the Reformers with French support in 1560.

When young Mary, Queen of Scots, arrived at Leith from France in 1561 Morton was made a Privy Councillor and when John Knox urged

Mary 'to forsake that idolatrous religion' Morton was heard to advise Knox to "hold your peace and go away."

In 1563 he was appointed Lord High Chancellor and whilst he supported the marriage between Mary and Lord Darnley he disliked Darnley. Mary did not trust Morton because of his friendship with the Earl of Moray and the Marquis of Argyll both of whom had rebelled against her marriage in the 'roundabout raid.' It was rumoured that the office of Lord Chancellor was to be given to Mary's Italian secretary, Rizzio, and Morton now joined the conspiracy to murder him.

He organised his men to surround the Palace of Holyroodhouse, while he held the staircase leading to the Queen's apartments and Darnley allowed the murderers entry through his apartment to stab Rizzio to death in the presence of the Queen. Morton took charge of the Palace while Mary and Darnley rode off to Dunbar.

In his house in Blackfriars Street, Morton with Moray and Ruthven discussed Mary's proposals for reconciliation but Darnley astounded them by his denial of any involvement and they were summoned before the Privy Council. Morton sailed for Flanders on 16th June 1566 but after Darnley's treachery was confirmed to Mary, Morton and the other conspirators were pardoned.

Morton's return signalled the end for Darnley. The 4th Earl of Bothwell, in whom Mary placed her trust, now conspired to murder Darnley and tried unsuccessfully to involve Morton and Moray. After the murder of Darnley at Kirk-o'-Field, Morton refused to serve on the jury of Bothwell's farcical trial at which he was acquitted.

After Mary's seemingly arranged abduction and marriage to Bothwell, Morton dropped any pretence of friendship and formed a 'secret council' to capture Bothwell and the Queen at Holyrood. However, they surrendered at Carberry Hill on 14th June 1567. Bothwell was allowed to escape and Mary was taken to Edinburgh where Morton insisted on sparing her life and she was taken to Loch Leven Castle where she abdicated.

Morton claimed to have taken possession of the 'casket letters' implicating Mary in the death of her husband and confirming that Bothwell had committed the crime. Claims of forgery cast doubt upon the authenticity of the letters.

Mary's son was one year old and the Earl of Moray was chosen as Regent. At the coronation Morton took the oath on behalf of the infant king promising to maintain Protestantism. Morton was once again Lord Chancellor. Mary escaped from the Castle of Loch Leven and her army was defeated at Langside on 13th May 1568 by Regent Moray and Chancellor Morton. Mary escaped to England and Morton accompanied

Moray to York where they received little encouragement from Elizabeth I. She disliked the triumph of rebels and even after the 'casket letters' were produced she took no action.

After the assassination of the Earl of Moray, the 'Good Regent', Morton swore vengeance on the Hamiltons and demanded assistance from Elizabeth I to punish them. Morton and John Knox were now close. Morton was determined to end the occupation of Edinburgh Castle by Kirkcaldy of Grange and Maitland of Lethington, two devotees of Mary.

The Earl of Lennox, Darnley's father, was now chosen as Regent and at Stirling, Kirkcaldy of Grange, a clever soldier, planned a surprise night attack on the king's lords. Morton awoke in time and barricaded himself indoors. However he was captured when forced out of the house which had been set alight. Regent Lennox was shot dead as he rode off and Morton escaped with the other lords when Kirkcaldy's men turned to looting. The Earl of Mar was chosen as Regent and Morton was appointed Lord General of the Kingdom.

Scotland was now under the firm grip of Morton, the Reformers were in ferment and in England pressure was increasing for Mary's execution. Elizabeth proposed to hand over Mary to her enemies in Scotland for secret execution. Morton insisted on openness but negotiations were suspended on the sudden death of Regent Mar on 29th October 1572. John Knox died on 24th November and on that day Morton became Regent. However, he delayed acceptance until Elizabeth agreed to assist him with money and troops for the siege of the Castle. Its eventual surrender and the execution of Mary's faithful Kirkcaldy of Grange in 1573 was a severe blow to Mary.

Morton was now in supreme control to become 'the most able man in Scotland to govern.' He was detested by Catholics and had little regard for his personal safety. He walked the streets of Edinburgh without a guard and hunted at his estates at Dalkeith alone. Scotland was at peace at last.

As far as the Church was concerned Morton followed Elizabeth's policy, his aim being a Protestant alignment with England preparatory to a union of the two crowns and his tendency towards Episcopalism antagonised the General Assembly of the Church of Scotland. He insisted that Church monies be collected by the government and he reduced the number of ministers by assigning one minister to several churches. Morton's achievements in placing the king's finances on a proper footing, repairing the king's palaces and restoring Edinburgh Castle won him 'both love and reverence, with the opinion of a most wise and prudent governor.' However, Catholics claimed that he was in the pay of Elizabeth and had accepted bribes to follow her policy. In fact he received 'not one penny for himself' and he refused large bribes from the French to try to arrange for Mary's freedom.

Morton's enemies were numerous and devious, he was accused of greed and rumours were spread of imaginary stores of treasure. He had alienated the Church and many nobles. The English nobility were jealous of his relationship with Elizabeth and Morton, now aged fifty-three, indicated his desire to demit office.

James VI was now twelve years old and Argyll and Atholl conspired against Morton at the Stirling convention. The council of twelve, of which Morton was not a member, meant government of the king but Morton was soon aware that his safety could not be assured unless he took charge again. From Stirling Castle, he, with the Earl of Mar, took charge at the head of the Council. Argyll and Atholl combined their forces against him but the mediation of the English ambassador effected a compromise.

With the sudden death of the Earl of Atholl on 25th April 1579, Morton was suspected of poisoning him and when Atholl's place in the leadership was filled by Esme Stuart, son of the king's great-uncle, this was the beginning of the end for Morton. The king much preferred the wit and friendship of this attractive Frenchman whom he created Earl of Lennox.

Morton had been accused of Darnley's murder and, having protested his innocence to the Privy Council, he declared that his accusers were guilty of forgery and malice. Lennox had arranged secret correspondence between the James VI and his mother and he exposed Elizabeth I's communication with Morton over the threat to take the king to Dumbarton Castle and then to France. When Elizabeth learned that Dumbarton was in the hands of Lennox, she encouraged Morton to 'lay violent hands on him.' However, she promptly withdrew her support of Morton and Lennox now informed the king of the plot. Morton was charged with treason and tried by his enemies. He was again accused of complicity in Darnley's murder. Only one witness, Sir James Balfour, could be found to speak against him. All that could be proved was that Morton knew of Bothwell's intentions.

The day of the trial was 1st June 1581, Morton was beheaded on the 2nd June by the 'Maiden'. His head was fixed to the highest point of the Netherbow Port between the High Street and the Canongate. The young king lost a good servant that day.

31. Paisley Close - William Fettes

In 1711 this property was purchased by one Henry Paislie from the Henderson family of Fordell. They were an old and respected family of Fife once visited by Mary Queen of Scots.

Near John Knox House a small wine and tea merchant's business was opened at **Paisley Close** (formerly East Bailie Fyfe's Close and Smith's Close) by a young man still in his teens - his name was **William Fettes** and the year was 1768. He was to become a highly prosperous businessman and Lord Provost of the City of Edinburgh. He left a fortune for the establishment of a school for orphans; it became the prestigious Fettes College. But before embarking upon some aspects of his life, an explanation of the motto above the entrance of the close must be given.

In 1861, a most terrible tragedy occurred: the whole building collapsed, killing thirty-five people. While rescuers were clearing the rubble the voice of a small boy was heard, "Heave Awa' Chaps, I'm no' Dead Yet" - this is carved in stone above the entrance. The boy, Joseph McIvor, was saved and the event was commemorated in stone with the portrait head of a boy and the inscription by sculptor John Rhind (1828-92).

William Fettes amassed a considerable fortune from the sale of military stores during the Revolutionary and Napoleonic Wars (1793-1815). He left £166,000 for the establishment of what was to become one of the most highly prestigious schools in Scotland - Fettes College.

William Fettes was born on 25th June 1750 and educated at the High School in Edinburgh. He started work in a grocery shop in the High Street and, at age eighteen, he started his own business in the shop at Paisley Close.

As underwriter with firms in Newcastle, Durham and Leeds he expanded his business activities into contracting for military stores - a growing business in 1789 with the threat of war after the French had stormed their Bastille on 14th July of that year. Revolution throughout Europe seemed imminent. After the French had declared war on Britain and Holland in 1793, the demand for his military stores increased and his business grew rapidly. In addition he supplied whisky to London but it was thought to be slightly tasteless; he was reputed to have remedied the matter by adding a little dilute sulphuric acid!

In 1785 Fettes, now well-known in business circles, was elected to the Town Council and soon became fourth bailie. By 1799 he had been appointed first bailie and in 1800 he was elected Lord Provost. He is credited with the inauguration of the Police Force in Edinburgh in 1805. The Edinburgh Town Guard had become the subject of many jokes, having hardly changed their image since their formation in 1682. Fettes was aware of the jokes at their expense and he was partly instrumental in bringing about their disbandment after the removal of the Old Tolbooth in 1817. He was created a baronet by George III in 1804 and re-elected to his second term as Lord Provost in 1805.

Having invested in several estates, one of which was Comely Bank (the land between East Fettes Avenue and Crewe Road South), Fettes decided, in 1800, to spend more of his time in estate management. He had retired from business and moved from his house in Princes Street to Charlotte Square.

Tragedy struck Fettes at the end of the Napoleonic War, in 1815, when his only son, an advocate, died in Berlin. When his wife, Maria, died on 7th May 1836, he decided to execute a trust fund for the education of children whose parents had died or for children whose parents could not afford the cost of education.

Sir William Fettes died at his home, no.13 Charlotte Square, almost one month before his eighty-sixth birthday, on 27th May 1836, only three weeks after the death of his wife.

His trust fund totalled £166,000 which, after twenty-eight years, had grown sufficiently to finance the building of the magnificent college to be designed by the famous architect, William H Playfair. Sadly, Playfair died shortly after he started his design in 1857 and the work was taken over by David Bryce. The building, a masterpiece of Scottish baronial-French design, was completed in 1870 at a cost of £150,000, the residue being invested to allow up to fifty boys as boarders, with others paying fees. The trustees received some complaints that the number of beneficiaries could be increased but no action was considered possible.

The burial place of Sir William Fettes is the Canongate Churchyard where his mausoleum on the east wall is inscribed:

'Over the grave of its founder the Trustees of the Fettes Endowment have erected this monument in grateful recognition of the enlightened benevolence which devoted the acquisition of an honourable life to the useful purpose of providing for the children of his less fortunate fellow countrymen the blessing of a sound and liberal education.'

The gravestone is inscribed:

'Sacred to the Memory of Sir William Fettes of Comely Bank. Baronet Lord Provost of the City of Edinburgh in 1801 and 1802 and a second time in 1805 and 1806.
Born 25th June 1750 died 27th May 1836 also of Maria Malcolm his wife who died 7th May 1836 and William Fettes, Advocate their only son who died at Berlin 13th June 1815 aged 27 years.'

Moubray House, High Street

32. South Gray's Close - Henry Erskine

An early name for **South Gray's Close** was Coyne-House Close then Coynie Close and Mint Close, the Scottish Mint or 'Cunzie House' being situated here from 1574 until the Act of Union in 1707, but the Close is probably named after an Edinburgh Burgess called John Gray.

South Gray's Close, next to the Museum of Childhood, was the birthplace of the sons of Henry, the 10th Earl of Buchan, the three Erskine brothers; the eldest, David Stewart Erskine (1742-1819) inherited the title, 11th Earl of Buchan, founded the Society of Antiquaries of Scotland, the middle brother Henry Erskine (1746-1817) was twice Lord Advocate and the youngest, Thomas Erskine, 1st Baron (1750-1823) became Lord Chancellor of England.

Henry Erskine was the best known in Edinburgh and loved by all who were fortunate enough to know or to meet him. He lived and served the law in Edinburgh, becoming a leader of the Whig party, although he was a man of such wit and charm he was welcome anywhere, even in the staunchest of Tory residences.

Henry Erskine was born on 1st November 1746 at South Gray's Close. He was the second son of the 10th Earl of Buchan and his mother, Agnes, was the second daughter of Sir James Steuart of Goodtrees. Henry was educated at Richard Dick's School in St Andrews and he matriculated from the United College of St Salvador and St Leonards in 1760. He studied law at the universities of Edinburgh and Glasgow and was admitted to the Faculty of Advocates in 1768. He developed his unrivalled eloquence as a member of the Forum Debating Society and wrote several pieces of poetry of considerable merit.

There are many amusing anecdotes told of Henry Erskine's life, for example: Dr. Samuel Johnson (1709-84), the learned lexicographer, critic and poet, of *Dictionary* fame who was well-known for his sarcastic rudeness, was observed walking up the High Street accompanied by the revering James Boswell (1740-95), Johnson's biographer. Henry Erskine, smiling and quite unable to pass by without comment, approached the pair and pressing a shilling into Boswell's hand, he whispered:
"This is for the sight of your English bear!"

In court he was at his best. His humour, mixed with sublime charm, was such that on commencing his summing up, he had opened his remarks with the well-used legal exaggeration,
"I shall be brief, my Lords." The welcoming response from the bench, was:
"Hoots man, Harry, dinna be brief - dinna be brief." A compliment reserved only for advocate Henry Erskine.

When the self-effacing James Gillespie *qv*, the snuff-maker of Colinton, in an atypical moment of self indulgence, bought a brightly coloured coach, Henry Erskine found this irresistible when he penned a proposed motto for it:

> *Wha would hae thoucht it,*
> *That noses had bocht it?*

Erskine's literary work included his metrical translations from the classics, *The Emigrant* and several others which were published in 1773 during the first year of his married life to Christian, the only daughter of George Fullerton of Broughton Hall, comptroller of customs at Leith. They had several children, one of whom succeeded his uncle as 12th Earl of Buchan. Christian died in 1804 and a year later Henry Erskine married Mrs Turnbull, the widow of an Edinburgh advocate.

When he was appointed Lord Advocate for Scotland in 1783, succeeding the mighty Henry Dundas *qv* (ref.28 Bishop's Close), who became the 1st Viscount Melville, Dundas remarked, somewhat sarcastically, that there was little point in Henry Erskine bothering to make the purchase of a new silk gown:

"For all the time you will want it; you had better borrow mine." Erskine replied smartly:

"From the readiness with which you make me the offer, Dundas, I have no doubt the gown is made to fit any party; but it shall never be said of Harry Erskine that he put on the abandoned habits of his predecessor." But Dundas's prediction proved correct, the coalition ministry which appointed Erskine was suddenly changed and he was replaced within a few months.

In 1785 he became Dean of the Faculty of Advocates but his outspoken opposition to the Government's 'Seditious Writings' Bill, resulted in his deposition in 1796 to be replaced by Robert Dundas of Arniston, nephew of the powerful Henry Dundas.

Britain was at war with France and during the paranoia of Pitt's 'Reign of Terror' innocent men were given stiff sentences for sedition. Henry Erskine trod a wary tightrope. It was at this time that the young advocate Thomas Muir asked him to conduct his defence. Muir had been charged with 'exciting a spirit of disloyalty and disaffection, of recommending Paine's *Rights of Man*, of distributing seditious writings and of reading aloud a seditious writing.' Henry Erskine, quite rightly, insisted on conducting the case without interference but Muir decided to defend himself. This was a mistake on Muir's part. Henry Erskine was held in great esteem and was highly respected, even by the ascerbic and vitriolic Judge Braxfield. In the event Muir was sentenced to fourteen years transportation to Botany Bay.

The crass injustice of this and other cases created international outrage. The obelisk to the Political Martyrs at the Calton Burying Ground commemorates the events of these dark days.

The old town, that is the Royal Mile of Edinburgh, had become overcrowded, in fact the absence of any form of drainage caused such a stench that most of the better off were leaving to take up residence in fashionable George Square, built in 1766. In 1784 Erskine took his family away from the risk of disease in the High Street to live at George Square. In 1789, in spite of criticisms against the New Town development, he moved to No. 27 Princes Street.

Sir Walter Scott (1771-1832), whose parents lived at George Square, said of him,

> "He was the best natured man I ever knew.... wherever
> there was a litigant, civil, criminal, fiscal or ecclesiastic,
> there was a desire for Henry Erskine; despair if he was
> lost - confidence if he was secured."

In 1788 Henry Erskine had the unenviable job of defending the infamous Deacon Brodie. He tried to prove his innocence by means of an alibi in spite of the 'king's evidence' of one of Brodie's partners in crime, but the production of Brodie's letters of farewell to his mistresses was conclusive evidence of his guilt and Brodie was sentenced to be hanged. (Ref. 10. Brodie's Close).

In July 1799, Erskine defended the English minister, Rev Fitzsimmons, who had aided the escape of several French prisoners from Edinburgh Castle. The guilty minister was given a light sentence of three months in the Tolbooth.

Erskine was the toast of the Whigs - "The independence of the Bar and Henry Erskine." His popularity was described by Lord Cockburn in his 'Memorials' - *nothing was so sour as not to be sweetened by the glance, the voice, the gaiety, the beauty of Henry Erskine.*

It was the general expectation in legal circles that Erskine would be appointed Lord President of the Court of Session in 1811, but Charles Hope, fifteen years his junior, was appointed. Henry Erskine was invited by Charles Hope to take the office of Lord Justice Clerk but after consultation with his friends he declined the generous offer. His health had begun to deteriorate and he retired to Almondell in Linlithgowshire to spend his remaining years enjoying his garden and his music.

Scotland lost her most popular jurist when he died in 1817. A plaque, long since removed from South Gray's Close, summed up this 'man of handsome presence, fascinating manner, and sparkling wit - the most eloquent speaker at the Scotch Bar in his time', it was inscribed:
No poor man wanted a friend while Harry Erskine lived.

33. Hyndford's Close - Professor Daniel Rutherford

Hyndford's Close (formerly Charteris Close and Collington's Close) takes its name from the Earls of Hyndford whose mansion in the Close is now part of St Patrick's Church. The **3rd Earl of Hyndford**, John Carmichael, was Ambassador to Prussia, Russia and Vienna. He was known for his agricultural improvements in Lanarkshire and he introduced fifty-seven year leases for his tenants just before his death (the short-lease system of tenure had caused misery and uncertainty for farm tenants since medieval times). The Earldom became extinct in 1817 on the death of Andrew, the 4th Earl of Hyndford.

Chambers in his *Traditions of Edinburgh* records that by 1868 the Close was in such state that access to it was prevented by filth. Of course, today it is perfectly pleasant and well-preserved. An adjacent, tall-turreted mansion was that of the 4th Earl of Selkirk.

The house was next occupied by **Dr Daniel Rutherford**, the discoverer of the distinction between nitrogen and carbon dioxide. He was professor of botany in 1786 at the University of Edinburgh and an uncle of Sir Walter Scott.

Another well-known resident was **Jean, Duchess of Gordon**, the daughter of Sir William Maxwell of Monrieth. She married the 4th Duke of Gordon and lived in a house on the west side of the Close. An astonishingly beautiful woman, she was the leader of late 18th century fashion in Edinburgh and her five daughters inherited her good looks. Three of them married dukes - the Dukes of Richmond, Manchester and Bedford. The fourth daughter married the Marquis of Cornwallis and the fifth a Baronet. However, the Duchess is possibly best remembered for helping her husband in 1794 to raise a regiment to fight in the Napoleonic War - the Gordon Highlanders (now amalgamated with the Queen's Own Highlanders to become simply the 'Highlanders'). The Duchess promised a kiss to any man who would accept the 'King's Shilling.' The offer proved irresistible as she toured villages throughout the north-east of Scotland and the regiment was quickly formed on 24th June 1794 in Aberdeen.

Sadly, she became estranged from her husband and led a wandering life to die in comparative poverty in an hotel in Piccadilly, London.

The house in Hyndford's Close was the home of Dr Daniel Rutherford, Professor of Botany at the University in 1786. He was one of the many geniuses of what came to be called 'The Scottish Enlightenment'. His great contribution to this 'Golden Age' was his scientific work in his discovery of the distinction between nitrogen and carbon dioxide.

He was born in this old mansion on 3rd November 1749. His father was Dr. John Rutherford (1695-1779) who introduced a completely new method of teaching at the University, that of clinical medicine, and he was the first to insist that chemistry should be recognised as a subject in its own right. Daniel Rutherford's mother was Dr Rutherford's second wife, Anne Mackay, who was intensely interested and encouraging in the early education at home of her son. At the age of seven, he attended Mr Mundell's school in Edinburgh and afterwards an academy in England. He studied medicine at the University of Edinburgh under the great Professor William Cullen (1710-90) who was the first to discover the importance of the nervous system. Another of his professors was Joseph Black (1728-99) who evolved the theory of 'latent heat' and who succeeded Cullen as Professor of Medicine and Chemistry.

Daniel Rutherford proved his genius while still a student. In his dissertation which formed part of the work for his MD degree he was the first to make the distinction between carbon dioxide and nitrogen. He did not name the new gas nor did he realise that it was an element but after the publication of his discovery in 1772 he travelled extensively in Europe receiving the approbation of scientists in France and Italy. He returned after two years of travel and study to practise medicine in Edinburgh. Grant, in his *Old and New Edinburgh* describes Rutherford's discovery:

'he chose a chemical subject 'De Aire Mephitico', which, from the originality of his views, obtained the highest encomiums from Dr Black. In his dissertation he demonstrated, though without explaining its properties, "the existence of a peculiar air, or new gaseous fluid, to which some eminent modern philosophers have given the name of azote, and others of nitrogen."'

Rutherford was admitted a Licentiate of the Royal College of Physicians on 6th February 1776 and a Fellow on 6th May 1777. His work as a botanist gained him the Professorship of Botany at the University in 1786. Young Walter Scott (later Sir Walter) was fifteen years old at this time and often walked from his home in George Square to visit his uncle, the professor, at Hyndford's Close. Rutherford's sister, Anne, married Walter Scott WS, a respected Edinburgh solicitor, father of the famous novelist and poet.

Daniel Rutherford's death was sudden on 15th December 1819 at the age of seventy-one. Two of his sisters died during the same month, one of whom was Anne, Sir Walter Scott's mother, who died on Christmas Eve. Professor Rutherford was buried in the churchyard of St John's Church at the west end of Princes Street.

34. John Knox's House - John Knox

John Knox was supposed to have lived for a short period in the upper floor of this medieval house which had its third storey added in 1525.

The overhanging timbers and gables are modern copies of their originals. The ground floor was a jeweller's shop in the 16th century and was occupied by James Mosman, goldsmith and jeweller to Mary Queen of Scots.

The gilded sun with its rays has the word GOD in Latin, Greek and Scots and the initials JM (James Mosman) and MA (Mariota Arres, his wife) give the names of the occupants. She inherited the house after her husband's execution for treason. Above the shop front is the inscription:

LYFE.GOD.ABUFE.AL.AND.YI.NYCHTBOUR.AS.YI.SELF (love God above all and thy neighbour as thyself).

The house was threatened with destruction about 1830, so that the roadway could be widened but thankfully Lord Cockburn *qv* (ref. 24. Cockburn Street) saved it from destruction.

It is named after the man who led Scotland away from Catholicism and into Presbyterianism. He was the leader of the Reformation in Scotland and risked his life many times for his new beliefs.

Born near Haddington c1505, **John Knox** was educated at the Grammar School of Haddington and the University of Glasgow (from 1521). He was ordained as a Catholic Priest in 1529 but he surrendered his Orders in 1544 having witnessed the cruelties and corruption then prevalent in the Catholic Church. He had studied the works of John Calvin (1509-64) which had been forbidden by Act of Parliament and he grieved over the burning of his friend George Wishart on 1st March 1546. It had been ordered by Cardinal Beaton who was assassinated one month afterwards during Henry VIII's 'Rough Wooing'.

Knox, a friend of Wishart and a known enemy of Beaton, was thought to have been implicated and he had to take refuge at the Castle of St Andrews. The Scottish Catholic nobles sought assistance from the French and Knox was taken prisoner when the French fleet laid siege to the castle. With his fellow Reformers he was chained as a galley slave and taken to Rouen then to Nantes.

During Knox's absence the Scots had been defeated by King Henry's forces commanded by Protector Somerset at Pinkie Hill (1547) near Musselburgh and later with French assistance the English were driven out.

The six-year-old Mary Queen of Scots was sent to France to be affianced to the Dauphin whom she married in 1558. Knox, near to death, was released in 1549 but he dared not return to Scotland which was under the Regency of Catholic Mary of Guise. Knox remained in England as one of King Edward's Chaplains in Ordinary. The ways of the English court displeased him and no-one escaped his stern reproof. He made enemies, one of whom was the Duke of Northumberland who cunningly arranged that Knox be offered the Bishopric of Rochester. Knowing that this was a device to curtail his influence he declined it risking criticism and accusations of disloyalty, but he knew that Edward VI favoured him. However, Edward died on 6th July 1553 aged only fifteen years and Knox promptly left London on the day that Mary I, a staunch Catholic, was proclaimed Queen.

Queen Mary, or 'Bloody Mary' as she became known, exercised repressive and vindictive authority by penalising Protestants as heretics. Against advice Knox steadfastly refused to leave the country and he wrote his *First Blast of the Trumpet against the Monstrous Regiment of Women* as a strong denunciation of Mary's government - the word 'Regiment' meaning 'Government' and not women in general; this was the basis of the misunderstanding which quite wrongly branded Knox a misogynist.

After his marriage to Marjery Bowes, Knox was persuaded to travel abroad. In January 1554 he arrived in Geneva where he and John Calvin became friends. Knox's two sons were born there and after two years of preaching and teaching the Knox family returned to Scotland. He had been given the freedom of the city of Geneva where he was greatly respected.

The Protestant nobles of Scotland had formed themselves into the 'Lords of Congregation' and in 1558, with their help, Knox made a new translation of the 'Geneva Bible'.

Mary I of England died in 1558 and Protestant Elizabeth I reigned, but when Knox arrived home the Queen Regent, Mary of Guise, James V's widow and mother of Mary Queen of Scots, treated Knox with undisguised hostility. He was proclaimed an outlaw and a rebel. After a riot in Perth when monasteries were burned, Knox was told that he would be shot if he attempted to preach. Ignoring all threats he proceeded to denounce the Papacy in the Cathedral of St Andrews where he gained the strong support of the Provost, the bailies and the inhabitants. They agreed to Reformed worship and to strip the church of all of its Catholic images.

Knox's influence spread rapidly. He was called to a meeting of nobles, barons and burgh representatives in Edinburgh. They agreed to suspend the authority of the Queen Regent. She sought reinforcements from the French who attacked the fortifications at Leith. The Reformers, under the Earl of Arran, repelled the French from Fife and, for the first time in the history of Scotland, English troops were asked for their support against the French, although they were never required. In March 1560 the Reformers blockaded Leith and starved the French to surrender. However, Mary of Guise died suddenly and in July the Treaty of Edinburgh was signed between Queen Elizabeth and the French. It agreed to their withdrawal and a free Parliament in Scotland.

In December 1560 young Mary's French husband, the Dauphin, died and she, avoiding Queen Elizabeth's intercepting ships, landed at Leith on 19th August 1561. She was eighteen years old, tall, comely and beautiful. At first she promised not to interfere with the new Scottish Protestantism and she asked only to be left in peace to practise her religion. One of Knox's early rows with her was over land revenues, one third of which was shared between the Crown and the kirk. Dissatisfied, Knox claimed all of it, saying, "Two parts freely given to the devil and one third divided between God and the devil."

Protestantism was now formally established in Scotland and Knox, with four ministers, was commissioned by the Privy Council to plan ecclesiastical government. The result was *The First Book of Discipline* which averred that a school for every parish be erected and that all monies should support the universities and churches. This did not please the nobility; they had long enjoyed the rich revenues of the Catholic Clergy. Neither the *First* nor the *Second Book of Discipline*, compiled twenty years later, received legislative sanction.

The General Assembly of the Church of Scotland met in Edinburgh for the first time on 20th December 1560. There were forty members of which six were ministers. Knox now took Mary Queen of Scots under his special charge and from the start there were deep disagreements. Her sympathy lay with the Catholic Princes of Europe and they advocated universal extermination of Protestants. Knox badgered, argued, corrected and criticised her behaviour and public policy; she was often reduced to tears of exasperation.

The Scottish Parliament met in May 1563, the first meeting since Mary's return, and she cleverly blocked ratification of the Treaty of Edinburgh. Knox reacted angrily. He severed his old friendship with the Earl of Moray and he preached against the deep ingratitude among the Lords for their deliverance from the bondage of Catholicism. He predicted serious consequences for the Queen if she married a Catholic. She had him brought to trial on the pretext of a letter he had written supporting two Protestants accused of rioting. He was begged to plead for the Queen's mercy. Knox would hear none of it. After long arguments the Lords voted that they could find no fault. The queen and her flatterers were enraged and commanded a second vote. The nobility, highly offended, absolved Knox of any offence.

John Knox's wife died in 1564 and three years later he married the sixteen-year-old daughter of Lord Ochiltree. Knox was now accused of ambitions to the throne, the Ochiltrees being of Royal blood.

In June 1565 Queen Mary married her cousin, the odious, overbearing Henry, Lord Darnley. She proclaimed him king without consulting the Estates of the Realm and Darnley immediately set out to attack Knox. Finding fault in one of his sermons, Darnley demanded his arrest for an imaginary insult. Knox was ordered to stop preaching but he replied simply, that commands to speak or to abstain could be made only by the Church. The Queen and Darnley renewed their efforts to encourage Catholicism. Catholic ecclesiastics were restored to Parliament but they fled after the murder of the Queen's secretary, the talented Rizzio, by the jealous Darnley and several nobles. Knox had retired to Ayrshire to write his *History of the Reformation in Scotland*.

The year 1567 was a momentous one. Knox was out of the country having been given permission to visit his two sons in England. In his absence Darnley was murdered and the Queen was suspected of complicity with the Earl of Bothwell who was put on trial. He was found guiltless in his absence; it was farcical.

After a pretended abduction Bothwell took the Queen to Dunbar Castle and they married on 15th May. The scandal was too much. Several lords joined against Bothwell who fled to the Orkneys after his defeat at Carberry Hill in June. Mary was jeered on her return to Edinburgh. She was imprisoned in Lochleven Castle and compelled to sign a deed of abdication. Knox hurried back to Edinburgh and preached a sermon at the coronation of the one-year-old James VI in which he advocated that Mary should answer to the crimes of adultery and murder.

The Earl of Moray became Regent and immediately summoned Parliament to ratify all the Acts of 1560. He worked assiduously for peace, but he had his enemies - the family feud with the Argylls and the jealousy of the Hamiltons. He had to crush two revolts and his victory at Langside compelled Mary, who had escaped from Lochleven, to flee to England.

Moray was assassinated by the treacherous Hamilton of Bothwellhaugh. There was national mourning and Knox, overwhelmed with grief, preached the funeral sermon. Afterwards he had a stroke which affected his speech and he wrote that he would 'soon take his goodnight of the world'. But there was to be no rest for him. Leith was under attack from the Queen's forces, Protestants were harassed and assaulted and Knox was now accused of complicity in the murder of Darnley. He defended himself easily and discredited his accusers, Robert and Archibald Hamilton. Ironically, the latter was hanged for his part in the murder.

Knox, now 67 years old, was weakening physically, but he could still electrify his congregations. On 6th August 1572 he wrote a touching farewell to the General Assembly. By November he was dying. He asked to hear his evening prayers after which Dr Preston asked him if he had heard the prayers. Knox replied,
"Would to God that you and all men had heard them as I have heard them; I praise God for that heavenly sound." He lifted his hand and died peacefully. The day was 24th November 1572. He was interred in the Churchyard of St Giles Church; his burial place is under car park no.44. The newly elected Regent Morton summed up his character saying, "Here lies one who never feared the face of man."

35. Tweeddale Court, Tweeddale House - 1st Marquis of Tweeddale

Tweeddale Court (formerly Alexander Young's Court, James Brown's Court and John Laing's Court) almost at the foot of the High Street on the south side, has the atmosphere of quaint old Edinburgh and the advantage of restoration work by the most eminent of architects. **Tweeddale House**, at the end of the Court, was the home of Sir William Bruce (1630-1710), the King's Surveyor, who reconstructed Holyrood Palace for Charles II. But the house is much older: it was built during the 16th century and inherited in 1585 by Neil Laing, Keeper of the Signet. Note the inscription on the lintel of the moulded window, left of the doorway - 'NL' and 'ED' - Neil Laing and his wife Elizabeth Danielstoune.

Bruce purchased the property in 1664 and reconstructed it. Six years later he sold it to the 2nd Earl of Tweeddale. In 1671 Tweeddale bought the adjacent tenement and carried out extensive repairs to it. From then the court was called 'Tweeddale Court'.

Today, Tweeddale House is occupied by the publishers, Oliver and Boyd, and part of the ground floor of the tenement accommodates the Scottish Poetry Library which has branches throughout Scotland.

Tweeddale House was threatened with demolition in 1750 when John Adam (1721-92) reported: *there is not one single thing within the doors of it that can be of use in the repairs, or can be allow'd to stand as they are*. Fortunately, his advice was not taken and instead John and Robert Adam were given the work of its reconstruction in 1752-53.

The 'Tweeddale' of this Court is **John Hay, 2nd Earl and 1st Marquis of Tweeddale** (1626-97) who joined the Royalists at Nottingham on the outbreak of the Civil War in 1642. At first the Royalists had some success and there were fears that King Charles would reintroduce Episcopacy in Scotland. The English Parliament had agreed to Presbyterianism in both England and Scotland under the 'Solemn League and Covenant' of 1543 and the Covenanters joined the Parliamentarians against the king.

Tweeddale could not accept Charles's refusal of the Covenant and he felt compelled to take command of a Scots Regiment against the Royalist advance northwards. His command was part of the army under David Leslie which joined the Roundheads at the defeat of Charles at Marston Moor on 2nd July 1644. The Royalists lost almost 4000 men and their power in the north. However, the Marquis of Montrose, now a Royalist, created havoc in Scotland by defeating the Marquis of Argyll. Perth, Glasgow and Aberdeen had fallen and Leslie's army came north to defeat Montrose at Philiphaugh.

Charles was finally defeated at Naseby and made his way to the Scottish army near Newark. He was imprisoned on the Isle of Wight and agreed to the Solemn League and Covenant on condition that it would not be compulsorily imposed. Tweeddale was party to this 'Engagement'. He commanded the East Lothian Regiment for the king at the Battle of Preston in 1648. However, the 'Anti-Engagers' with Argyll and Warriston as leaders were in ascendancy, but all Scots were horrified when Charles I was executed on 30th January. Tweeddale was present when Charles II was crowned by the Marquis of Argyll at Scone in 1651 but he too could not accept the Covenant.

The 1st Earl of Tweeddale died in 1654 and John Hay succeeded as 2nd Earl. He was chosen the following year as Member of Parliament for East Lothian and he became a member of the committee which was set up to consider the situation if Cromwell became king. In the event Cromwell refused offers of kingship but he ruled the country, including Scotland, as Protector for nine years with one Parliament. Cromwell died in 1658 and Tweeddale was appointed a Scottish Commissioner and sat in the English Parliament of 27th January 1659.

After the rejoicing of the Restoration, Tweeddale was made a Privy Councillor under Charles II, but he was held in Edinburgh Castle because he had opposed the sentencing of James Guthrie, a minister of Stirling who, as one of the Covenanters, had met with Cromwell in 1648 at Moray House. Tweeddale wrote to Lauderdale saying that 'he was struck as with thunder by the order for committal.' He apologised to the King and petitioned the Council for his freedom which was duly granted but with a bond of £1000 and confinement to his house under a penalty.

However, he was soon in favour again and in 1663 he was chosen as President of the Council. In 1664 he was appointed a member of the High Commission 'for the execution of the laws in church affairs'. He was appointed an extraordinary Lord of Session but, in spite of his previous fall from favour over the Rev. James Guthrie, he expressed his deep concern over the Government's harsh treatment of the Covenanters. He convinced the new Commissioner, Lauderdale, to issue a 'Letter of Indulgence' in June 1669. It allowed the more peaceable of the 'outed' ministers to resume their ministry. The conventicles (open air preaching by Covenanter ministers) worried Lauderdale and he toughened the laws against them for their stubborn refusal to accept Episcopacy.

Inevitably, Tweeddale and Lauderdale clashed, and the latter wrote to Charles II on 20th November 1673 that Tweeddale was 'at first an underhand contriver and counsellor and has now shown himself openly against the government'. A few weeks later Tweeddale was deprived of his seat in the Privy Council.

The Covenanters now rebelled openly and marched against Charles II's illegitimate son, the Duke of Monmouth. At the Battle of Bothwell Bridge on 2nd July 1679 they were routed by an army of Borderers (who were to become the renowned Scots Greys); 400 were killed and 1200 taken prisoner to be held for five months in Greyfriars Churchyard where many starved to death. This brutality marked the end of Lauderdale and in 1680 Tweeddale was reappointed Commissioner of the Treasury. One of the conventicles had been held in the town barn of Inverkeithing of which Tweeddale was proprietor. However, he was absolved of responsibility because the barn was held within the tenure of the town. After two years the Earl of Tweeddale and the Duke of Hamilton were readmitted to the Privy Council (11th May 1682) and in June, Tweeddale was appointed Commissioner of the Mint.

Charles II died in 1685 and was succeeded by his brother James VII (II of England), a staunch Catholic, and the first year of his reign was so relentlessly cruel in hunting down Covenanters it became known as the 'killing time'. Tweeddale remained in office under James II but he was strongly against his policies in Scotland. To speak out could easily have meant the death sentence and he remained moderate. James had replaced many high offices in government with Catholics.

Catholic services were conducted in the Chapel of Holyrood and James issued a Letter of Indulgence which allowed Roman Catholics and Presbyterians to worship as they wished. This seemingly harmless action was a ploy to allow Catholic ascendancy and ultimately to make Scotland and England Roman Catholic again. Such was the outcry against him that William of Orange, who was married to James's daughter Mary, was invited to become Protestant king. Tweeddale supported the Revolutionary Party in support of William and Mary and in March 1689 with the Earl of Leven, he on behalf of the 'Estates', presented an order to the Duke of Gordon to hand over Edinburgh Castle within twenty-four hours.

Tweeddale was now sworn in as a Privy Councillor (18th May 1689) of King William, six months later he was appointed a Lord of the Treasury and a month afterwards he became Lord High Chancellor of Scotland. However, King William had his enemies in Scotland one of whom, John Graham of Claverhouse, Viscount Dundee, led the Highlanders to fight for the restoration of James VII. He was defeated at Killiecrankie but William was still apprehensive of rebellion; he distributed £12,000 among the clan chiefs to 'buy' their loyalty but some refused to take the money.

The government now proclaimed that all chiefs must take the oath of allegiance to the king before 1st January 1692. The clan chief of the Macdonalds of Glencoe was the only one not to have signed by the due date. He was an old man and had been delayed by snow and ice; he took the oath on 4th January at Inveraray, having been turned away from Fort William on 1st January. Sir John Dalrymple, the Secretary of State, arranged for William III to sign the 'Letter of Fire and Sword'. Dalrymple simply omitted to tell the king that the Macdonald chief had already signed the oath and he sent two Campbells, Major Duncanson and Captain Campbell, to wipe out the Macdonalds.

The whole nation was appalled. Tweeddale was one of the members of the commission of enquiry which reported to Parliament that this dastardly deed had been committed despite the fact that the Macdonalds had trustingly given their hospitality to the soldiers who, in the middle of the night, killed the Macdonald men, women and children in their sleep.

Tweeddale's conscientious and honest statesmanship was rewarded in his creation as 1st Marquis of Tweeddale on 17th December 1694. However, he was to fall from favour yet again. This time Tweeddale, as Commissioner, had given Royal assent in the absence of the king to 'The Company of Scotland trading to Africa and the Indies'. This would undoubtedly affect trade in England and the English Parliament denounced it. However, when William Paterson proposed his 'Darien Company' for a Scottish colony in Darien or Panama, the king was so dissatisfied that he dismissed Tweeddale from office in 1696.

A year later John Hay, the 1st Marquis of Tweeddale, now seventy-one years of age, became ill and died on 11th August 1697. He had served four kings as best his conscience and great patriotism would allow. He is recorded in history as among 'the most honourable and straight forward of his time.'

36. World's End Close - Sir James Stanfield

Before the Canongate was incorporated within the City of Edinburgh in 1856 the last Close within the City was **World's End Close** (formerly Stanfield's Close, Sweit's Close and Swift's Close) - this was the end of the world as far as the residents of Edinburgh were concerned.

In this close stood the town residence of **Sir James Stanfield**. This Englishman was a colonel of Cromwell's Parliamentarian army and after Cromwell's victory over General David Leslie at the Battle of Dunbar in 1650, Stanfield established a wool factory at New Mills in Haddington.

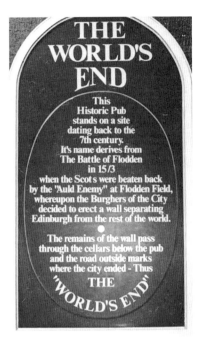

After the Restoration in 1660 the Scottish Parliament granted immunity to Colonel James Stanfield, to establish a company which prospered under the joint ownership of James Stanfield and Robert Blackwood of Edinburgh. They purchased the ecclesiastic land which surrounded the mill in Haddington and Colonel Stanfield became the principal partner of the New Mill Company.

Such was his success in manufacture and trade the Scottish Parliament and the Privy Council passed an Act to encourage trade and manufacture in Scotland and Colonel Stanfield was knighted by Charles II.

He became the Member of the Scottish Parliament for East Lothian and his success seemed assured when demand exceeded production. However, cheaper imports from England to supply General Dalzell's dragoons caused discontent among the 700 mill workers as did the importation of English weavers. The Privy Council agreed to burn imported cloth but dissolution was discussed among the shareholders and Stanfield proposed to sell his share of the company.

His financial difficulties were worsened by the spending excesses of his son, Philip; their relationship deteriorated into frustrated anger and the colonel disinherited his eldest son. Their quarrels were well known and talked about and when, in 1687, Colonel Stanfield's body was found in the River Tyne at Haddington it was, at first, assumed that he had committed suicide but when it became known that his wife had prepared his burial before his death, suspicion was aroused. When his body was exhumed it was discovered that he had been strangled. His son Philip was accused of patricide and after a trial he was hanged in Edinburgh on 24th February 1688.

In those days of mystery and superstition it was believed that the body of the person murdered bled at the touch of the murderer. This was considered as evidence of guilt at the trial of Philip Stanfield.

> *Young Stanfield touch'd his father's corpse,*
> *When rose a fearful wail;*
> *For blood gushed from the winding sheet,*
> *And every face grew pale.*
>
> James Miller

His head was displayed at the East Port in Haddington being the spot nearest to which the crime was committed.

The grave of Sir James Stanfield is at Morham Churchyard where his elaborately carved tombstone is near the church door.

Tour Walk 4 - The Canongate

37. St Mary's Street - St Mary
38. Flodden Wall - The Battle
    of Flodden
39. Jeffrey Street - Lord Jeffrey
40. Cranston Street
    - Sir Robert Cranston
41. New Street
- Henry Home, Lord Kames
and David Dalrymple, Lord Hailes
42. Mid Common Close/ Morocco Land
    - Andrew Gray
43. [Boyd's Close] - The White
    Horse Inn
    Chessel's Court
    Jack's Land
    Old Playhouse Close
44. St John's Land/Street
    - Lord Monboddo
45. Moray House
    - Marquis of Argyll
    Bible Land/Shoemakers'
    Close
46. Gladstone Court
    - W.E.Gladstone
47. Canongate Tolbooth
48. Canongate Church
49. Huntly House
    Bakehouse Close
    Acheson House
50. Panmure House
    - Adam Smith
51. Milton House
    - Lord Milton
52. Haddington's Entry/Nisbet
    of Dirleton's House
    - Sir John Nisbet
53. Clarinda's Tearoom
    - Mrs Agnes Maclehose
    Golfers' Land & Brown's
    Close, Jenny Ha's
54. Queensberry House
    - 1st Duke of Queensberry
55. Whitefoord House
    - Dugald Stewart
56. White Horse Close
    - William Dick
    Russell House
57. Edward VII statue
58. Palace of Holyroodhouse
59. Holyrood Abbey - David I
    Queen Mary's Bath,
    Abbey Strand

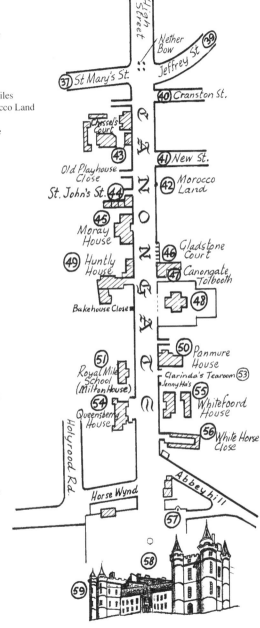

Tour Walk 4 - Summary

The Canongate

The name **Canongate** derives from 'canon gait' - the walk or way of the canons - this was the route taken by the canons of Holyrood to the gates of the old town at the **Netherbow**. The August-inian canons arrived in 1128 when David I founded the Abbey of Holyrood. They left during the troubled time of the Reformation, about 1570. Houses began to appear outside the city early in the 14th century.

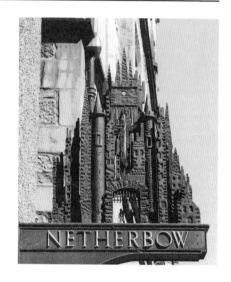

After 1513 the **Flodden Wall** was built and entry to the city was through any of the six ports. Entry at the Canongate was through the Netherbow Port the approximate position of which is marked in outline by means of brass studs on the roadway almost opposite World's End Close.

The Canongate was absorbed into the Edinburgh boundary in 1856.

37. St Mary's Street was part of an old Roman Road and takes its name from the Chapel and Convent dedicated to the Virgin Mary. The chapel was destroyed in 1572 during the Reformation when windows and doors of the houses were walled up, even the roofs were removed, so that no shelter could be given to the supporters of the infant James VI and Sir William Kirkcaldy of Grange, the faithful devotee of Mary Queen of Scots, defended the town. In 1650 cannons were mounted on the Netherbow Port to repel Cromwell's army.

38. The **Flodden Wall** was built after the Battle of Flodden in 1513. After this disastrous defeat of the Scots army there were fears of invasion by the English, but it was to take over thirty years to build the wall which was never needed. Part of it can be seen at the foot of St Mary's Street. Its route followed the Castle rock to the foot of the Grassmarket, up the Vennel to Laurieston Place, alongside Greyfriars Churchyard to the foot of Drummond Street where it turned north down the Pleasance and up St Mary's Street to Cranston Street at the foot of which it came to an end having reached the Nor Loch - a total length of 2420 yards (2213m).

39. Jeffrey Street, linking the Canongate to Market Street and the Waverley Station, was built in 1888-92. It was named after **Francis Jeffrey** (1773-1850) who was appointed a Judge of the Court of Session in the year of the Scottish Reform Bill, 1834. As MP for Perth (1830) he was heavily committed to the success of the Reform Bill (1832) and when Earl Grey became Prime Minister Jeffrey was appointed Lord Advocate for Scotland. He had been editor of *The Edinburgh Review* for twenty-seven years and, much to his surprise, he was elected Lord Rector of Glasgow University in 1820.

40. Cranston Street, formerly Leith Wynd, was the main road to the Port of Leith and now merely links the Canongate to East Market Street. It is named after **Sir Robert Cranston** (1843-1923) the highly decorated and honoured part-time soldier and Lord Provost of Edinburgh from 1903 to 1906. He was a successful hotelier, a founder member of the total abstinence movement and a keen participant in the Volunteer Movement in which he attained the rank of Brigadier-General.

41. New Street was a private cul-de-sac when it was built in 1760. Its name was changed in 1819 from Young Street (after a resident, Dr Young) when it was extended to meet Calton Road. This street was the address of two of the *literati* of the 'Golden age' - **Henry Home, Lord Kames** (1696-1782) and **David Dalrymple, Lord Hailes** (1726-92).
  Henry Home, Lord Kames became a judge in 1752 and wrote six law books plus several on philosophy. He then wrote several books on agriculture.
  David Dalrymple was elevated to the bench in 1776. He was a distinguished historian best known for his *Annals of Scotland 1057-1371*. His great uncle was Sir John Dalrymple, 1st Earl of Stair, who ordered the 'Massacre of Glencoe' to eliminate the Macdonald clan in 1692.

42. Mid Common Close / Morocco Land (formerly Vietche's Land), now demolished, is represented by a Moor figure on the wall of the tenement at Mid Common Close. It reminds us of a romantic story of young **Andrew Gray** who fled the city and the law to return many years later from Morocco during the plague in Edinburgh of 1645. He used an Eastern medicine to cure the Lord Provost's daughter. They fell in love, married and set up home at Morocco Land. Another version relates to the kidnapping of a young lady who was sold to the Emperor of Morocco. She was treated with kindness and her reassuring letter home suggested trading which flourished thereafter.

43. [Boyd's Close] - White Horse Inn was named after James Boyd who owned the Boyd's Inn or "The White Horse Inn" commemorating a white horse which brought Boyd good fortune at the races on Leith Sands. 'Boyd's' was a favourite inn in the Royal Mile and was patronised by many eminent people such as the ascerbic Dr Samuel Johnson (1709-84) who berated a waiter for using his fingers instead of tongs while sweetening his lemonade which he then tossed out of the window.

Chessels Court accommodated the Excise Office after its removal from the Cowgate. Its attractive arcades lead to Chessels Buildings, built in 1745 by Archibald Chessel who was Excise Officer from 1769. It was here that the infamous Deacon Brodie perpetrated his last robbery (ref. 10. Brodie's Close) on 5th March 1788. It was a total fiasco with Brodie fleeing the scene much to the annoyance of his partners in crime, one of whom, John Brown, turned king's evidence which resulted in Brodie's execution on 1st October 1788.

Jack's Land, built by a slater called Robert Jack, was the residence of David Hume (1711-1776) from 1753 to 1762 during which he finished his *History of England* in six volumes. Another eminent resident was the strikingly beautiful Countess of Eglinton who entertained Prince Charles Edward Stuart during his occupation of Edinburgh in 1745.

Old Playhouse Close was the venue of an early theatre from 1747 to 1769 and is credited as 'the cradle of legitimate drama in Scotland.' The Church and City Magistrates strongly disapproved of such activity, fearing that it would 'inflame the minds' of ordinary people. The Rev. John Home (1722-1808) of Athelstaneford had to resign his ministry for daring to write the tragedy, *Douglas*. It was an immediate success at this theatre on 14th December 1756, and prompted a shout from the audience, "Whaur's your Wullie Shakespeare noo?"

44. St John's Pend was the site of the Priory of the Knights of the Order St John. A Cross of St John is represented in the roadway to signify the site of the Cross from which proclamations were made. Lord Provost Sir Alexander Clark was knighted here by Charles I in 1633. The Canongate Kilwinning Lodge, the oldest Masonic Lodge in the world, had its rooms here. The notorious burglar and Deacon of Wrights, Deacon Brodie (ref. 10. Brodie's Close), was a member and Robert Burns was made 'Poet Laureate' of the Lodge during his visit to Edinburgh in 1787.

St John's Street was the address of several eminent people during the 'Golden Age' of intellectual genius in Edinburgh (1760-90), one of whom was the kindly but eccentric judge **James Burnett, Lord Monboddo**, whose 'learned suppers' attracted many of the *literati* to his house. At the rear, a stone tablet informs us that the novelist Tobias Smollett (1721-1771) visited his sister, Mrs Telfer who lived here in 1766.

45. Moray House was built in 1625 for Mary, Dowager Countess of Home but it was named after her daughter, the Countess of Moray, who inherited it in 1643. Oliver Cromwell took over the house in 1648 and met with several Scottish nobles. Its frontage faces south and is best viewed from Bakehouse Close. It was in this house in 1650 that Lord Lorne, son of the 8th Earl of Argyll, married the daughter of the Countess of Moray. During the reception, the wedding party looked down from the balcony to jeer his old adversary, the Marquis of Montrose, who had been captured and was being taken to his trial and subsequent execution. Ironically, both Argyll and Lorne were to meet the same fate some years later.

Bible Land; Shoemakers' Land with its Bible quotations contained within a shield: Psalm 133, v.1: *Behold how good a thing it is, and how becoming well, Together such as brethern are in unity to dwell* and from Proverbs XX, v.20: *It is an honour for a man to cease from strife.* This building, of '1677' above the door, accommodated the hall of the Incorporation of Cordiners whose shield contains a shoemaker's paring knife and St Crispin's crown, the patron saint of shoemakers.

46. Gladstone Court is easily recognised from its covered arches. It was formerly known as Bowling Green Close from the bowling green overlooked by prisoners in the Tolbooth gaol. The Close was also named Magdalene Entry leading to the asylum of that name. It was renamed in honour of the eminent Liberal statesman **William Ewart Gladstone**, four times Prime Minister: 1868, 1880, 1886 and 1892 whose legacy of successful legislation is unequalled in the history of Parliament.

47. The Canongate Tolbooth was built in 1591 which is the date above the entrance arch with the Burgh motto 'Patriae et Posteris' and the initials 'SLB' - Sir Lewis Bellenden the lay Abbot and superior of the burgh. The Tolbooth was a Council Chamber, Police Court and Prison in which Covenanters were imprisoned in 1661-8. It was restored in 1875 by Robert Morham. Its overhanging clock is dated 1884 and has the Burgh Coat of Arms facing the street.

48. The Canongate Church was built at the instigation of James VII from money left to the crown by a rich merchant, Thomas Moodie. It was completed in 1690 and is a place of worship for the Royal family whilst in residence at Holyrood. It is the Military Church of Edinburgh having been adopted by the Royal Scots as their Regimental Kirk. Its Churchyard of 1688 has many interesting monuments: Lord Provost George Drummond (1687-1766), philosopher and economist, Adam Smith (1790); poet, Robert Fergusson (1774); philosopher and teacher, Professor Dugald Stewart (1828); Sir William Fettes (1836), who founded Fettes College; 'Clarinda', Mrs Maclehose (1909), the platonic loved-one of Robert Burns.

49. Huntly House is a museum of olden Edinburgh complete with a model of mediaeval Edinburgh and an attractive shop. The house, built early in the 16th century, takes its name from the fact that the Duchess of Gordon (the Gordons of Huntly) had a flat there in the middle of the 18th century. Its front faces south and is best viewed from Bakehouse Close. The restoration work was carried out from 1927 to 1932 when the conversion to a museum was made.
Bakehouse Close (formerly Cordiner's Close and Hammerman's Close) dates back to the 16th century when it was known as Huntly Close. The house was purchased by the Incorporation of Hammermen in 1647 but it was named Bakehouse Close in 1832 when the Guild of the Incorporation of Bakers bought the property.
Acheson House, immediately east of Huntly House, was built in 1633 for Sir Archibald Acheson of Glencairnie, a Secretary of State during the reign of Charles I. Its side faces the Canongate; and its frontage faces Bakehouse Close. It was purchased by the Marquess of Bute in 1935 and its restoration was completed in 1937.

50. Panmure Close (formerly McKell's Close) in which Panmure House (1691) was the town house of the 4th Earl of Panmure, a brave soldier during the Austrian Succession War, a Privy Councillor to James VII and an ardent Jacobite. He was attainted after the 1715 Rising.
  Adam Smith, the great philosopher and economist, author of *Wealth of Nations*, lived here from 1778 until his death in 1790. He was buried nearby in the Canongate Churchyard.

51. Milton House School, now called the Royal Mile Primary School, stands on the site of the mansion of **Andrew Fletcher, Lord Milton** (1692-1766) a Lord of Session who, as Lord Islay's chief executive, exerted great power in Scotland but with fairness and discretion.

52. Nisbet of Dirleton's House was the residence of **Sir John Nisbet** (1609-1687) a Lord of Session who severely persecuted Covenanters after the Pentland Rising of 1666. He was matched in his severity by his successor and friend, Sir George Mackenzie ('Bluidy Mackenzie').

53. Clarinda's Tearoom at No. 69 Canongate is a welcome stopping place for refreshments and takes its name from **'Clarinda', Mrs Agnes Maclehose**, so beloved of her 'Sylvander', Robert Burns who wrote a series of inspired love-letters to her; a page from one of them is displayed in the tearoom. Her grave, in the Canongate Churchyard, is marked with a beautiful bas relief bronze erected by the Ninety Burns Club
Golfers' Land at Brown's Close (the latter was known as Paterson's Close and Sommerville's Close) was the residence of Bailie John Paterson, a shoemaker, who played golf with the Duke of York (who was crowned James VII) when he was Commissioner in Scotland in 1681 for his brother, Charles II. The wall-plaque is the Paterson Coat-of-Arms with the motto: 'Far and Sure'.
Jenny Ha's is a popular hostel in the Canongate. The plaque nearby is a bas relief representation of the old Change House with the description: *JENNY HA'S CHANGE HOUSE On this site stood a well-known tavern which was the rendezvous of the poets Gay & Allan Ramsay and other congenial spirits of the period 1600 - 1857.*
Its claret was as famed as its Younger's Ale for its potency.

54. Queensberry House was built in 1681-86 by Charles Maitland, Lord Hatton who sold it to the **1st Duke of Queensberry**. The duke supported the enthronement of William III and Mary when James VII (II of England) was deposed in 1688. His son, the 2nd Duke, inherited the house in March 1695. He was a strong Unionist and because of this he was very unpopular. Edinburgh people considered that he was punished for his support of the Union of the Scottish and English Parliaments in 1707 when his insane son escaped from his locked room to roast and eat a kitchen boy. The house was sold by the Earl of March to the Government in 1801 to pay off his gambling debts and became a barracks. It was then converted to a home for the destitute. It became a Nursing Home for the elderly during the 1970s and is now closed and for sale.

55. Whitefoord House was built for Sir John Whitefoord of Blairgunan and Ballochmyle in 1769. It was designed by Robert Mylne, son of the King's Master Mason of Mylne's Court in the Lawnmarket. It was Sir John's sister, Maria, who was immortalised by Robert Burns in his song: *The Lass of Ballochmyle*. Sir John, a patron and admirer of Burns, died in 1803. The house became the home of the popular and inspiring teacher and philosopher, **Professor Dugald Stewart** (1753-1828). His monument, by William H. Playfair, stands on the Calton Hill. Whitefoord House is now a hospital and residence for Scottish War Veterans. After its renovation in 1984 it was opened by Her Majesty the Queen.

56. Whitehorse Close (formerly Davidson's Close and Laurence Ord's Close) was built in 1623 and rebuilt in 1961-4. The Close was named from a white palfrey (a lady's saddle-horse) when the stables were used as the royal mews. This was the starting point for the horse-drawn coaches to London and it became a famous hostelry. In 1639 the Royalist nobles attempted to set out from this Close in support of Charles I who was in Berwick. They were prevented from leaving by a mob of Covenanters who had no faith in the king. The Marquis of Montrose escaped them to give his support to his king.

After 1742 Lord Milton used the house as a coach-house when he lived at Milton House. In 1745 during the Rising, when Prince Charles Edward Stuart occupied the City, the Highland Chiefs and officers used the accommodation of this Close.

William Dick (1793-1866), founder of the 'Dick Vet' College, was born and apprenticed to his father, an ostler, at White Horse Close where he gained his love of animals.

Russell House, at the foot of the Canongate, was saved from demolition by Sir Patrick Geddes (ref. 7. The Outlook Tower). The wall plaque reads:

> *A 17th century tenement preserved by Sir Patrick Geddes (1854-1932). This building was rescued from demolition and restored again in 1976 by the perseverance and endeavours of a number of bodies and individuals including Sir Robert Russell (1890-1972) after whom it is named.*

57. Edward VII Statue, by Henry Snell Gamely in the Palace Yard of Holyroodhouse, commemorates the nine-year reign (1901-10) of a king who was known by the nicknames 'Edward the Peacemaker' for his efforts to maintain peace and 'Edward the Caresser' for his numerous amours. The magnificent screens and gates by George Washington Browne is the **Scottish National Memorial to Edward VII**.

58. Palace of Holyroodhouse, the official residence in Scotland of H.M. Queen, was started by James IV in 1501-05; the northwest tower was built for James V by his Master Mason, John Ayton, from 1528 to 1532. The rest of the frontage with the north west tower was built for Charles II in 1671-6 by Sir William Bruce, the King's Surveyor.

Mary Queen of Scots' second marriage to Lord Darnley and her third, to the Earl of Bothwell, took place at the Palace. Her secretary was murdered and thrown out of a window of the Palace. The importance of the Palace diminished after James VI left Scotland in 1603 to become James I of England. After the Union of the Scottish and English Parliaments in 1707 the Palace was the residence of the nobility. George IV's visit to Edinburgh in 1822 meant extensive repairs and when Queen Victoria became a regular visitor to Scotland the Palace regained its status as a Royal residence. Tours of the interior are regularly available; this is a key historical visit.

59. Holyrood Abbey was built for **David I** in 1128; it is the ruin at the north east corner of the Palace. David II (1329-71) was buried here; James II (r.1437-60) was born, crowned and married in the Abbey and Kings James III, IV and V were married here. James VII (II of England) who revived The Most Ancient and Most Noble Order of the Thistle in 1687 planned to use the Abbey for its chapel but after his dethronement in 1688 the Magistrates, the City Guard with many enraged citizens destroyed the King's Chapel and burned the Abbey complete with furnishings and service books; even the bones of long dead kings were put to the flame.

Queen Mary's Bath in Abbey Strand, although not strictly in the Royal Mile, cannot be omitted. It is often described as the bath-house of Mary Queen of Scots during her six-year reign (1561-1567). It was in fact a summer house in the Palace Physic Garden which stretched over the roadway and now leads to the north gate.

37. St Mary's Street

St Mary's Street, at the cross-roads of High Street, Canongate and Jeffrey Street, runs from the Netherbow Port (its outline is marked in brass studs on the roadway) along the line of the Flodden Wall, part of which can be seen at the end of St Mary's Street looking across to the Pleasance. St Mary's Street was named after a chapel and convent which was dedicated to the Virgin Mary and was destroyed about 1572 during the rampage of destruction by the Reformers.

Little is known of the early life of **St Mary**, the Blessed Virgin, mother of Jesus Christ but each Christmas the story of the birth of Christ is enacted in many primary schools and in church Nativity plays. Mary with her husband Joseph arrived in Bethlehem and being turned away from the inn, their son, the baby Jesus was born in the stable, wrapped in swaddling clothes and laid in a manger. The angel of the Lord appeared to them and said,

"Fear not: for, behold, I bring you good tidings of great joy, which shall be to all people. For unto you is born this day in the city of David a Saviour, which is Christ the Lord.....Glory to God in the highest, and on earth peace, good will toward men".

The three wise men, who had followed the star of David, brought gifts of gold, and frankincense and myrrh. The flight of Mary and Joseph to Egypt to save the baby Jesus from King Herod, are all part of the Christmas story.

The Gospels describe Mary as humble, obedient, candid and prudent at the Annunciation, when the Archangel Gabriel came to her to declare that she was chosen to be the Mother of God. The miracle of Mary 's virginal conception is clearly stated in the Scriptures and Mary is pre-eminent among the saints. Thomas of Aquinas describes her as 'hyperdoulia', meaning that she is venerated above all other saints but infinitely below the adoration due to God alone. Her special cult is called Hyperdoulia - the highest of God's creatures.

Throughout the life of Jesus, Mary remained in the background sharing in the suffering of her son; she did not involve herself in teaching and preaching but her feast days signify the main events in her life:

8th December - her Immaculate Conception
8th September - her birthday
12th September - her most holy name of Mary
21st November - her Presentation to God by her parents in the temple of Jerusalem
25th March - the Annunciation

2nd July - the Visitation to her cousin Elizabeth, mother of St John the Baptist.

11th October - her Divine Motherhood; Mother of God

2nd February - the Purification when Mary took Jesus to the temple of Jerusalem

19th September and the Friday after Passion Sunday - the Seven Sorrows of Our Lady: the flight into Egypt, the three days of disappearance of the boy Jesus, the ascent of Calvary, the crucifixion, the taking down from the cross and the entombment.

15th August - Mary's Assumption soul and body into heaven

5th August - the dedication of Mary's principal Roman basilica "of the snow"

16th July - Our Lady of Mount Carmel

24th September - the apparition of Our Lady on Ransom

7th October - the Most Holy Rosary

11th February - Our Lady's miraculous apparitions to St Bernadette Soubirous at Lourdes.

At a marriage in Cana of Galilee, to which Mary and Jesus were invited, she said to Jesus,

"they have no wine", and Jesus, initially reluctant, performed his first miracle for his mother. She said to the servants,

"whatsoever he saith unto you, do it". Jesus asked them to fill six stone pots with water and when the 'ruler of the feast' tasted the water he found it to be wine.

Mary suffered her greatest anguish when, standing at the Cross on which Jesus was crucified, he said,

"woman behold thy son" and then to the beloved disciple,

"behold thy mother"; he was the loving son making provision for his mother.

Mary lived so quietly and kept in the background to such an extent that there is little record of her life and none of her death; it was thought that she died in Ephesus in Turkey but Jerusalem was claimed as her last abode by the Eastern Fathers. Nations and diocese of the Catholic Church venerate the Blessed Virgin fulfilling her prophecy: "from henceforth all generations shall call me blessed."

38. Flodden Wall

The building of the **Flodden Wall** around Edinburgh was considered to be urgently required as a defence against a possible invasion by the English after the Battle of Flodden on 9th September 1513. This dramatic defeat, in which the King, James IV, and many Scottish nobles were killed, was the saddest day in Scotland.

The wall, which was built over a period of almost fifty years, was never required as a defence and it served to define the boundary, or Royalty, of the city for over two hundred years.

Grant's *Old and New Edinburgh* describes the route:

'Descending from the castle in a south-westerly direction, it crossed the Portsburgh at the foot of the Grassmarket, where there was a barrier called the West Port; and ascending the steep Vennel - where much of it still remains - to Lauriston, it turned due eastwards to the corner of Teviot Row, from whence it ran acutely northward to the Bristo Port. Thence it ran nearly eastward by the south of the present University and Drummond Street to the Pleasance, crossing the Cowgate foot, where stood the Cowgate Port. From there to the Nether Bow Port the enclosure was completed by the west side of St Mary's Wynd (now St Mary's Street), and perhaps part of the old wall of 1450. Descending Leith Wynd (now Cranston Street), which was also closed by a port, the wall ended at the foot of the Nor Loch (now Princes Street Gardens), then, as yet, the artificial defence of the city on that side, the waters of it being regulated by a dam and sluice. These walls were added to and strengthened from time to time as suspicions occurred of the English; at Leith Wynd by Act of Parliament in 1540; another addition in 1560 to the foot of Halkerson's Wynd, near the present North Bridge; and in 1591 all were repaired with bulwarks and flankers; the last addition being, in 1618, at the Greyfriars Port. They had all become ruinous by 1745. The whole length of the old wall was about one mile, that of the new was one mile three furlongs (2420 yards)'.

The battle from which the wall takes its name - the **Battle of Flodden**.

There had been aggravation between the Kings of England and Scotland for many years - Henry VIII of England and James IV of Scotland - but the reason for war was that James decided to honour a long-standing alliance between Scotland and France. Henry VIII had attacked the French to win the Battle of the Spurs in 1513 and the Queen of France had asked James to step one pace into England and to break a lance in her honour and in defiance against the English. However, James, in spite of portents of disaster, declared war on the

English and his army of 20,000 men and boys from all over Scotland assembled in the Lammermuir Hills.

In spite of terrible premonitions of doom he crossed the River Tweed at dusk on 22nd August and by 9th September he had taken up a strong position on Flodden Hill; a position, in retrospect, he ought never to have given up. Instead, he felt that the English, commanded by the Earl of Surrey, had an even stronger position on Branxton Hill, about one mile away. James IV ordered that fires be lit and, behind the smoke, he advanced towards Branxton, but the English were waiting with their light and manoeuvrable artillery.

King James continued his march in schiltrom formation but the mud underfoot caused the disarray of his force. His men were armed with 18-foot pikes which proved to be unwieldy to handle in comparison to the English soldiers' shorter halberd - a pointed spear with an axe head, about ten feet shorter than the pike. However, the Scots gained supremacy on their left wing but, instead of following through with their success, they scattered to loot and plunder. On their right the Scots were overcome and the English continued their attack on the King's division. He was pierced by arrows and his neck was slashed by an English halberd only a few feet from the English commander.

The Scots fought on until darkness made it impossible to continue. At first light it was clear that the Scots had left; their losses were very heavy. The King was dead, nine Earls, fourteen greater Lords, an Archbishop, a Bishop, three Highland Chiefs and thousands of men lay dead. The 9th September 1513 was Scotland's saddest day. The old ballad, *Edinburgh after Flodden* describes the anguish:

Woe and woe, and lamentation, what a piteous cry was there!
Widows, maidens, mothers, children, shrieking, sobbing in despair!
Through the streets the death-word rushes, spreading terror sweeping on -
Jesu Christ! our King has fallen - Oh, great God, King James is gone!
Oh, the blackest day for Scotland that she ever knew before!
Oh, our King, the good, the noble, shall we never see him more!
Woe to us, and woe to Scotland! Oh, our sons, our sons and men!
Surely some have 'scaped the Southron, surely some will come again!
Till the oak that fell last winter shall uprear its withered stem,
Wives and mothers of Dunedin ye may look in vain for them!

The Flodden Wall was not needed. Henry VIII was too pre-occupied in fighting his wars in France to be bothered to follow up his advantage over the defeated Scots.

39. Jeffrey Street

Jeffrey Street, at the crossroads of the High Street, Canongate and St Mary's Street, runs from the Royal Mile to Market Street. Jeffrey Street, with its baronial tenements, crow-stepped gables and conical-roofed turrets, was built from 1886 and named after the literary jurist, **Francis Jeffrey**, a contemporary and friend of Lord Cockburn (ref. 24. Cockburn Street).

Francis Jeffrey was a formidable opponent in court, an uncompromising critic, a strong Whig champion of Reform, Judge of the Court of Session, Lord Advocate and Member of Parliament. He was the editor of *The Edinburgh Review* for twenty-seven years from which he resigned on his appointment as Dean of the Faculty of Advocates in 1829.

It seems perfectly appropriate that two streets, each named after judges should be linked at each end of Market Street - Cockburn Street, named after Lord Henry Cockburn (1779-1854), at the west end of Market Street and Jeffrey Street and the east end of Market Street. These men of eminence were good friends, their political aims coincided in their enthusiasm over reform and in their criticism of the old self-perpetuating Councils.

Francis Jeffrey was born on 23rd October 1773 in Charles Street (now demolished) in Edinburgh, the eldest son of George Jeffrey, Depute Clerk of the Court of Session. He was educated at the High School and he studied law at the universities of Glasgow and Oxford. His father had refused to allow him 'to attend the lectures of so dangerous a teacher' as Dugald Stewart, the Professor of Moral Philosophy at Edinburgh (ref. 55 Whitefoord House). To the old Tory establishment this new Whig reforming radical was a dangerous disturbance in the established order.

In 1794 Jeffrey was called to the Scottish Bar. In Edinburgh he joined the Speculative Society, a literary society of the university, where he met Walter Scott, a fellow law student, Henry Brougham, a future Chancellor and many others who sharpened his wit and perfected his oratory.

The proliferation of clubs in Edinburgh was part of the 'Golden Age' in what came to be called the 'Scottish Enlightenment' when fortunate young men such as Jeffrey were exposed to such great names as Dugald Stewart (1753-1828) the brilliant teacher and common sense philosopher, Adam Smith (1723-90) economist and philosopher, Joseph Black (1728-99) chemist, John Playfair (1748-1828) mathematician and geologist, Francis Horner (1778 -1817) economist; to name only a few.

Jeffrey's early years in court were dominated by the sedition trials presided over by the feared Lord Braxfield (ref. 21. Covenant Close) who meted out stiff sentences to any who dared to preach reform. Jeffrey learned some sharp lessons in injustice and seeming disregard for the law. This was Pitt's 'Reign of Terror'. France had declared war, there were fears of riot, Henry Dundas 'ruled' Scotland with an iron hand and many were sent to the gallows or given long sentences of transportation, often on the flimsiest of evidence. However, Jeffrey's spirited defences made his reputation as a future force with which to be reckoned.

In 1801 he married his second cousin, they set up house at No. 18 Buccleuch Place and within a year they moved to No. 62 Queen Street where they lived happily for the next eight years. He was a devoted husband and father who loved children - his own and their friends. In 1810 they moved to No. 92 George Street where they remained for the next eighteen years. In 1815 he purchased the old country keep of Craigcrook from the publisher Thomas Constable. In a letter to his friend Lord Cockburn he was to write of it:

'It is an infinite relish to get away from courts and crowds, to sink into a half slumber on one's own sofa, without fears of tinkling bells and importunate attorneys; to read novels by a crackling wood fire, and to go leisurely to sleep without feverish anticipations of tomorrow; to lounge over a long breakfast, looking out on glittering evergreens and chuckling thrushes, and dawdle about the whole day in the luxury of conscious idleness.' (Grant's *Old and New Edinburgh*, vol. III p.110).

Only a very hard-working man could cherish thoughts of such blissful leisure. But Jeffrey's description of idleness is deceptive; Craigcrook was a hive of social activity. Jeffrey entertained many literary and legal friends: Scott, Lockhart, Dickens, Thackeray, Tennyson, Carlyle and any visitor of eminence who happened to visit the City found himself in the stimulating atmosphere of Jeffrey's country retreat.

In 1820 he was surprised to be elected Lord Rector of the University of Glasgow; this was his first honour and it was the first election at Glasgow based on literary or scientific merit since that of Adam Smith in 1787. Jeffrey's speech and his Whig politics delighted the students but dismayed several professors.

As a writer, reviewer and critic he, with Henry Brougham, Sydney Smith and Francis Horner, started the Whig periodical, *The Edinburgh Review* in 1802 and for the next twenty-seven years Jeffrey was its editor. Between them, they zealously pursued their Whig aims and fairly flailed the most pretentious of London authors. They attacked the frivolity and opulence of the aristocracy and scorned the Tories of the

Edinburgh Town Council for the undemocratic self-perpetuation of their merchant Deacons and Bailies as well as Councillors. In 1829, bowing to the preference of the legal establishment, he resigned the editorship of *The Edinburgh Review* on his appointment as Dean of the Faculty of Advocates.

In 1830 he was elected Member of Parliament for Perth and when Earl Grey became Prime Minister in 1832 he was appointed Lord Advocate. Jeffrey was heavily committed to the success of the Reform Bill of 1832 with Henry Cockburn, Henry Brougham, and Lord Grey. The Bill passed through Parliament and the Lords after three attempts. Joyous celebrations followed and when Jeffrey was elected Member of Parliament for Edinburgh he quickly prepared the Scottish Burgh Reform Bill which was passed in 1834. That year he was appointed a Judge of the Court of Session to become Lord Jeffrey.

His town house at No. 24 Moray Place was almost a social and literary centre for friends but he was a devoted family man who loved children. On one occasion Sydney Smith (1771-1845), one of the co-founders of *The Edinburgh Review*, arrived to find Jeffrey playing with the children on a donkey. Smith, highly amused to see this normally stern judge in such a joyful state, immediately composed these lines:

> *'Witty as Horatius Flaccus,*
> *Great a Jacobin as Gracchus,*
> *Short but not as fat as Bacchus,*
> *Riding on a little Jackass!*

Jeffrey was passionately fond of Edinburgh; he hated to be away for too long and during his visit to America to marry his second wife, Miss Wilkes of New York, he wrote longingly for home. It was during this visit he dined with President Madison during the British-American War of 1812.

The year 1843 was that of the great 'Disruption' when 120 ministers accompanied by 350 other churchmen walked out of the General Assembly of the Church of Scotland in protest against patronage in the Church; Jeffrey expressed his delight:

"Thank God for Scotland! there is not another country on earth where such a deed could be done."

In his later years, when he retired from the Bench, his tough exterior seemed to soften from that of an uncompromising critic to an almost, but not quite, tender-hearted soul whose writings were less censorious towards mediocre attempts at authorship.

He died peacefully on 26th January 1850 in his seventy-seventh year. He was taken from his house at Moray Place to be buried in 'Judges Row' in Dean Cemetery. The 'Golden Age' of literature, philosophy and science had petered out some years before and now seemed suddenly dead.

40. Cranston Street

Cranston Street which links the Canongate to East Market Street was the main road to Leith when it was called Leith Wynd. The Cranston family had their residence here and Robert Cranston was the City Councillor of the Canongate who started the Cranston Temperance Hotels. His son, **Sir Robert Cranston KCVO, CB, CBE, LLD, DL, JP, VD**, became Lord Provost of the City from 1903 to 1906. He was a highly decorated and honoured part-time soldier. Cranston Street was renamed in 1874.

The Lord Provost Cranston was born on 2nd June 1843 in Edinburgh, son of Bailie Robert Cranston. He was educated in Edinburgh, Tillicoutry, Wilmslow and Paris. In his early years his father's influence led him to sympathise with the six Chartist aims of Parliamentary reform - annual Parliaments, universal male suffrage, equal electoral districts, the ballot, payment of members and no property qualification.

Having been inspired by the great oratory in the sermons of Dr. Thomas Guthrie (1803-73), Cranston became a founder member of the total abstinence movement, believing that alcohol was the major contributor to the abject poverty and squalid living then painfully evident in the Royal Mile. Thomas Guthrie, the co-founder of the Free Church, the founder of the Ragged Schools and powerful preacher of temperance and social reform, was the inspiration of the day. Successful businessmen of influence, such as Cranston and Charles Jenner (of Jenners in Princes Street), became his devoted supporters.

Robert Cranston carried on the hotel business of Cranston and Elliot in North Bridge started by his father. This hotel was moved to the more prestigious site in Princes Street in 1883; it is now the Old Waverley Hotel which commemorates its founder with the 'Cranston Restaurant'. He managed, with extraordinary success, the Cranston Hotels in Edinburgh and London; the name Cranston was synonymous with excellence in hotel practice.

In 1868 he married Elizabeth, daughter of James S Gilbert of Edinburgh and their family consisted of two sons and two daughters. Cranston's interest in education led to his elected membership of the Edinburgh School Board in 1887 which had been set up following the 1872 Education (Scotland) Act. This great landmark in education had transferred responsibility for education from the church to Local Authorities. For his services to education, the Educational Institute of Scotland made him a Fellow (FEIS). He was elected to the Town Council in 1892 becoming City Treasurer in 1899 for three years when the City Rate was 2s.5d (12p) in the pound.

In 1900 Cranston fought a close contest for the Lord Provostship against the gregarious house-builder James Steel who won by a small majority of seven votes. However, Cranston was elected Lord Provost in 1903. An outward-looking Provost, he encouraged many French dignitaries and visitors and entertained several overseas visitors and civic leaders. He was awarded the French Legion of Honour in 1904 and made a Knight Commander of St Olaf of Norway in 1906.

As a young man, Cranston was attracted by the ceremony, the discipline, the uniform - the whole ethos of military life. He joined the Volunteer Movement as a lieutenant of the Queen's Edinburgh Rifles and marched with pride and vigour at the first large Review held for Queen Victoria on 7th August 1860. Such was his enthusiasm and dedication he reached the rank of Brigadier-General of the 1st Lothians Brigade. For his outstanding service he was knighted in 1903 by Edward VII. His enthusiasm was infectious and his continuous concern for the welfare of his men, especially at camps and during long route marches, was repaid with their spontaneous congratulation when he was made a Knight Commander of the Royal Victorian Order at the Volunteer Review of 1905.

After his retiral from active service he became a member of the Territorial Force Association and he was invited to become a member of the War Office Advisory Council. At the outbreak of war in 1914 he, at the age of seventy-one, raised the 15th Battalion of the Royal Scots of which he was Colonel. In recognition of this he was again honoured, being made a Commander of the newly founded (1917) Most Excellent Order of the British Empire (CBE) by George V. Sir Robert Cranston received his last honour in his eightieth year - the Freedom of the City of Edinburgh. He died shortly afterwards, in October 1923 at his home, No.10 Merchiston Avenue. The Cranston pillar in St Giles commemorates the family name.

41. New Street -
Henry Home, Lord Kames,
Sir David Dalrymple, Lord Hailes

New Street was built in 1760. Its name was changed in 1819 from Young Street (after a resident, Dr Young) when it was extended to meet Calton Road.

This private and secluded little 18th century cul-de-sac was the residence of two of the 'literati' of the 'Golden Age' - Henry Home, Lord Kames (1696-1782) and David Dalrymple, Lord Hailes (1726-92).

Henry Home was born in 1696 at Kames in Berwickshire. He became a judge in 1752 and took the title **Lord Kames**. Known for his eccentricity of manner and speech, he wrote six law books plus several on philosophy including his *Essays on Morality* (1751), *An Introduction to the Art of Thinking* (1761) - his best known work, the two-volume *Principles of Criticsm* (1762) and *Sketches of the History of Man* (1774).

His house in New Street faced the Canongate and was deemed to be the best in the Royal Mile. It was demolished with other self-contained houses when New Street ceased to be a private street about 1819.

Although something of a jovial practical joker most of his works were published by the witty conversationalist William Creech from whom came almost all the great literature of the day and included the works of William Cullen (1710-90), John Gregory (1724-73), Adam Smith (1723-90) *qv*(50), Robert Burns (1759-96), Dugald Stewart (1753-1828) *qv*(55), Henry Mackenzie (1745-1831), Hugh Blair (1718-1800) and many others. These men of the *literati* met often at Creech's printing office which was situated at the east end of the Luckenbooths on the north side of St Giles Church and was previously the shop of Allan Ramsay *qv*(6).

Lord Kames had a style of writing which was fluent and elegant with the complacent intellectual ease of the privileged but he lacked the disciplined scholarship of James Burnett, Lord Monboddo *qv*(44) and the brilliance of David Hume *qv*(8), and was perhaps subtly summed up by the former when asked, "have you read my *Elements of Criticism*?" To which James Burnett, Lord Monboddo, replied, "No, my Lord, you write much quicker than I can read."

In addition, he wrote several books on agricultural improvements on his estate at Blairdrummond in Perthshire. His *The Gentleman Farmer* (1776) gave impetus to the agricultural revolution taking place.

In contrast to his elegant writings his speech was often coarse; he had a propensity to racy conversation and on leaving court for the last time, shortly before his death, he was heard to remark, "Fare ye a' weel, ye bitches." He died aged 87 in 1782.

Sir David Dalrymple, Lord Hailes, resided at New Street towards the end of his life and was another distinguished member of the 'literati' of Edinburgh's 'Golden Age'. His learned and accurate *Annals of Scotland 1057-1371* (1776-79) was the most exhaustive and scholarly work of its day. Such was his reputation, Europe's greatest philosopher and historian, David Hume, asked him to revise his *Enquiry into the Human Mind* in 1753 - even before Dalrymple had published anything of note.

He was born on 26th October 1726 in Edinburgh, the eldest of sixteen children of Sir James Dalrymple of Hailes. His grandfather, Sir David Dalrymple, was the MP for the Haddington Burghs and Solicitor-General to Queen Anne and his great-grandfather was Sir James Dalrymple, the 1st Viscount Stair, President of the Court of Session and author of the famous *Institutes of the Law of Scotland*. But possibly his most illustrious relation was his great-uncle the Master of Stair, Sir John Dalrymple, 2nd Viscount Stair and 1st Earl of Stair who as Secretary of State for Scotland gave the order for the extermination of the clan Macdonald in the 'Massacre of Glencoe' on 13th February 1692.

Sir David Dalrymple was educated at Eton and studied civil law at Utrecht. He returned to Scotland just after the Battle of Culloden and was admitted to the bar in 1748. His father died when he was 24 years old and he inherited a tidy fortune; he was therefore able to follow his literary interests and to amass a great library of some 7000 books at Newhailes House which was built in 1686 and had been bought by his grandfather in 1707 - even the normally critical Dr Samuel Johnson of *Dictionary* fame referred to the library as "the foremost room of learning in Europe". Today Newhailes House remains almost exactly as it was during the Scottish Enlightenment and when restored to its former glory by the National Trust for Scotland it will be open to the public by the year 2000.

David Dalrymple proved to be a punctiliously accurate lawyer which won him many cases through his written pleadings such as the cause of the Countess of Sutherland in her claim for her title through the female line. He was raised to the bench of the Court of Session in 1766 and took the title Lord Hailes. In 1776 he became a judge of the criminal court distinguishing himself for his humane sentencing in comparison to many disgraceful judgements of the day. He was unsurpassed in his knowledge of the history of law.

He was a member of the Select Society in Edinburgh but he distanced himself from fellow members David Hume, Adam Smith and Principal Robertson by his devotion to study at Newhailes; he preferred to correspond with English scholars such as Samuel Johnson (1709-84), Edmund Burke (1729-97), William Warburton (1698-1779), Bishop Richard Hurd (1720-1808) and others.

The list of his published work is prodigious, learned, critical and completely free of prejudice and covers a wide range of subjects - legal, religious, philosophical, political, linguistic and historical.

His first wife, Anne Brown, was a daughter of the Scottish judge, Lord Coalston. She died giving birth to twins. His second wife, Helen, was the daughter of Sir James Fergusson, Lord Kilkerran, another judge.

He died at Newhailes House on 29th November 1792 and was survived by two daughters, one from each marriage. After his death Dr Alexander Carlyle, minister of Inveresk Church and Moderator of the Church of Scotland in 1770 spoke of him in his sermon:

> 'His knowledge was accurate and profound and he applied it in judgement with the most scrupulous integrity. In his proceedings in the criminal court, the satisfaction he gave the public could not be surpassed. His abhorrence of crimes, his tenderness for the criminals, his respect for the laws, and his reverential awe of the Omniscient Judge, inspired him ...'

Opposite: John Knox House

42. Morooco Land - The Moor Figure

The effigy of a Moor figure which appears on the wall of the tenement of Mid Common Close on the north side of the Canongate at the corner of Jeffrey Street has a curious story associated with it. In fact, there are two versions of the story:

The house, long since demolished, was called **Morocco Land** by a young man who had been in the service of the Emperor of Morocco in North Africa. His name was Andrew Gray, a young Edinburgh born son of the house of Moray, who was sentenced to death for his part in a riot against an unpopular Lord Provost shortly after Charles I was crowned in 1628.

Gray was imprisoned at the Old Tolbooth and with the help of a friend who had drugged the guard and provided a rope, he escaped on the eve of his execution and fled the country. The tentacles of the Scottish establishment reached out for him in Europe but he found a safe haven in Morocco. He was something of a curiosity there and he became a trusted servant of the Emperor.

In 1645 Edinburgh was devastated by plague, so many had died that the defence of the town was seriously weakened. It was during this vulnerable state that a pirate ship arrived at Leith. Its captain, with several armed men demanded entry to the town at the Nether Bow Gate. They scoffed at threats of infection from the plague and demanded a huge ransom. During the negotiations the ship's captain, on being made aware that the only daughter of the Provost was seriously ill, suddenly changed from belligerence to concern. He then consulted his men and, producing an Eastern medicine, he demanded that the girl be placed in his care. He further promised that if he failed to cure her then he would depart without the ransom.

Opposite: The Canongate Tolbooth

The ship's captain was Andrew Gray who, with unhappy memories of the tyrannical Lord Provost and his death sentence, had intended vengeance. However, the young woman's father, Lord Provost Smith, was a friend of his father. She was carried to a house at the head of the Canongate where Andrew tended her and administered his potion. During her gradual improvement Andrew fell deeply in love. They were married and Andrew Gray bought the house in which he had cured her. He was now a rich and respected citizen of the burgh of Canongate. He named the house Morocco Land and on the wall, just below the second floor, he placed the effigy in memory of the Emperor of Morocco who had treated him so kindly.

Evidence of ownership of the property, Morocco Land, is referred to by Grant in his *Old and New Edinburgh:*

> *a disposition of 1731, so far confirms the tale that the Proprietor at that date is John Gray, merchant, a descendant, it may be of the Algernine Rover (pirate ship) and the Provost's daughter.*

An alternative story which is attributed to Morocco Land concerns a young lady who was said to have been kidnapped by an African slave-trader and sold to the Emperor of Morocco for his harem. He was attracted not simply by her fairness but by her stately demeanour. He treated her with respect and kindliness. Many years passed and her parents who lived in the house at the top of the Canongate were surprised to receive a letter from her. In it she advised them of her good state of health and her good treatment. She suggested that trade between the two countries could benefit both. Her brother immediately set sail for North Africa, trading began and she returned home with her brother and had the effigy of the Emperor placed on the wall of her father's house.

43. [Boyd's Close] -
White Horse Inn

Boyd's Close has now disappeared but the little pub, originally known as "Boyd's Inn", named after its innkeeper, James Boyd, became known as the White Horse Inn when he had a sign painted with his winning white horse. This was one of 'the great hostelries of Edinburgh, in the days when "hotels" were unknown.' (Grant's Old and New Edinburgh). It is possibly the oldest surviving tavern in the Royal Mile.

Boyd was a devotee of the turf and his many wins on Leith Sands were the talk of the town and the subject of many articles written in the journals of the day. However, when his winning streak came to an end and he was on the brink of ruin, he placed the last of his funds on a white horse. This white horse was so successful Boyd recouped his losses and made a tidy profit. He was so grateful to the white horse, he kept it in blissful retirement for the rest of its life. In addition he had its portrait painted for the sign above his inn which was thereafter known as "The White Horse Inn."

The White Horse Inn dates back to 1742. A large room at the rear was often used for marriage ceremonies for eloping couples from England; one of its windows bore the inscription:

"Jeremiah and Sarah Bentham, 1768"

which was doubtless engraved with the diamond ring of the bride.

In the year 1771 the inn with its adjacent stables and sheds with stabling for 100 horses and 20 carriages was owned by Peter Ramsay who became very rich from the patronage of his eminent guests among whom was the chief patriot of Corsica, Pasquele de Paoli, who had fled from the invading French. He arrived at the inn on 3rd September 1771 with the Polish Ambassador; they were invited by James Boswell (1740-95, the biographer of Samuel Johnson) to be his guests at his home at James Court in the Lawnmarket.

Another visitor was the cantankerous Englishman, Dr Samuel Johnson (1709-84), of *Dictionary* fame. He arrived in Edinburgh on 17th August 1773 on his memorable *Journey to the Western Isles* and from the inn he sent his curt note to James Boswell - "Saturday night:- Mr Johnson sends his compliments to Mr Boswell, being just arrived at Boyd's." It was here at the White Horse Inn that Johnson raged and stormed at a waiter when he used his fingers instead of tongs to sugar Johnson's lemonade which, in his fury, he tossed out of the window - the waiter being threatened with a similar mode of exit.

44. St John's Street -
James Burnett, Lord Monboddo

St John's Street was named from the cross of St John which marked the boundary of Edinburgh and the Canongate, a separate burgh until 1856 when it was merged with the city. The markings in the roadway opposite the entrance to **St John's Pend** represent the site of the actual cross from which pro-

clamations were made; Charles I knighted Lord Provost Sir Alexander Clark here in 1633. The premises of the Masonic Lodge, Canongate No.2 Kilwinning, were in St John's Street where Robert Burns was made Poet Laureate of the Lodge in 1787.

St John's Street was the address of several well-known and interesting people: James Ballantyne (1772-1833) the printer of Scott's novels, Dr James Gregory (1753-1821) Professor of the Practice of Physic at Edinburgh University (Gregory's Mixture was a household name and panacea of many stomach ailments), Tobias Smollett (1721-1771) the Scottish novelist visited his sister, Mrs Telfer, for a few months here in 1766.

A popular resident of St John's Street was **James Burnett** who succeeded Andrew Fletcher (Lord Milton) *qv* (51) as a Lord of Session to become **Lord Monboddo**. His amiable eccentricity and his writings: *Of the Origin and Progress of Language* and his *Ancient Metaphysics* earned him a place in the 'Golden Age' of the Scottish Enlightenment. His 'learned suppers' at St John's Street were popular events which promoted discussion and inspired argument among those of the *literati*.

James Burnett was born towards the end of 1714 at his father's estate of Monboddo in Kincardineshire. His tutor, Dr Francis Skene, gave him his early education and his love of Greek philosophy which became an obsession for the rest of his life. When Dr Skene was appointed Professor of Philosophy at Marischal College, Aberdeen, James Burnett followed him to study Greek philosophy in depth. However, he decided that law should become his profession and after graduating at Edinburgh he studied Civil Law at Groningen in Holland. He was admitted a member of the Faculty of Advocates on 17th February 1737.

During the '45 Rising when Prince Charles Edward Stuart, the 'Young Pretender', occupied Edinburgh, Burnett's legal work diminished to almost nothing and he decided to go to London where he thoroughly enjoyed the company of several literary figures of the day. On his return to Edinburgh he played a prominent part in the 'Douglas Cause' - a dispute in which the surviving son, a twin son of Lady Jane Douglas, was deemed not to be the true heir to the Dukedom of Douglas in 1761. Burnett travelled to France several times to prove the birthright which had been denied by the Duke and Duchess of Hamilton as claimants. The Scottish courts decided in favour of the Hamiltons but the House of Lords upheld the claim of the remaining twin who became Baron Douglas of Douglas Castle.

In 1764 Burnett was appointed Sheriff of Kincardineshire and, following three years of brilliance in the courts, he succeeded Andrew Fletcher, Lord Milton, as an ordinary Lord of Session assuming the title of Lord Monboddo. He was an excellent judge, his statements were both profound and direct but he had one small eccentricity, he insisted on sitting with his clerks rather than with the other judges on the Bench. This was said to have been a protest against his fellow judges who had found against him in his case against a blacksmith who had caused the death of his favourite horse. There were other occasions too, when he found himself in a minority of one in legal decisions.

It was Burnett's interest in the study of Greek philosophy which consumed him. He was said to have declined a seat in the Court of Justiciary because it might interfere with his studies. Between 1773 and 1792 he published his six volumes entitled, *Of the Origin and Progress of Language*, the first of which was largely the work of his secretary, Professor John Hunter of St Andrews. The last volume, Burnett's own work, caused a furore - he contended that the orang-utan was a class of human species and that it was a mere accident that this animal could not speak. His *Ancient Metaphysics*, also written in six volumes, was a veneration of Greek philosophy. This work was derided as much as his previous work but, no matter how voluble his jeering critics, he never became perturbed. He maintained an amiable detachment which almost seemed as if he were observing their behaviour as would an anthropologist studying human behaviour. Seventy or so years after his death, in 1799, his work might not have been so loudly scorned when Darwin's *Origin of Species* (1859) and his *Descent of Man* (1871) argued that Homo Sapiens was derived from a colateral branch of the orang-utan, the chimpanzee and the gorilla.

James Burnett was one of the privileged who lived during the era of the great intellect of the 'Scottish Enlightenment'. Edinburgh seemed to attract geniuses; it was known too, as the 'Age of Reason'. There was an air of optimism that reason could somehow perfect human nature. James Burnett, a brilliant conversationalist, was one of those who believed that an adherence to Greek philosophy was intellectually liberating and that anything modern was contemptible. He loved to entertain and to debate through his 'learned suppers' which became a forum for the *literati* of the day. Among his guests at his house in St John's Street were: Joseph Black (1728-99) the chemist, James Hutton (1726-97) the geologist, David Hume (1711-1776) philosopher and historian, Adam Smith (1723-90) economist and philosopher, William Robertson (1721-93) historian and Principal of the University. Scotland's famous poet, Robert Burns, was a frequent guest and admirer of Burnett's extremely attractive daughter who died, aged twenty-five, of consumption and prompted the poet to compose his *Address to Edinburgh*, the fourth verse of which makes clear reference to her:

> 'Thy daughters bright thy walks adorn.
> Gay as the gilded summer sky,
> Sweet as the dewy, milk-white thorn,
> Dear as the raptured thrill of joy!
> Fair Burnet strikes th' adoring eye,
> Heav'n's beauties on my fancy shine;
> I see the Sire of Love on high,
> And own his work indeed divine!'

Burnett revelled in the debates of the Select Society which met weekly at the Advocates' Library, founded over seventy years before by Sir George Mackenzie, 'Bluidy Mackenzie' (ref.29 Strichen's Close). The society was founded by the portrait painter to George III, Allan Ramsay (1713-90) and counted among its members such eminent men as Hume, Smith, Robertson, Home and Wedderburn who thrashed out their ideas in sparkling debate. Burnett especially was the cause of much heated and wide-ranging discussion but he was well respected as the one of its best scholars.

The income from his estate at Monboddo was small because he could not bring himself to increase the rents. He spent many holidays at Monboddo where he worked happily as an ordinary farmer with his tenants. He knew them well and simply could not deprive any of their houses who could not pay their rents. At a time of the conscienceless 'Clearances' in the Highlands he boasted, with justifiable pride, that his estate was the most densely populated in the area. During one such holiday, he received a visit from Dr Johnson of *Dictionary* fame. This was a deviation by Boswell during their tour of the Hebrides and he knew perfectly well that Johnson and Monboddo would be sure to disagree; Johnson had a reputation for scornful argument and was known for his impatient outbursts of anger. He had the annoying habit of being right most of the time. The two men did indeed argue and in spite of Johnson's invective Monboddo never once raised his voice beyond an agreeable response.

Up to the age of sixty-six Monboddo's annual visits to London were made on horseback. He regarded the modern coach to be an effeminate affectation. In London, he conversed with men of letters and frequently attended the Court of George III who thoroughly enjoyed the company of this eccentric learned Scotsman.

He was over eighty when he made his last journey to London on horseback. On his way home to Edinburgh he became ill and was found on the road by a friend who tried to convince him to accept a lift in his coach. At first Monboddo refused but after a day in the coach he continued his journey on horseback, arriving in Edinburgh eight days later.

This lovable, generous character departed the Edinburgh scene at the age of eighty-five on 26th May 1799. He died at his home in St John's Street after a stroke.

45. Moray House

Moray House is easily recognised from the sharp pyramidal finials of its gate-posts and its heavily corbelled balcony in the Canongate.

The house was built in 1625 for the Countess of Home and became the residence of the Countess of Moray who had inherited it in 1643 from her mother, the Dowager Countess of Home. Her initials 'MH' are carved on various parts of the building and the balcony, on the street-facing gable at first floor level, is supported by huge carved corbels; it was added by Lady Home.

It was from this balcony in May 1650 that the bridal party of Lord Lorne, son of the Marquis and 8th Earl of Argyll, jeered and scorned his enemy, James Graham, the Marquis of Montrose, on his way up the Canongate to his execution outside St Giles.

> *Then as the Graham looked upward,*
> *He met the ugly smile,*
> *Of him who sold his king for gold,*
> *the master-fiend Argyle!*

Montrose, with Argyll, had supported the National Covenant and both had been created Marquises by Charles I, but Montrose abandoned the Covenanters when they went against the king who had declined to accept the Covenant.

At the start of the Revolution in 1642 Argyll decided to support the English Parliament against the king and the Treaty of the Solemn League and Covenant was signed in 1643 agreeing that Presbyterianism would become the religion of Scotland and England. Montrose therefore left Scotland to support the king and so Argyll and Montrose became bitter enemies.

The Royal Mile was filled with spectators, some weeping and others full of hatred; the latter being inspired by the clergy. Montrose was tied to a cart which was accompanied by the City Guard under the command of Major Weir (ref.9 Riddles Court). He too jeered his captive as "a dog, atheist and murderer" and ordered a pause at Moray House so that the bridal party could observe the plight of their adversary. But the calm, almost peaceful, stare of Montrose disturbed them. The Marchioness of Argyll broke the spell by spitting on Montrose. Shocked, the Marquis of Argyll turned away while his son, Lord Lorne, and his bride, Lady Mary Stuart, daughter of the Earl of Moray, continued to laugh little realising that Argyll himself would meet the same fate after the Restoration, to be sentenced as a traitor to the king in 1661.

Montrose was a brilliant general, he marched his army of Highlanders and Irishmen such great distances they continually surprised their enemies. At Tippermuir, near Perth, he easily defeated the Covenanters. He marched his army to Aberdeen where his men sacked and plundered the town. Next, he ignominiously defeated Argyll at his stronghold, Inverlochy. Montrose's final victory, his greatest, was fought at Kilsyth in 1645. Glasgow surrendered without a fight and now Montrose was master of Scotland. He had denied his men the plunder of Glasgow and most of them left for their harvests at home. Montrose now marched those who remained to the Borders in the hope of raising another army. This was unsuccessful and he was defeated by General Leslie at Philiphaugh near Selkirk. Charles I was executed in 1649 and Montrose, now in support of Charles II, was taken prisoner and executed on 21st May 1650.

Oliver Cromwell visited Argyll at Moray House and, in the 'Cromwell Room' on the south side of the building, he was said to have discussed the proposal to execute the king. In 1651, when Charles II was proclaimed king by the Scottish Estates, Argyll, as the chief noble, placed the crown upon his head at Scone. Cromwell used Moray House as his headquarters during the Battle of Dunbar.

In 1707 the Lord High Chancellor, the Earl of Seafield, lived at Moray House. He was one of the commissioners who negotiated the Treaty of Union and received a payment of £490 for his services. There were thirty-two payments made by the English Treasury which were described as bribes by the opponents of the Treaty. After the Union of Parliaments most of the Scottish nobility left for London. Edinburgh, having lost its Parliament, lost its status.

Moray House became the office of the British Linen Bank until it was purchased shortly after the 'Disruption' of 1843 by the Free Church of Scotland. In 1849 Moray House became a school and Moray House College of Education at Holyrood Road was built in 1910-13.

46. Gladstone Court

Gladstone Court, (formerly Bowling Green Close and Magdalene Entry) on the north side of the Canongate is easily recognised by its attractive arches. It was known as Bowling Green Close when prisoners in the Tolbooth jail could overlook the bowling green nearby.

The Close was re-named about 1867 after the eminent Liberal statesman, **William Ewart Gladstone**, four times Prime Minister; 1868, 1880, 1886 and 1892. He was an unrivalled orator and debater whose legacy of successful legislation is probably unequalled in the history of British politics but Queen Victoria detested him.

William Ewart Gladstone was born in Liverpool in 1809. His father, Sir John Gladstone, after whom Gladstone Place, near Leith Links, is named, was a successful corn merchant in Leith. William was educated at Eton and Oxford where he took a double first class degree.

He stood for Parliament in 1833 and won his Parliamentary seat at Newark. As a devout Christian his original intention had been to enter the Church but he took his religious beliefs into political life. His workload was formidable and from his entry into Parliament, aged only twenty-four, his opponents soon discovered his ability as an outstanding debater.

Within a year of his arrival in Parliament he was appointed a Lord of the Treasury in Sir Robert Peel's government of 1841-46 with its powerful statesmen - Wellington, Stanley, Aberdeen, Goderich, Hardinge, Ellenby, Dalhousie and Canning. In 1841 Gladstone was appointed Vice President of the Board of Trade and Master of the Mint and in 1843 he was again President of the Board of Trade - all before the age of thirty-four.

In 1844, the age of railway mania (1847-48), he led the Railway Bill through the House of Commons - the 'Parliamentary' train fare was a penny a mile for third class and the train had to achieve a speed of twelve miles per hour. The great engineers - Joseph Locke, George Hudson, Robert Stephenson (son of the great George Stephenson), and Isambard Kingdom Brunel could continue to push ahead with their new railways.

Four ministries had fallen since 1852, Napoleon III started the war of Italian liberation and Queen Victoria's choice of Palmerston as Prime Minister was that of public opinion and not her preference. Lord Russell was given his choice - the Foreign Office - and Gladstone, to pacify the Peelites, was appointed Chancellor of the Exchequer.

He had to struggle with his conscience to serve under Palmerston but his budget of 1853 was masterly - he got rid of 140 excise duties and lowered another 150, and, in his belief that income tax was evil, he cut it to 7d with intention of reducing it to zero within seven years. In 1865 his budget reduced income tax to 4d, halved the tea duty and reduced expenditure from £72 million to £66 million.

He created the Post Office Savings Bank and reiterated his preference to avoid State interference with the maxim: 'God most helps those who help themselves'. He was the power behind the University Act of 1854 which abolished close fellowships and close scholarships; he allowed the government of universities by their teachers, opened their halls of residence to men of poorer means and reduced the requirement to take Holy Orders.

In 1868, with the people shouting 'Gladstone and liberty', he formed his first Ministry with a majority of 112 - this Government lasted until 1874 during which the 1870 Education Act was passed and the Acts of reform he passed met many of the demands of earlier Liberalism - disestablishing the Irish Church; the abolition of Church rates, religious tests for entry to Oxford and Cambridge and the purchase of army commissions (in 1871). He legislated on Irish land and on Education in England and Scotland. He opened the Civil Service to entrance by competitive examination and an independent commission; he made capital relatively safe for the investor by introducing limited liability and trade finance.

In 1874 he dissolved Parliament and lost the subsequent election to his old rival Disraeli which pleased the Queen who much preferred his courtly concern to the stern and austere Gladstone. When Disraeli put through the Royal Titles Bill of 1876 describing the Queen as 'Empress of India', Gladstone opposed it as 'flummery'. There were times when the Queen came near to open hatred and undisguised enmity of Gladstone; she used all her influence against him and he, in turn, did nothing to assuage her. But Gladstone was by no means beaten, he became Prime Minister again in 1880. Five years later the Irish problem contributed to his resignation.

During Gladstone's election campaign *The Scotsman* of 18th June 1886 reported; "It is estimated that between 40,000 and 50,000 people assembled on the Waverley Bridge and in Princes Street to receive the Premier on his arrival, and the enthusiasm of this assemblage knew no bounds."

In 1886, for the third time, he returned to the Premiership and, with the same, apparently inexhaustible, supply of energy at the age of seventy-five he tried again to get the Home Rule for Ireland Bill through Parliament but it just failed.

In 1892 Gladstone, ageing, half blind and partially deaf formed his last Government. It was a sorry business, he could not withstand the pressures of Cabinet dissension. One faction, the Imperialists, wanted to keep Uganda and Egypt; the others, old Radicals, thought this tyrannical. Rosebery, the Foreign Secretary and Harcourt, Chancellor of the Exchequer, were at each other's throats, but Gladstone was single-minded for Irish Home Rule while the country was plagued with strikes. His Irish Bill got through the Commons but failed miserably in the Lords - this was the end of Gladstone's political life. He resigned in March 1894 and retired, with approbation from both sides of the House, to write his memoirs in Wales. He died, aged eighty-nine, in 1898 and was buried at Westminster.

47. Canongate Tolbooth

The projecting clock, tower and spire, the turrets and dormer windows of the Canongate Tolbooth make it an easily recognisable landmark in the Canongate. Its tower and court room to the east were built in 1591 and the clock is dated 1884. The inscription above the arch entrance is: 'S.L.B. Patriae et Posteris 1591' (For Country and Posterity). The initials, SLB for Sir Lewis Bellenden, a Lord of Session, Council and Exchequer and the lay successor of the Abbots of Holyrood was said to have exorcised a warlock; Richard Graham was so terrified, he died soon after the experience.

On the clock side which faces the street is the coat-of-arms of the Burgh of the Canongate with its stag head and cross between its antlers with the motto, *Sic itur ad astra* (this is the way to Paradise). The stag and cross derive from the fable of David I and Holyrood. On Holy Cross day, 14th September in the year 1128 King David, while hunting in the forest near the present ruin of the Abbey of Holyrood at the north east corner of the Palace of Holyroodhouse, was attacked by a white stag. The miraculous appearance of the cross or rood frightened the stag and David's life was saved. After a 'visitation' that night, by St Andrew, Patron Saint of Scotland, David founded the Abbey of Holyrood on the spot where his life was saved.

The Canongate Tolbooth was originally a booth at which tolls were collected from travellers entering the town. It had various functions: Council Chamber, Police Court and Prison. Oliver Cromwell's guard held several Scottish prisoners in the Tolbooth in 1654, but they escaped using strips of their blankets to lower themselves to freedom from an upper floor.

After the completion of the Calton Jail in 1817 the Canongate Tolbooth accommodated only seventeen debtors (in 1834). The old Magdalene Asylum, which accommodated sixty women in 1797, was situated in an adjoining court.

Today, the Canongate Tolbooth accommodates a most interesting museum called *The People's Story* with fascinating exhibits of many facets of late 18th century life and the condition of ordinary folk during the two World Wars to the present day.

Coat of Arms of the Burgh of the Canongate
Sic Itur ad Astra - *This is the way to paradise*

48. Canongate Church and Churchyard

The Canongate Church is not only the Parish Church of the Canongate, which encompasses the Palace of Holyroodhouse, it is a Church of the Royal family while in residence at Holyrood.

How was it that this beautiful but unpretentious, almost plain little church became a place of worship of royalty? The story starts in 1686 when James VII (II of England) ordered that the Council Chamber of the Palace be converted into a Roman Catholic Chapel and, one year afterwards, he ordered that the Abbey of Holyrood, adjacent to the Palace, be converted into a chapel for the newly recreated, *The Most Ancient and Most Noble Order of the Thistle* (it is considered by some authorities to have been created in 787). In 1688 a Protestant mob sacked the Abbey and the Chapel Royal. King James decided that money from a fund left to the crown in 1649 by a rich merchant, Thomas Moodie, should be used to build a new church - the Canongate Church.

The Lords of the Treasury appointed James Smith (1645-1731) to design the new church and ordered the Town Council to have it built under Smith's supervision. His design, in the form of a Latin cross, has an S-shaped frontage with the curved skews of the aisles on each side.

Above its Roman Doric porticoed entrance is an inscribed tablet with the arms of Thomas Moodie. At the top, above the circular window, is the Royal Arms of William III who succeeded the dethroned James II in 1688.

The church was completed in 1691 at a cost of £1900. The antlers of a stag provide a theme throughout the interior and this is emphasised in the King David Aisle and with Stanley Cursiter's painting as well as the superbly embroidered panel of the communion table. Each is a reminder of the story behind the antlers. It is, of course, that of David I's deliverance from certain death while hunting near the site of the ruined Holyrood Abbey. His horse had reared as a magnificent white stag rushed to the attack. Lying on the ground and about to be gored, he was saved by the brilliance of a cross (or rood) which appeared above the antlers of the stag. The animal took fright and fled. That evening, David awoke from a dream in which it was made clear to him that his gratitude should be shown in the foundation of an Abbey - Holyrood Abbey.

Royal Arms of William III

Restoration work for the Canongate Church was carried out internally by Ian G Lindsay in 1946-54 when 19th century additions were replaced with new vestries. The Royal Pew, the Governor's Pew, Choir Stalls and new furniture were installed in 1991 when the restoration of the 1817-ceiling was completed in time for the 300th anniversary of the Church when Her Majesty Queen Elizabeth II unveiled the Royal Coat of Arms and quarterings of Scotland which were presented by past Governors of Edinburgh Castle.

The Canongate Church is the Military Church of Edinburgh and commemorates servicemen of many regiments who gave their lives in war. In 1951 the Governor of Edinburgh Castle opened the Memorial Chapel in memory of forty men of the Canongate who were killed in World War II. The memorial to the Dunkirk Veterans' Association, on the west side of the communion table, contains sand from the French

Opposite: *Moray House, Canongate*

beaches. The 606 (City of Edinburgh) Squadron Roll of Honour was unveiled by H.M. The Queen in 1989. The Old Colours of the 1st Battalion The King's Own Scottish Borderers were laid up in 1979 and those of the 7th/9th Battalion of The Royal Scots (The Dandy Ninth) in 1986. The 350th anniversary of the raising of The Royal Scots (The Royal Regiment) was celebrated in 1983 with the adoption of Canongate Church as their Regimental Kirk.

The Canongate Churchyard dates back to 1688 and contains tombstones of several famous people of Edinburgh:

George Drummond (1687-1766), six times Lord Provost who dreamt of and planned for the New Town of Edinburgh and personally raised the money for the Royal Infirmary.

Adam Smith (1723-90), the illustrious philosopher and economist famed for his *Wealth of Nations* .

James Gregory (1753-1821), Professor of Medicine of the University of Edinburgh whose 'Gregory's Mixture' was the panacea of stomach complaints.

George Chalmers (1773-1836) obelisk, an Edinburgh plumber who left £30,000 for the building of Chalmers Hospital in Lauriston Place.

Robert Fergusson (1750-74), the young poet so admired by Robert Burns who paid for his gravestone in 1789 and had it inscribed:

> *No sculptur'd Marble here, nor pompous lay,*
> *No storied Urn, nor animated Bust;*
> *This simple Stone directs Pale Scotia's way*
> *To pour her sorrows o'er her Poet's Dust.*

Dugald Stewart (1753-1828) a mausoleum at the north-west corner commemorates this great teacher and philosopher who was Professor of Moral Philosophy of the University of Edinburgh. His Grecian monument is prominent on the Calton Hill.

Sir William Fettes (1750-1836) a successful merchant who left £166,000 to found Fettes College.

James Ballantyne (1772-1833) the publisher of Sir Walter Scott's novels who lived at St John's Street.

Mrs Agnes McLehose (1759-1841), **'Clarinda'** to Robert Burns who, as her 'Sylvander', wrote the heart-rending love song to her: *Ae Fond Kiss.*

David Rizzio (c1533-66), the talented secretary of Mary, Queen of Scots who was murdered at Holyrood by Lord Darnley and a few nobles who stabbed him fifty-six times.

Opposite: Octagonal Fountain, 1858-9 by Robert Matheson, around which masses of Floral tributes to Diana, Princess of Wales, were laid in September, 1997 following her tragic death.

The Burgh Cross at the south west corner facing the street is of great antiquity; its octagonal shaft is of 16th century origin but its head and base date from 1888. Its original position was at the foot of the Canongate on the traffic island opposite Russell House. From here royal and civic proclamations were made and executions were carried out by means of the 'Maiden' (Edinburgh's guillotine). Grant's *Old and New Edinburgh* (Vol.III p.99) gives a description of one such execution: that of the youthful and beautiful Lady Warriston whose husband had ill-treated her and she conspired in his murder. At her summary trial she was sentenced to death; 'the lady to have "her heade struck frae her bodie" at the Canongate Cross.' [1]

49. Huntly House

Huntly House Museum was originally three small but separate houses in 1517. They were made into a single stone-built house in 1570 when a block was added bringing the front ten feet (3m) closer to the street.

The old timber houses were probably destroyed during the sacking of Edinburgh in 1544 by the Earl of Hertford under orders of Henry VIII. There is no record of its inhabitants at that time and the first reference to the Gordons of Huntly, from whom the house takes its name, is about 1762 when the Duchess of Gordon had a flat there.

The house was previously owned by the Incorporation of Hammermen, who bought it in 1647 and enlarged the front block into flats for letting in 1671. Two storeys were added, their three broad gables facing the street.

The Hammermen's seal was issued by the Provost, Sir Patrick Baron, in 1483 and incorporated blacksmiths, goldsmiths, lorimers (makers of the metal parts of horse harnesses), saddlers, cutlers, buckle-makers, armourers and "all others within the said burgh of Edinburgh."1 After 1581 the goldsmiths separated from the Hammermen but others joined - gunsmiths, watchmakers, founders, braziers and coppersmiths. The first locksmith arrived in 1586, then the trade of pewterer in 1588 to be followed by a clockmaker in 1647. The first maker of surgical instruments, a French Protestant refugee, arrived in 1691. Pinmakers appeared in 1720 and 1764 saw the first edge-tool maker and fish hook maker. The Hammermen left the house in 1762.

The present-day interior of **Huntly House** contains many panelled rooms the woodwork of which is original in some and others, on the south side, have the panels of some demolished Edinburgh houses. The 16th century painted beams came from Pinkie House in Musselburgh.

On the street- facing wall are some quaint inscriptions:
Antiqua Tamen Juven Esco. TBW 1932 - In old age I grow young. Sir Thomas B. Whitson (Lord Provost 1929-1932).
Hodie Mihi Cras Tibi Cur Igitur Curas - Today its me; tomorrow you. Worrying achieves nothing.
Vt Tu Linguae Tuae Sic Ego Mear Um; Avir Dominus Sum - You decide what to say, I choose what to listen to.
Constanti Pectori Res Mortalium Umbra - A well-balanced person takes the long term view.
Spes Altera Vitae - There is hope of another life.

Huntly House was purchased by the Corporation of the City of Edinburgh in 1924 and extensive restoration work was carried out by Frank C. Mears in 1927 when the local history museum was formed. The museum was extended into the adjoining 17th century tenement when further restoration work was completed in 1965 by Ian G, Lindsay & Partners. The exhibits consist of old trades of Edinburgh, glass and silverware and military memorabilia of Earl Haig *qv*(5), the Commander-in-Chief of the British Army during the 1914 - 18 War.

50. Panmure House - Adam Smith

After the Canongate Church, **Panmure House** is behind Panmure Close (formerly McKell's Close) but entry is gained from Little Lochend Close. It is a late 17th century L-shaped house with crow-stepped gables and takes its name from the Earls of Panmure who used the property as their town house.

The 4th Earl of Panmure, a brave soldier, distinguished himself at the Siege of Luxembourg (1684). He was appointed a Privy Councillor to James VII but he was bitterly opposed to the Union of Parliaments of 1707. A strong supporter of the 'Old Pretender', he fought valiantly for the Jacobite cause at Dunblane in 1715 during the reign of Protestant George I. For this allegiance to the House of Stuart he was attainted, losing his title and suffering exile in Paris where he died.

His nephew, William Maule, was the last of the Panmures to live at Panmure House. He served in the Scots Guards at Dettingen in 1743 under George II (the last monarch to actually lead in battle) during the Austrian Succession War and he was rewarded that year with the Earldom Panmure of Forth of the Irish peerage. At the defeat of Fontenoy in 1745 he served under the Duke of Cumberland but he was recalled when the army had to return home to quell the '45 Rising and Cumberland finally defeated Prince Charles Edward's Jacobite army at Culloden in 1746.

The Countess of Aberdeen was the next resident of Panmure House from about 1750 until 1778 when the illustrious philosopher and economist **Adam Smith** took up residency on his appointment as Commissioner of Customs, an appointment obtained through the patronage of the Duke of Buccleuch.

Adam Smith is the 'father of economics', a reputation he gained after the publication of his magnum opus, *Inquiry into the Nature and Causes of the Wealth of Nations.* It was this which gave birth to 'political economy' as a study in its own right. Smith was one of the

geniuses to whom James Mitchell referred in his *Scotsman's Library* of 1825 when he reported that Mr Amyatt, the King's Chemist, in conversation with William Smellie the printer of Burns's poems, described the Edinburgh scene:

> "Here stand I at what is called the Cross of Edinburgh,
> and can in a few minutes, take fifty men of genius and
> learning by the hand." [3]

Adam Smith was a contemporary of those of the 'Golden Age' of intellectual stimulation - a thirty year period (1760-90) of scintillating brilliance in Scottish scholarship which was centred mainly in Edinburgh. Clubs and societies abounded in the Royal Mile and their membership included such geniuses as: David Hume, James Hutton, John Gregory, William Robertson, Joseph Black, Adam Ferguson, William Cullen, Hugh Blair, Henry Home (Lord Kames), James Burnett (Lord Monboddo), Robert Burns and many others.

A remarkable difference between the Edinburgh *literati* and those of the other great cities of Europe, was in their accessibility. Mitchell in his *Scotsman's Library* of 1825, explains that it was 'not only easy, but their conversation and the communication of their knowledge, are at once imparted to intelligent strangers with the utmost liberality.'[3]

It was the 'Age of Reason' during which firmly held beliefs were questioned and the intellectual emancipation of Hume displeased the church; humanism was uncomfortable and therefore unacceptable.

Adam Smith was born on 5th June 1723 at Kirkcaldy in Fife. His father, comptroller of customs, died shortly before Adam was born. The bond with his mother was greatly strengthened after he was kidnapped by gypsies when three years old. His early education was at the Burgh School of Kirkcaldy where he befriended the Adams brothers of architectural fame. He studied at the University of Glasgow and Balliol College, Oxford where he was a Snell exhibitioner. He made the journey from Kirkcaldy to Oxford on horseback in 1740 and stayed there until 1746 taking his B.A. degree in 1744.

This was supposed to lead him into the church but his preference was an academic life. Life at Oxford was lonely, Scots were disliked there and he was severely reprimanded when caught reading David Hume's *Treatise of Human Nature*. Smith and Hume were to become firm friends in later life.

One of Smith's great teachers was Francis Hutchison (1694-1746), Professor of Moral Philosophy and a pioneer of the 'common sense' school of philosophy at Glasgow. Smith became a private tutor and lecturer in rhetoric and belles lettres (literature - poetry, fiction, criticism, aesthetics). His reputation grew and he was unanimously elected to the Chair of Logic at Glasgow on 9th January 1751. Within a year he succeeded Professor Craigie in the Chair of Moral Philosophy. His lectures became famous with the publication of his *Moral Sentiments*. He became Dean of the Faculty and Vice-Rector in which capacity he was a patron of James Watt (1736-1819) of steam engine fame. Smith was a member of the Anderston Club and was elected to membership of the Philosophical Society of which David Hume was secretary. In 1754 he was one of the fifteen members of the Select Society founded by Allan Ramsay (1713-84) who became portrait painter to George III.

In 1759 Smith published his *Theory of Moral Sentiments* which was greatly praised by Hume and received favourably in London where he visited for the first time in 1761.

His Professorship of Moral Philosophy at Glasgow was a thirteen-year period of near bliss. It came to an end when Smith was offered and accepted a travelling tutorship with the 3rd Duke of Buccleuch at £300 a year for life. He resigned his professorship and arrived in Paris in February 1764 where he met David Hume, Voltaire, Rousseau (with whom Hume quarrelled) and many other eminent Frenchmen. The Duke's young brother, Hew Campbell Scott, joined them in Paris and Smith was devastated when the young man was murdered during his visit. He returned immediately with the body, reaching Dover on 1st November 1764.

Smith remained in London to supervise the third edition of his *Moral Sentiments*. He was elected a Fellow of the Royal Society (FRS) in May 1767 and he returned to Kirkcaldy to write his *Wealth of Nations* which was published on 9th March 1776; it was an immediate success and soon became the authoritative work for politicians and philosophers. He had given new life to a hitherto mediaeval approach to the subject of economics. Smith paid not only careful attention to historical change but dissected each argument into the theory of free enterprise. William Pitt studied it carefully and used it in the 1786 Treaty with France, mutually agreeing lower tariffs. Smith met Pitt many times and on the occasion of a dinner at the house of Henry Dundas (ref. 28. Bishop's Close), Pitt invited Smith to be seated first, saying, "we are all your scholars!"

His happy days of discussion and debate with his old friend David Hume came to an end in August 1776 when Hume died after a year-long illness. The two great men had followed almost parallel paths, in fact Hume's reputation as an economist excelled that of Smith in his lifetime.

In January 1777 Smith was appointed Commissioner of Customs at £600 per year. This was probably due to the influence of the Duke of Buccleuch and Smith offered to forego his £300 per year pension from the Duke; he insisted that Smith keep his pension. Smith was now relatively well off and could afford to buy Panmure House to which he brought his mother and two cousins from Kirkcaldy. He emulated Lord

Monboddo (ref.44 St Johns Street) in giving Sunday suppers to his literary friends.

His mother died in 1784 aged ninety; he was grief-stricken to such a degree that his health was affected. His recovery was slow and in 1787 he was elected Lord Rector of Glasgow, an honour he received with humble gratitude in a letter to the Principal; he was unable to give an inaugural address.

Early in 1790 his health was poor and realising that death was near, he asked his friends James Hutton and Joseph Black to burn sixteen volumes of his manuscripts. This was done and Smith seemed to be relieved. Some of his essays were published after his death by his executors, Black and Hutton. He was buried in a modest grave in Canongate Churchyard, a few metres from his last abode at Panmure House.

51. Milton House -
Andrew Fletcher, Lord Milton

Milton House School (now the Royal Mile Primary School) in the Canongate was built in 1886 on the site of John Adam's Milton House which was owned and built, between 1755 and 1758, by Lord Milton; the previous owner of the site being the Duke of Roxburgh. The red sandstone school building was designed in Scots tradition by Robert Wilson, the architect of the Edinburgh School Board in the 1880s.

The School and the old House were named after **Andrew Fletcher** who became a Lord of Session, **Lord Milton**, in 1724 succeeding Sir John Lauder of Fountainhall. James Grant, in his *Old and New Edinburgh* (Vol. II, p. 34) describes him:

> 'a senator of the Court of Session till his death. He was the nephew of the noble and patriotic Fletcher of Salton, and was an able coadjutor with his friend Archibald, the great Duke of Argyle, during whose administration he exercised a wise control over the usually-abused Government patronage in Scotland. He sternly discouraged all informers, and was greatly esteemed for the mild and gentle manner in which he used his authority when Lord Justice Clerk after the Battle of Culloden.'

Lord Milton is perhaps best known in local history as the judge who presided over the trial of Captain Porteous in 1736 and sentenced him to be hanged for murder. The Town Guard, under the command of Porteous, had fired on threatening rioters at the hanging of a horse-stealer who, by sheer brute strength, had held off three guards while his accomplice made his escape. The assembled crowd cheered the prisoner. Captain Porteous was so angry, he grabbed a gun and shot a ring-leader. He ordered his men to open fire, some fired above the heads of the crowd, with the result that several people in the crowd and others, spectating from their windows, were killed.

Queen Caroline, who was acting as Regent, (George II being in Germany) ordered Porteous's reprieve, pending a pardon. This caused such a furore in Edinburgh that a well-armed group of rioters stormed the Tolbooth jail, hauled Porteous from his hiding place, (he was cowering with fear in a chimney), marched him through the streets and hanged him from a dyer's pole. The Government ordered the arrest of Lord Provost Wilson who was released after three weeks and Lord Milton was examined at the bar of the House of Lords where he aquitted himself effortlessly.

Andrew Fletcher was born at the family seat in East Lothian, Salton Hall, in 1692, the year of the Massacre of Glencoe. He was the eldest son of Hendry Fletcher of Salton and his mother, the daughter of Sir David Carnegie, was an active and enterprising lady who secretly brought the art of weaving and dressing linen (called holland) from Holland to Salton (an early example of industrial espionage!). His uncle, Andrew Fletcher, 'The Patriot', was the great statesman who resolutely opposed the Union of the Scottish and English Parliaments in 1707, and left Scotland with the words, "I leave Scotland to the slaves who sold it."

After completing his legal studies in Edinburgh young Andrew Fletcher was admitted as an advocate on 26th February 1717. He replaced James Hamilton of Pencaitland as a Lord of the Court of Justiciary in 1726, was appointed a Commissioner for improving the fisheries and manufacture of Scotland, succeeded James Erskine of Grange as Lord Justice Clerk in 1735 and was appointed Principal Keeper of the Signet in 1746.

Lord Islay (who became 3rd Duke of Argyll), knowing of Milton's vast knowledge of the law of Scotland and his sound judgment, made him his confidential agent or chief executive. George II, not intending a compliment, described Islay as 'Vice Roy in Scotland'. As uncrowned King of Scotland Islay dispensed his favours to over half of the Scottish judiciary who owed him their appointments. Milton was a prime example. He acted with discretion and with leniency during and after the '45 Rising, and he worked energetically to improve trade and agriculture in Scotland. The Islay-Milton team exerted its influence over many important institutions - the Convention of Royal Burghs, Edinburgh Town Council, the General Assembly of the Church of Scotland and many new boards and commissions; their function was not so much to create new policies but to ameliorate and to pacify troubles. They could guarantee 30 out of 45 Parliamentary seats for Britain's first Prime Minister, Sir Robert Walpole (1676-1745), but this reduced to 19 seats and consequently they were powerless against the punitive laws passed in Parliament against Jacobites who lost their estates and tartans; even the bagpipes were prohibited.

Lord Milton married Elizabeth, a daughter of Sir Francis Kinloch of Gilmerton. Their daughter, Miss Betty Fletcher married Captain Wedderburn of Gosford at Milton's manor-house of Brunstane in 1758.

Lord Milton was not simply a stuffy Law Lord and Chief Executive, he was the beloved guardian of the six beautiful daughters of the Countess of Eglinton from the time of the death of his friend, the Earl of Eglinton. A mark of the affection in which he was held was humorously described by the daughters in their *Petition of the six vestal virgins of Eglinton*; this was signed by each of them and sent to Milton.

He retired from the bench in 1767 and was succeeded by James Burnett, Lord Monboddo. Lord Milton, in spite of a long illness, continued to preside as a judge until his death, aged seventy-four, at Brunstane Manor House near Musselburgh on 13th December 1766.

52. Haddington's Entry - Nisbet of Dirleton's House

The street-facing, crow-stepped gable at Nos. 82-84 Canongate is Nisbet of Dirleton's House, a 1953 replica of the 1624 version with the inscription above the door:

1619 Pax Intrantibus DZK Salus Exeuntibus (In the Lord I put my trust, let nothing harm me). Another stone has the motto of the City:

16 Nisi 19   *Blissit be*
Dominus   *God in all*
Frustra   *His Gifts*

Sir John Nisbet of Dirleton who lived here until his death in 1687 was Lord Advocate of Scotland and a Lord of Session during the persecution of Covenanters in the reign of James VII (II of England). Nisbet's reputation was almost as bad as that of his successor, Sir George Mackenzie ('Bloody Mackenzie') - ref. 29 Strichen's Close.

John Nisbet was born on 1st July 1610, the son of Patrick Nisbet, Lord Eastbank, an ordinary Lord of Session who was knighted by Charles I in 1638. John Nisbet was admitted to the Faculty of Advocates on 30th November 1633 and appointed Sheriff-Depute of the county of Edinburgh in 1639.

The Marquis of Montrose, having been imprisoned in Edinburgh Castle as one of the 'Plotters' in 1641, asked Nisbet and John Gilmore to defend him against a charge of treason. Montrose had become alarmed at the Covenanters' proposals to strip the King, Charles I, of much of his power. Montrose left the Covenanting cause to support the King - for this he was imprisoned. Nisbet obtained his release and Montrose became a loyal Royalist and proceeded to wreak havoc when he raised the 'fiery cross' in the Highlands to conquer almost the whole of Scotland for Charles I, until his capture in 1650.

Nisbet built up a lucrative law practice, so much so, that he was able to purchase the Dirleton estates said to have been 'a great bargain' of the time. His fortune had grown with his reputation and, on 14th October 1664, he was appointed Lord Advocate of Scotland and a judge of the Court of Session with the title of Lord Dirleton.

Nisbet's dual appointment was the last in which the Lord Advocate served simultaneously as a judge. He presided over the court with such confidence in his own power it became eminently clear that his verdicts were not unbiased but he was a valuable servant of the Crown. He literally persecuted the Covenanters, always falling back on government policy rather than the letter of the law.

By 1666 the Covenants had been declared unlawful but the Covenanters insisted on attending the services of the 'outed' ministers; this was dealt with by simply passing another law which forbade ministers from going within twenty miles of their Parishes. The Covenanters rose in rebellion at Dumfries. They gathered support in Ayrshire and in Lanark, but on reaching Rullion Green in the Pentland Hills they were routed by Sir Thomas Dalziel's troops. Fifty were killed and another fifty were taken prisoner and Nisbet prevailed upon his colleagues to try them in their absence. Their death sentences were clearly contrary to law and in order to satisfy complaints an Act was passed, in retrospect, declaring that the sentences were lawful - such was justice in these threateningly brutal times.

Robert Wodrow (1679-1734), in his *Sufferings of the Church of Scotland 1660-88* relates another example of Nisbet's dubious legal methodology in the case against Robert Gray. Gray had refused to divulge the hiding-places of fellow Covenanters and Nisbet simply removed a ring from Gray's finger and had it sent to Gray's wife with a message: 'that her husband had revealed all that he knew, and had sent the ring to her as a token that she might do the same.' She told all, and Gray was so sickened by this despicable action, he died of depression a few days later. This story, although never substantiated, was a measure of the opinion against Nisbet.

In 1670, Nisbet was appointed to a Commission sent to London to consider the union of Scotland and England. He was completely against the loss of the Scottish Parliament and clashed with Charles Maitland, brother of the Duke of Lauderdale, the virtual ruler of Scotland. Nisbet was expected to resign but he refused. However his day of reckoning arrived when his cousin was accused of perjury before the Privy Council and Nisbet had advised him to pay off his accuser in order to settle the case; however, Nisbet's involvement was never proved.

In the case of the Leven estates, Nisbet was accused by Lord Halton of taking fees from both sides for his advice. In the ensuing investigation, by three judges of the Court of Session, Nisbet resigned as Lord Advocate. In 1677, he was replaced by Sir George Mackenzie ('Bloody Mackenzie') who, at first, refused the appointment and offered his assistance to Nisbet, advising him to defend himself. Nisbet felt that he could not rely on sufficient support and duly resigned.

Aged seventy-eight, he died in April 1687 at his house in the Canongate. Gilbert Burnet (1643-1713) in his *History of the*

Reformation described Nisbet as 'one of the worthiest and most learned men of his age', but Omod's *Lord Advocates* paints a quite different picture - 'At a time when bad men were common, he was one of the worst; and it does not appear that, in the course of his public career, he ever did one deed which lightens the darkness of his servile and mercenary life.'

53. Clarinda's Tearoom, No. 69 Canongate - Mrs Agnes McLehose - Clarinda

Opposite Milton House School there is a welcoming tearoom called 'Clarinda's' which takes its name from the lady idolised by Scotland's national poet, Robert Burns. Nearby, in the Canongate Churchyard, the attractive plaque, on the east wall, is a romantic bas relief of her beautiful face.

She was Robert Burns's *Clarinda* whilst he was her *Sylvander*. Romantic nonsense perhaps, but it inspired poetical masterpieces which immortalised this genteel lady. They left an extraordinary series of love letters which were written between 6th December 1787 and 25th June 1794; forty of them, by Burns, were written in the first four months.

She, Agnes Craig, was born only three months after Burns in April 1759. Her father was Mr Andrew Craig, a well-respected Glasgow surgeon. On her mother's side she was a grandniece of the mathematician Colin Maclaurin (one of the geniuses of the 'Scottish Enlightenment'). In her youth she was known as 'pretty Miss Nancie.'

She met James Maclehose, a lawyer, on a journey from Glasgow to Edinburgh. She was young and impressionable, he was struck by her beauty; they imagined that they were in love. Their courtship was short and she married him when she was seventeen years old, in July 1776. He was a jealous man and treated her badly. After five years of unhappy marriage, she could tolerate him no longer. She returned to her father's house with her two sons while he (Maclehose) left Glasgow for the West Indies.

After her father's death in 1782 she came to Edinburgh and lived at General's Entry in Potterow, with her two boys. Her income was a small annuity from her father's estate and she received some financial help from her cousin, Lord Craig, the judge.

Burns was introduced to her at a tea-party on 7th December 1787 given by Miss Nimmo, the sister of a customs official; Burns had probably accepted the invitation in the hope of obtaining a customs post. Instead, he found a stunningly beautiful lady whose interest in poetry displayed a critical intelligence; Burns, as was his wont, was captivated by her. She was genteel but fascinating, irresistible and provocative; he was intoxicated by her; she inspired him to write some of the world's greatest love letters and poems, of which R. W. Mackenna, in his 1929 Introduction to *Robert Burns, The Letters of the Poet*, wrote:

> "he struts and swaggers, poses and makes fine gestures, pleads and reproaches, flatters and cajoles. This windy braggart, this loud-mouthed actor, this pietist frothing at the lips with the airy bubbles of religiosity, this mean spurner of poor Jean Armour, is not the manly Robert Burns we know and love." [28]

But this was new to Burns, he had never before pursued a love affair with a lady of gentility. She kept him at a tantalising distance but at the same time enjoyed his ardour.

Two days after their first meeting Burns wrote, "I have never met with a person whom I more anxiously wished to meet again than yourself. Tonight I was to have had that very great pleasure - I was intoxicated with the idea; but an unlucky fall from a coach has so bruised one of my knees, that I can't stir my leg off the cushion. So, if I don't see you again, I shall not rest in my grave for chagrin". Her reply, sympathising, was subtlety itself: "... were I your sister, I would call and see you." She enclosed a poem: *When first you saw Clarinda's Charms,* and from then, they corresponded as *Clarinda* and *Sylvander*. Burns praised her poems, and with some amendments and additional stanzas they were published in her name. Their meetings were increasingly romantic and his letters were powerful declarations of his love.

Throughout this brief, passionate but platonic affair Burns was engaged to be married to Jean Armour; but Clarinda's love for Burns was truly genuine; she loved her *Sylvander* with that special love that 'knows not death'. Many of his letters contain respectful references to her deep feelings of religion and, although regarded as imprudent in her passion for Burns as a married lady, she was above suspicion of intimacy.

In an attempt to cool his over-powering ardour, she wrote,
> "I believe nothing were a more impracticable task than to make you feel a little of Gospel humility. Believe me,

I wish not to see you deprived of that noble fire of an excellent mind which you eminently possess, yet a sense of your faults - a feeling sense of them - were devoutly to be wished."

Then on Sunday morning of 3rd February 1788, Burns's letter:

"I have just been before the throne of my God, Clarinda; according to my association of ideas, my sentiments of love and friendship, I next devote myself to you. You are an angel Clarinda you are surely no mortal that the earth owns. To kiss your hand, to live on your smile, is to me far more exquisite bliss than the dearest favours that the fairest of the sex, yourself excepted, can bestow."

Then on Sunday evening:

"You are the constant companion of my thoughts. Clarinda, the dear object of my fondest love; there, may the most sacred inviolate honour, the most faithful kindling constancy, ever watch and animate my every thought and imagination!"

When Burns left Edinburgh to visit Glasgow and Kilmarnock his scientific analogy of his love for her was contained in his letter of 18th February 1788, the first day of his journey:

"The attraction of love, I find, is an inverse proportion to the attraction of Newtonian philosophy. In the system of Sir Isaac, the nearer objects are to one another, the stronger is the attractive force. In my system, every milestone that marked my progress from Clarinda, awakened a keener pang of attachment to her."

In spite of his engagement to Jean Armour, Burns wrote from Mossgiel on 23rd February 1788:

"Now, for a little news that will please you. I, this morning, as I came home, called for a certain woman (Jean Armour). I am disgusted with her - I cannot endure her! I, while my heart smote me for the profanity, tried to compare her with my Clarinda; 'twas the expiring glimmer of a farthing taper beside the cloudless glory of the meridian sun. Here was tasteless insipidy, vulgarity of soul and mercenary fawning; there polished good sense, Heaven-born genius, and the most generous, the most tender passion. I have done with her and she with me."

But Clarinda reproached Burns for his fickleness; Jean Armour gave birth to his twins nine days after that letter was written.

He had signed the lease of Ellisland Farm on 18th March to marry Jean. He acknowledged her as his wife in late April and they moved to the hundred-acre farm in June 1788. Clarinda was undoubtedly hurt. She wrote forbidding any further correspondence. Her natural reserve had hidden her true love and she remained silent for over a year. She wrote again during the summer of 1791 and Burns visited her in November. She had decided to join her husband in Jamaica and Burns's last parting with Clarinda on 6th December 1791 was sad and tearful. He wrote his most heart-rending love song:

Ae Fond kiss, and then we sever!
Ae fareweel, and then for ever!
Deep in heart-wrung tears I'll pledge thee!
Warring sighs and groans I'll wage thee!

Who shall say that Fortune grieves him,
While the star of hope she leaves him?
Me, nae cheerfu' twinkle lights me,
Dark despair around benights me.

I'll ne'er blame my partial fancy:
Naething could resist my Nancy!
But to see her was to love her,
Love but her, and love for ever.

Had we never lov'd sae kindly,
Had we never lov'd sae blindly,
never met - or never parted -
We had ne'er been broken-hearted.

Fair-thee-weel, thou first and fairest!
Fair-thee-weel, thou best and dearest!
Thine be ilka joy and treasure,
Peace, Enjoyment, Love and Pleasure!

Ae fond kiss, and then we sever!
Ae fareweel, alas, for ever!
Deep in heart-wrung tears I'll pledge thee,
Warring sighs and groans I'll wage thee.

James Maclehose, having invited his wife to join him, now tried to dissuade her by false reports of a rebellion and an outbreak of yellow fever. It is probable that he was looking for a way out of supporting her further. She left for Jamaica in March 1792 but life with him proved as unbearable as before; his brutal behaviour and her illness forced her return to Edinburgh in August 1792.

Burns and she corresponded spasmodically but Burns found it impossible to write as a 'friend' as she wished. In his last letter, dated 25th June 1794, Burns wrote: "So, my lovely Clarinda I devote this glass of wine to a most ardent wish for your happiness".

Her husband died in 1812 and having previously obtained a judgment against him for aliment of £100 per year she was now able to make a claim on his estate.

Thirty-five years after Burns's death (1796), Mrs Maclehose wrote in her diary on 6th December 1831 -

"This day I can never forget. Parted with Robert Burns in the year 1791, never more to meet in this world. Oh, may we meet in Heaven!" Three years later, at the age of seventy-five, her doctor recorded that he - "heard Clarinda express the same hope to meet in another sphere the one heart that she had ever found herself able entirely to sympathise with, but which had been divided from her on earth by such pitiless obstacles."

Burns's letters to Clarinda were published without her permission in 1802 and the whole correspondence was arranged and edited, after her death, by her grandson, W.C.Maclehose, in 1843.

Clarinda died in her house on the Calton Hill on 22nd October 1841, in her eighty-third year. In her dying breath she said one word: "Sylvander." She was buried in Canongate Churchyard where the Ninety Burns Club erected the beautiful bronze relief by J.H.Gamely 1909 on the east wall.

The menus of Clarinda's Tearoom are adorned by a sketch of the bronze relief in the Canongate Churchyard and a facsimile page, in Burns's handwriting, of one of his many letters is displayed on a wall of the tearoom.

54. Queensberry House - Duke of Queensberry

Queensberry House was built in 1681 and completed in 1686 for Charles Maitland, Lord Hatton. He was a brother of John Maitland, the 1st Duke of Lauderdale (1616-82). Maitland sold the house to William Douglas, 1st Duke of Queensberry, only four years after its completion. He was created Duke of Queensberry by Charles II in 1684 as a reward for his support to the Government in the suppression of Covenanters; from then the house became known as Queensberry House. He was a man of many contradictions: a great miser and yet he built fine houses and pleasure grounds; illiterate and yet a great collector of books.

The **1st Duke of Queensberry** was born in 1637 and was to become Lord High Treasurer and the chief power in Scotland from 1682 when he was made Constable and Governor of Edinburgh Castle. His high office was renewed when James VII was crowned James II of England in 1685.

James's first 'black' year was the 'killing time' against the Covenanters. Queensberry was now granted the 'new gift' of the lead mines within his earldom but, a year later, he was deprived of all his offices and forbidden to leave Scotland, because of his less than whole-hearted support for the king's 'Dispensing Power'in which James VII (II) gave himself power to change the law and to replace the highest offices with Roman Catholics. However, in 1688 the king informed the Council that Queensberry 'had given satisfaction' and that he was now 'taken under protection.'

By the summer of 1688 James II's reign was nearing its end, he had ignored his Parliament and the Church for too long. Queensberry now supported the Revolution when the English Parliament offered the crown to William of Orange and Mary (James's son-in-law and daughter).

William of Orange landed in the south of England on 5th November 1688 and Queensberry took the oath of allegiance six months later, having sent his son James Douglas to meet the Prince of Orange at Sherborne.

The Duke was now appointed Extraordinary Lord of Session (1693-95) and Commissioner of the Treasury in the year of his death (28th March 1695, aged fifty-eight). His only daughter, Anne, who married the 4th Earl of Wemyss, died in 1700 following a horrific accident in which she was burned to death at Queensberry House.

His son James, the **2nd Duke,** was a Privy Councillor (1684) and Lord of the Exchequer (1685) under James VII (II of England). He resigned his Royal appointments and joined William of Orange at Sherborne in November 1688. He was welcomed with open arms and promptly made a Captain of William's Dutch Guards, a Privy Councillor (1689) and Lord of the Bedchamber (1689 - 1702 at £1000 per year), Lord of Exchequer (1690), Lord of Treasury (1691-1707), Acting Lord High Treasurer (1694), Lord Privy Seal, (1606-1702) and Extraordinary Lord of Session (1696-death). For his services to Parliament he was given a KG (Knight of the Most Noble Order of the Garter) in 1701.

Queensberry was Lord High Commissioner four times between 1700 and 1706 and was the power behind the Act of Union (of the English and Scottish Parliaments of 1707). A most horrific tale is told of the day on which he left Queensberry House to go up the High Street to Parliament House for the final debate on the terms of the Union. He was jeered and threatened by a mob on his way and had to take a valet for protection. Chambers in his *Traditions of Edinburgh* and Grant in his *Old and New Edinburgh* relate the horrific tale of the Duke's insane eldest son, Lord Drumlanrig. The valet had, as part of his duty, responsibility for the security of this insane giant of a man, Lord Drumlanrig, who was left unattended in the house. He escaped from the locked room in which he was kept and found his way to the kitchen where he seized a terrified kitchen-boy. He stripped him and killed him and fixed him to the spit over the kitchen fire and roasted him.

The Duke on his return, found him eating the remains of the corpse. The ghastly event was hushed up but the ordinary people of Edinburgh blamed the Duke, saying that this was his punishment for his part in the unpopular Union.

William III was succeeded by Queen Anne in 1702 and Queensberry was stripped of his offices in 1704. He was wrongly accused of complicity in what came to be called the 'Queensberry Plot' but in spite of Queen Anne's dislike of him, Queensberry was again appointed Lord Privy Seal for Scotland and a Lord of the Treasury. He was made third Principal Secretary of State of Scotland in 1708 and a Privy Councillor of Great Britain in 1709.

His personal finances were severely dented with his investment in the disastrous Darien Scheme. However, he received compensation in the sum of £12,325 in secret from Lord Godolphin, the Treasurer of England. A total of £20,540 was distributed to thirty-two members of the last Scottish Parliament, described at the time as 'the grossest bribery and corruption.' An even larger sum (£400,000 - the 'Equivalent') was distributed to those who had invested and lost in the disastrous 'Darien

Expedition' of 1698. This too, was described as bribery and its late arrival in Edinburgh was greeted by a jeering mob who stoned the Dragoon Guards who guarded it on its way through the Royal Mile.

In 1706 the Duke of Queensberry resigned his peerage titles and nominated his second surviving son, Charles (1698-1778) to be his heir, thus excluding James (1697-1714/5) the eldest insane son. The Dukedom was therefore inherited by the second son, Charles, whose eccentric wife lost £3000 at cards against the infamous Colonel Charteris, a known cheat. She patronised the English poet and playwright John Gay (1685-1732) and entertained him at Queensberry House. Their eldest son, Lord Drumlanrig, showed signs of instability verging at times on madness; he was committed to one lady and married another, a daughter of the Earl of Hopetoun. After army service in Holland he shot himself in 1754 on his way to London with his wife. His brother Charles died in 1755 and the title and estates were inherited by a distant cousin, the Earl of March, Francis Charteris, who became 6th Earl of Wemyss.

As 4th Duke, Grant describes him as 'an old debauchee, better known as "Old Q"', he stripped Queensberry House of its decorations and sold it for £900 in 1801 to pay off gambling debts. He was famous for his patronage of horse racing. He died unmarried in 1810 leaving over a million pounds.

Queensberry House was now owned by the Board of Ordinance and was converted to an army barracks, a storey being added in 1808. In 1832 it was converted into a People's Refuge. In 1971 it was renovated to become a nursing home for the care of the elderly. Today it lies empty awaiting a further renovation and transformation, possibly into offices.

55. Whitefoord House - Dugald Stewart

Whitefoord House was built in 1769, on the site of the ruins of the Earl of Winton's house, for Sir John Whitefoord of Blairgunan and Ballochmyle. It was designed by Robert Mylne, son of the King's Master Mason of Milne's Court in the Lawnmarket. Sir John's sister, Maria, was immortalised by Robert Burns in his song: 'The Lass of Ballochmyle'.

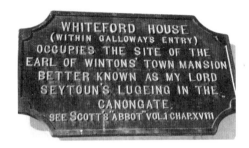

Sir John, who was an army Major, was an early patron and admirer of Burns. He had to sell his idyllic estate of Ballochmyle to pay his debts after the failure of the bank in which he had invested much of his fortune. He died in 1803.

The next owner, Sir William Macleod Bannatyne, died in 1832 at the age of ninety-one and the house became a type foundry for a time.

Another resident, before he moved to Lothian Hut (demolished in 1825 to make way for the brewery) in Horse Wynd was the popular and inspiring teacher and philosopher, **Professor Dugald Stewart** (1753-1828). He lived at Whitefoord House from 1806 to 1812 and his monument, the circular colonnade enclosing the Greek urn by William H. Playfair, stands on the Calton Hill.

Whitefoord House is now a hospital and residence for Scottish War Veterans which was opened after its renovation by H.M. The Queen in 1984.

Dugald Stewart was undoubtedly one of the fifty geniuses that the King's Chemist, Mr Amyatt, claimed he could meet within the space of a few minutes at the Cross of Edinburgh. 'Edinburgh enjoyed a noble privilege not possessed by any other city in Europe.' 36 This was the 'Golden Age' when men sharpened their wits and honed their arguments to fine degrees of excellence in the numerous clubs and societies of Edinburgh which met in the taverns of the Royal Mile.

Had he had any say in the matter, Dugald Stewart could hardly have chosen a better place for his birth, on 22nd November 1753, for his future distinguished academic career - he was born in an old house attached to the Old College of the University, where his father, Matthew

Stewart (1717-85) was Professor of Mathematics. Young Dugald was educated at Edinburgh's famous High School (1761) and at Edinburgh University under the great philosopher and historian, Adam Ferguson (1723-1816), the 'father of sociology'. He attended Glasgow University in 1771, under the revered head of the Scottish School of Philosophy, Thomas Reid (1710-96) with whom he became a lifelong friend and admirer.

In 1773, barely twenty years of age, Dugald Stewart read his essay, *On Dreaming* to the Literary Society of Glasgow and to the Speculative Society of Edinburgh.

He was appointed an assistant in mathematics under his father's professorship and in 1775 he was elected joint-professor with his father whose health was failing. Dugald Stewart took over Ferguson's lectures on morality plus three hours each day on mathematics plus a course on astronomy and he published many articles. To cope with his formidable workload he rose at 3.0 a.m. every weekday and was often so exhausted at the end of a day he had to be lifted into his carriage.

In 1783 he accompanied Lord Ancrum to Paris and on his return he married Helen Bannatyne. He succeeded Adam Ferguson to the chair of Moral Philosophy in 1785. His lectures were inspiring, students flocked to hear him from all over Britain - the young men of means being sent to Edinburgh, their 'grand tours' having been cancelled due to the threat of war with France. Edinburgh rivalled even London as the place of intellectual stimulation.

Lord Cockburn eulogises him in his *Memorials*:

> "the voice was singularly pleasing; a slight burr only made its tones softer. His ear, both for music and for speech was exquisite; and he was the finest reader I have ever heard .... his whole manner was that of an academical gentleman .... Stewart dealt as little as possible with metaphysics, avoided details, and shrank, with a horror which was sometimes rather ludicrous, from all polemical matter. Invisible distinctions, vain contentions, factious theories, philosophical sectarianism, had no attractions for him; and their absence left him free for those moral themes on which he could soar without perplexing his hearers or wasting himself, by useless and painful subtleties .... Stewart was uniformly great and fascinating. Everything was purified and exalted by his beautiful taste .... he breathed the love of virtue into whole generations of pupils."[5]

His summers were spent at Catrine near Mossgiel where he met and conversed happily with Robert Burns who had just published the 'Kilmarnock' edition of his poems (1786). Stewart's wife died in 1787 and his next two summers were spent in France. The Bastille was stormed in July 1789 during one of his visits and he met with several influential men to whom he expressed his strong sympathy for the Revolutionary movement. But his liberal views were not shared by all, for example Francis Jeffrey's father forbade his son, the future Lord Jeffrey (ref.39 Jeffrey Street), 'to attend the lectures of so dangerous a teacher', and Sydney Smith, the clergyman, journalist and wit, referred to him as a 'humbug' in metaphysics, although he held him 'in the highest terms of his moral and literary merits'.

In July 1790 he married Helen D'Arcy Cranstoun, a lady of immense charm. His home life was idyllic, she was his intellectual equal and Stewart 'submitted all his writings to her judgement'. Grant, in his *Old and New Edinburgh* describes her: 'the best essence of beauty, expression, a bright eye beaming with intelligence, a manner the most distinguished, yet soft, feminine, and singularly winning.' Students were especially appreciative of her welcoming warmth when they visited the venerable professor at home, which was Lothian Hut at Horse Wynd.

Some of those who benefited from her hospitality and his tuition and wisdom included: Henry Brougham (1778-1868) (later Lord Brougham), Sydney Smith (1771-1845), Francis Horner (1778-1817), Francis Jeffrey (1773-1850), Henry Erskine (1746-1817), Lord John Russell (1792-1878), Henry Temple (1784-1865) later Lord Palmerston; Lords Dudley, Lansdowne, Kinnaird, Ashburton - naming only a few.

In 1810 Dugald Stewart became ill and retired with great regret. There was genuine sorrow among students and staff of the university. Cockburn again paints the scene:

"We could scarcely bring ourselves to believe that the voice was to be heard no more. The going down of such a luminary cast a foreboding gloom over the friends of mental philosophy, and deprived the college of its purest light." 5

He was succeeded by Thomas Brown for whom Stewart had canvassed the Town Council. However, when Brown dared to criticise the work of Stewart's old master, Thomas Reid, Dugald Stewart was greatly disappointed. He had promulgated Reid's doctrine of 'common-sense' philosophy to an even greater degree than Reid himself.

Brown died in 1820 and Stewart took over the Chair for the second time but he was unable to lecture and soon felt too infirm to continue; he resigned in June 1820. He was unable to canvass for his friends Macvey Napier and Sir William Hamilton. The Tories won the day with the appointment of John Wilson (1785-1854), 'Christopher North', who knew little of philosophy and whose statue is in East Princes Street Gardens.

Dugald Stewart died at his house in Ainslie Place on 11th June 1828; his passing seemed to bring to an end the magical days of the 'Scottish Enlightenment'. He had suffered from palsy for the last seven years of his life, but his mental faculties remained in sparkling form. He corrected and revised the last two volumes of his last book only two months before his death.

His body was taken from the Western New Town to the Canongate Churchyard. The service was not public but it was attended by the Principal and the Professors of the University and the Magistrates of the City.

56. White Horse Close - William Dick

White Horse Close (formerly Davidson's Close and Laurence Ord's Close), a delightfully picturesque restoration of 1964, has the date 1623 carved in stone on its inner wall. It is thought to be named from Mary Queen of Scots' white palfrey (a lady's saddle-horse) when its stables were used as the Royal Mews.

This Close was the starting point for the horse-drawn coaches to London and it became a popular hostelry. In 1649 several Royalist nobles of Scotland met at the Close and when it became known that they intended to set out in support of Charles I, who was in Berwick at the time, they were prevented from leaving by an angry mob of Covenanters who had no faith in the king. The Marquis of Montrose escaped them to conquer all Scotland for his king.

After 1742 Lord Milton *qv*(51) used the inn as a coach-house when he lived at Milton House in the Canongate. In 1745, during Prince Charles Edward's occupation of Edinburgh, his Highland Chiefs and officers used the Close as their quarters.

A young man called **William Dick** worked and lived with his blacksmith father at White Horse Close when it accommodated stables. From this humble beginning he would become the founder of the now internationally famous Royal (Dick) School of Veterinary Studies which is the Faculty of Veterinary Medicine of the University of Edinburgh, best known in Edinburgh as the 'Dick-Vet College'.

The plaque on the west wall of the close is inscribed:

Within this close on 6th May 1793 was born
WILLIAM DICK
1793-1866
Founder of the Edinburgh Veterinary College
incorporated in the University of Edinburgh
in 1951 as the Royal (Dick) School of Veterinary Studies
and in 1964 instituted the Faculty of Veterinary Medicine.

William Dick was born barely three months after France had declared war on Britain; his formative years and early manhood therefore were influenced by the death and destruction of over twenty years of the Revolutionary and Napoleonic Wars. There was of course a great demand for horses and his father's forge at White Horse Close was kept in constant work. A hard-working intelligent man, he insisted that his son received the education which had been denied him.

Young William Dick was therefore sent to a charity school of St Paul. He watched his father at work and listened to his explanations of how to shoe horses so that the animal felt no discomfort. What interested him was the great care that his father took to ensure that the animal should not experience pain and this led, almost naturally, to William's interest in animal welfare. He attended lectures on the subject given by the Perthshire born anatomist, John Barclay (1758-1826). Barclay was at once taken with William Dick's intense interest; Dick's curiosity and his stream of questions brought the two men to a lifelong friendship.

John Barclay guided his keen young scholar to further study in London but after three months Dick found that his studies were confined only to horses; Barclay's teaching had given the young man a much broader view and he wanted to study the animal world, not simply one species. He therefore returned to Edinburgh. However, he had sufficiently impressed the London College directors to receive the award of the college diploma. This was his credential to give his own lectures, firstly in rooms at Nicholson Street, not far from the University, which were soon to become inadequate for his needs. He moved his 'college' to Clyde Street (between North St Andrew Street and Elder Street). His students included many farmers because his lectures covered all farm animals and his visual aids included diagrams and skeletons.

His greatest encouragement was to come from his sister Mary and from his old teacher, John Barclay, who had so convinced the Highland Society of the worth of William Dick that they decided to make a grant of £50 to set up an Examination Board; the Society itself having powers to award diplomas and certificates in agriculture.

The Dick-Vet College was born from these beginnings and by 1833 the demand was such that Dick, out of his own finances, put up £10,000 to finance a new extension. This was eventually recouped from fees and further extensions, including the college library, laboratories and an animal hospital, were added.

William Dick had his own rooms above the college which he shared with his sister, Mary. He was now the Professor of a highly successful College, but his activities for the community had broadened with his reputation; he was appointed a Justice of the Peace, a member of the Board of George Heriot's School and the Board of the old Asylum at Morningside Park.

William Dick, having devoted his life to veterinary science, died in April 1866 and in his Will he bequeathed the College to the Town Council of Edinburgh. He was buried almost in the centre of the New Calton Burying Ground.

Fifty years after his death the college built new premises at Summerhall Place - Causewayside. In 1951 its name change, 'The Royal (Dick) School of Veterinary Studies', coincided with its incorporation within the Faculty of Medicine of the University of Edinburgh and in 1964 it gained Faculty status as the Faculty of Veterinary Medicine.

57. Edward VII Statue, Holyrood;
Scottish National Memorial to
Edward VII

The bronze statue at the north-west corner of Holyrood Palace Yard is that of Edward VII; it was sculpted by H.S. Gamely in 1920-22. The Scottish National War Memorial to Edward VII consists of magnificent wrought iron gates and screens at each end of the Palace Yard. These were designed by Sir George Washington Browne in 1920-22.

Edward VII, the only monarch of the House of Saxe-Coburg, was born on 9th November 1841 at St James Palace. Known as 'Bertie', his parents, Queen Victoria and Prince Albert, tried every device they could think of to interest their ill-tempered son in his education and training for kingship.

In childhood he was impossible; he bullied his younger brothers and sisters. He kicked and spat at his tutors until his father took over his education. In spite of his abominable behaviour he could be quite charming, especially when young ladies were present. His visit to Canada and the USA in 1860 was an unexpected success, especially with the ladies.

His father died (of typhoid) shortly after an incident which greatly angered him and which the Queen always considered to have shortened her husband's life. It occurred during military manoeuvres in Ireland; the Prince's brother officers, knowing of his fondness for female company, smuggled an actress into the Prince's tent during the night. The joke seriously backfired but the Prince resolutely refused to name the officers involved. The Queen never forgave him nor did she ever trust him again.

In 1863, the Queen fervently hoped that her wayward son would settle down after his marriage to the beautiful Princess Alexandra of Denmark. She was welcomed by the British Royal family but the Queen became annoyed when, in 1864, she and her new husband supported the Danes in their war against Prussia and Austria over Schleswig-Holstein. She was even more annoyed when the Prince supported Prime Minister Lord Palmerston and Lord Russell, the Foreign Secretary, against the German States and, when the Prince agreed to meet the Italian revolutionary Guiseppi Garibaldi, who also supported Denmark, she was exasperated to the point of despair.

Prince Edward and Princess Alexandra had three sons and three daughters. Their eldest son, Prince Albert Victor died in 1892 shortly after he had become engaged to Princess Mary of Teck. It could be said that she had a fortunate escape. Prince Albert had led a dissipated life and died of syphilis. A year later she married his younger brother Prince George who became George V.

Contrary to ministerial advice, Queen Victoria jealously refused to allow Prince Edward any access to State papers. She confined his activities to the opening of bridges and public buildings - in fact, it was this which started the practice of Royalty accepting such engagements. However, the Prince's favourite pastimes were quite different and included eating (five huge meals each day, on one occasion at least, he ate a twenty-course meal), hunting, shooting, gambling and beautiful women - he loved female company. He was known to have had six mistresses and dozens of casual affairs.

His friends had to be very rich to afford his company; they included not only the aristocracy but rich businessmen, politicians and trade unionists. He became involved in several scandals and managed to have them covered up, except for two court cases in which he was subpoenaed. One was a divorce case in which he was involved with the wife of Sir Charles Mordaunt and the other, his participation in an illegal game of baccarat, in which Sir William Gordon-Cumming had been accused of cheating and sued the players for slander.

Curiously the public seemed either not to notice or to forgive his indiscretions; he was cheered more often than jeered. Even his wife tolerated his mistresses with detached amusement, referring to one of them, Miss Chamberlayne, as "Chamberpots". Another, Lily Langtree, was introduced at Court and received frostily by Queen Victoria. The

Princess was known to enjoy conversing with Mrs Keppel, her husband's last mistress.

He succeeded Queen Victoria in 1901 at the age of fifty-nine and in spite of her predictions of disaster his nine-year reign was not at all unsuccessful. It coincided with an era of great intellect in government and the 1906 General Election gave the Liberals an eighty-strong majority under Sir Henry Campbell-Bannerman. He gave South Africa the right to govern itself, the trade unions the right to picket peacefully and he forbade the Courts from taking civil action against them. The social changes included the introduction of the old-age pension, National Insurance and the embryo of the modern welfare state. However, Edward VII supported the Conservatives and was against votes for women.

His tours of Europe, especially France, gave him the epithet 'Edward the Peacemaker', but his nephew, Kaiser William II of Germany, viewed his activities with suspicion. The French Foreign Minister, Delcassé, was well pleased when Edward became king; Queen Victoria had favoured Germany, and now the two men were anxious to achieve friendship between Britain and France and, in 1904, the 'Entente Cordiale' was reached. The Socialists and some Liberals were openly critical of the king's meeting with Czar Nicholas II whose regime of oppression in Russia was detested.

In 1909, when Lloyd George was Chancellor of the Exchequer, the House of Lords turned down his 'War Budget' (war against poverty). This was a constitutional catastrophe not equalled since the Reform Bill of 1832 and Edward VII at first refused Prime Minister Asquith sufficient additional Peers to give him a majority in the Lords, preferring instead to try to negotiate. In the end Edward insisted on a General Election, and in the midst of the crisis he died - on 6th May 1910 aged sixty-eight. Never a degenerate, he lived life quite simply, as he wished, deserving perhaps of his media title 'Edward the Caresser'.

58. Palace of Holyroodhouse

Before the Palace of Holyroodhouse was built kings of Scotland made use of the guesthouse of the Abbey as a Royal residence; it stood on the site now occupied by the north range of the Palace.

It was not until the year 1501 that building of a new Palace began. James IV (r.1488-1513) built it in 1501-05 for his newly-wedded wife, Margaret Tudor, daughter of Henry VII. Their marriage took place at Holyrood on 8th August 1503 and twenty-five years later, their son, James V (r. 1513-1542) added the north-west tower and the royal apartments on the north side. In addition he rebuilt the west and south sides of the quadrangle. A new chapel was built during his reign, the old one being transformed into a Council Chamber.

Holyrood and the town were burned and looted by the army of Henry VIII under the command of the Earl of Hertford in 1544 as revenge against Cardinal Beaton (1494 -1546) who had persuaded the Scottish Parliament to break the marriage-treaty of 1543 between Prince Edward, son of Henry VIII, and the one-year-old Mary, daughter of James V. Again Holyrood was repaired and restored but the Abbey was destroyed by the Reformers in 1559. The nave was used for worship but the choir and transepts were destroyed in 1570.

In March 1566 a horrendous murder took place at Holyrood Palace. Mary Queen of Scots' talented secretary, Rizzio, was the victim. Her husband, the worthless Lord Darnley, jealous of Rizzio's popularity and exceptional talent, had conspired with some of the nobility to surprise Rizzio in the presence of the Queen. They seized the harmless secretary and brutally stabbed him to death and, but for the presence of mind of the Countess of Argyll who grasped a candle, Mary herself might have been murdered in the confusion of darkness. She screamed and the assailants fled the small supper-chamber. Mary, who was six months pregnant, was fortunate not to lose her baby.

The visit of James VI in 1617 prompted redecoration of the chapel and major repairs were made to the Church and Palace for Charles I's Coronation as king of Scotland (not of Scots) in 1633. In November 1641, at a time of dire disagreement with his English Parliament, he entertained the Scottish Peers at a banquet in the Palace in the hope of winning their allegiance.

In 1650, after Cromwell's victory at the Battle of Dunbar (3rd September 1650), his troops used the Palace as a barrack and through their carelessness it was badly damaged by fire. Cromwell paid for inferior repairs which were executed properly after the Restoration of Charles II in 1660.

In 1670, £30,000 was voted for the repair of Holyroodhouse and Stirling Castle. Charles II disliked the initial proposals for Holyrood but he approved a revised plan. During the reconstruction, the Earl of Lauderdale, as Commissioner to Parliament was in residence and his brother, Lord Hatton who was Lord Treasurer Depute, was given administrative oversight of the reconstruction. After its completion in 1679 by Sir William Bruce, the King's Surveyor-General, the Duke and Duchess of York took up residence at the Palace when he became Royal Commissioner. The Duchess ordered that a Catholic Chapel be fitted in the Queen's Presence Room and when he became king James VII (II of England, 1685-88) ordered that the Council Chamber be converted into a Roman Catholic Chapel.

James VII revived the Order of the Thistle in 1687 and ordered the fitting out of Holyrood Abbey as the Thistle Chapel. However, a Protestant mob destroyed the Chapel Royal and the Abbey Church for James's persecution of the Covenanters. He was dethroned in 1688 and his son-in-law and daughter, William and Mary were crowned.

The Act of Union brought an end to the Scottish Parliament and the Scottish Privy Council. The Palace ceased to be used and was occupied by the Hereditary Keepers of the Palace and of the Household, the Dukes of Hamilton and Argyll and other favoured nobles.

During the 1745 'Rising', Prince Charles Edward Stuart, the 'Young Pretender', occupied the Queen's apartment after the ten- minute Battle of Prestonpans. He proclaimed his father King as James VIII and held a grand ball. He lived at the Palace like a king for a little over a month.

Another seventy-seven years were to pass before Holyrood Palace was again used by Royalty. The great occasion, orchestrated by Sir Walter Scott, was the Royal visit to Scotland by George IV in 1822. The Palace had been allowed to fall into disrepair and the king ordered its refurbishment. It took two years to plan (by Robert Reid) and a further ten years to execute at a cost of £25,000. A new Presence

Chamber replaced the Guard Hall of the Great Apartment, the King's Privy Chamber replaced the Council Chamber and Queen Mary's Apartment remained untouched. The garden was extended to be viewed from each side and from the back, the buildings and the south front were refaced but restoration of the Abbey Church was considered to be too expensive.

Queen Victoria visited Holyrood in 1842 and during her reign the Crown obtained repossession of the rooms occupied by the Officers of State but the Duke of Hamilton was allowed to keep his apartment. Holyrood thus became a Victorian Palace by 1871, the Queen having had the Duke of Argyll's rooms made into a private apartment on the second floor.

The entry to the Palace from Abbeyhill was completed in 1857 by cutting through the Privy Garden in which the late 16th century 'Queen Mary's Bath' stands on its own. The magnificent wrought-iron gates, designed by George Washington-Browne in 1920-02, at the Palace Yard form a memorial to Edward VII. In the north-west corner is H.S.Gamely's bronze statue of Edward VII. The octagonal fountain with its gnome-like historical figures, its crown spire and its lion masks form an impressive centre piece in the Palace forecourt.

59. Holyrood Abbey - David I

The name Holyrood is said to be derived from a miracle perceived by David I (r.1124-1153), King of Scots. Finding himself alone in the forest, where the ruined Abbey now stands, he was attacked by a magnificent white stag. His horse reared and as he lay on the ground death seemed imminent. Miraculously, a gleaming rood or cross appeared between the antlers of the stag. Frightened by the brightness of its light, the stag turned away and ran off. Shaken but thankful to be alive, David returned to Edinburgh Castle and that night a vision of St Andrew appeared to him and counselled that he should show his gratitude by founding an Abbey and Monastery on the spot where he had been saved from death.

Craftsmen were brought from Flanders to build the Augustinian Monastery and the Abbey of the holy rood. Canons of the Order of St Augustus came from St Andrews Priory in 1128 and were given the right to found a burgh. The canons walked regularly between their Abbey and the gates of the town. Their pathway came to be called 'Canon Gait' - the word *gait* meaning way of walking. The burgh was called Canongate and the Burgh Arms consist of antlers between which is the cross or holy rood.

The Abbey, founded in 1128, contained accommodation for the monks and a guesthouse for the kings of Scotland which gave it great prestige.

Another explanation for the derivation of the name Holyrood is: King David's mother was Queen Margaret, a saintly queen who gave succour to the poor and reformed the Scottish church from its "Celtic idiosynchrasies". Her husband, King Malcolm Canmore, had given her a bejewelled black rood which young David called her 'Holy Rood'.

The earliest factual record of Holyrood Abbey is that of the Papal Council held at the Abbey in 1177. A few years later, in 1189, the Scottish nobles met at the Abbey to arrange the payment of the 10,000 mark ransom demanded by King Richard for the release of William the Lion, King of Scots. William had been captured at Alnwick in 1174 and was held prisoner by Henry II. His successor Richard, Coeur-de-Lion, needed the money for his Crusade to the Holy Land.

At the end of the 12th century the Abbey was extensively rebuilt after its sacking by Edward II in 1322. Four years later King Robert the Bruce held his parliament there and used it as a Royal residence. In 1370 David II, son of Robert II, was buried in the Abbey (1371) and James II was born (1430), crowned (1437), married (1449) and buried (1460) at Holyrood.

The Abbey was destroyed during the Earl of Hertford's rampage of destruction in 1544. This was Henry VIII's revenge against Cardinal Beaton (1494-1546) who had persuaded the Scottish Parliament to break the marriage-treaty of 1543 between his son, Prince Edward, and the one-year-old Mary, daughter of James V. Again the Abbey was repaired and restored only to be destroyed again; this time by the Reformers in 1559.

The last Royal personage to be buried at the Abbey was odious Lord Darnley, the overbearing husband of Mary, Queen of Scots; he was murdered in 1567 at Kirk o' Fields. Further destruction of Holyrood Abbey took place in 1570 when the choir and transepts were burned by order of the General Assembly of the Church of Scotland. James VII (II of England) intended that the Abbey should be converted into a Chapel for the newly recreated Most Ancient and Most Noble Order of the Thistle but a Protestant mob finally destroyed the Abbey and the Chapel Royal in 1688 when James was deposed and replaced by his son-in-law William III.

The Abbey's founder, David I, was the sixth and youngest son of Malcolm Canmore and Queen Margaret; she was canonised in 1251 by Pope Innocent IV. David was born in 1080 and at the age of nine he was orphaned. Four years later he, with his elder sister, Matilda, was sent to the Court of William II (1087-1100) to escape from his uncle Donaldbane who reigned in Scotland for a year from 1093. Matilda remained in England where she married William's fourth son who became Henry I.

David, who was a great favourite at court, returned home to Scotland after a few years. He had become well-versed in Norman ways, he spoke fluent French and had many friends at the English court.

His step-brother, Duncan, was killed by his brother Edmund in 1094 and the next brother, Edgar the Peaceable, became king in 1097 having superseded Donald Bane. He died in 1107 and Alexander, David's eldest surviving brother (fourth son of Malcolm and Margaret) succeeded to the throne of Scotland north of the Clyde and the Forth. With the help, possibly at the insistence, of King Henry, David now became Prince of Cumbria including part of Cumberland and southern Scotland but not the Lothians.

In 1113/4 David married the widow of Simon de Senlis, the Norman Earl of Northampton. She was the forty-year-old daughter of the Saxon Earl of Northumbria and David became Earl of Huntington. His elder brother died in 1124 and he succeeded him as David I.

The early part of his reign was spent in quelling the opposition of the powerful Moray family; this took him five years with the help of Norman barons. They were never actually involved in the fight, but the threat was sufficient to gain Moray's submission. In England, King Henry had named his daughter, Matilda (David's niece), as his successor and David, with other English barons including Henry's nephew, Stephen, swore fealty to her. However, when Henry died in 1135, Stephen rushed across from Normandy to claim the English throne. Much to the annoyance of David I, Stephen was received with enthusiasm and crowned king. David, faithful to the late king and to his niece, Matilda, now raised an army to invade England.

David, having been educated at the English court, was regarded as a civilised knight and was probably more Norman than Scots in his thinking. His arrival at the head of a huge army of ill-trained and brutal hirelings from France, Germany, Cumbria as well as from Galloway to the Western Isles, was treated as insulting by the Archbishop of York.

David's army had marched unchecked through Northumberland and Durham, which he regarded his own, but when he reached Yorkshire the Archbishop Thurston of York had so inspired the barons, they amassed an army of well-armed, mail-clad soldiers. They raised a mast (or standard) with the banners of three saints and stood against their foe, inspired as if fighting a holy war. David's tactics were spoiled by internal squabbling and he was defeated at the Battle of the Standard on 11th August 1138. He retreated to Carlisle and King Stephen, preoccupied in fighting Matilda's supporters, was glad to make a treaty with King David.

David now ruled all of Scotland which included parts of England and the greater barons, or earls, in whom he could place his trust, were given lands in return for their support in times of trouble.

His unification of Scotland marked the end of Celtic life and the beginning of the feudal system in which greater vassals, vassals, free-tenants and serfs served the king. The vassals received land from the greater vassals in return for their loyalty and supply of fighting men when needed in times of war. Free tenants paid rent to their lord in the form of produce and men. Their serfs were literally owned and could be bought or sold. This system existed in Scotland for hundreds of years. King David obtained annual payments through his creation of Royal Burghs which were permitted to trade, and taxes from exports brought handsome sums to the crown. In addition, fines collected from criminals were paid to the crown. To ease the system of collection he created his coinage; the first of its kind in Scotland.

In addition to the creation of Royal Burghs, David extended the monasteries created by his mother, Queen Margaret, and his brother Alexander I, and he created several new religious orders. The monasteries of Dunfermline, Scone and Selkirk existed by 1124; Dunfermline was elevated from a Priory to an Abbey in 1128 and Augustinian Abbeys were founded at Holyrood, Cambuskenneth (near Stirling), Jedburgh and St Andrews. His 'Border Abbeys' were built as if to show his English neighbours the skill of Scottish craftsmen and the level of civilisation of the country.

By 1153, the year of David's death, Kelso and Lesmahagow Abbeys had been founded, but of course, many decades were to pass before their completion. King David was responsible for the development of the system of parishes with compulsory tithes (a tithe being one tenth of the livestock and produce of the land) for the church. Bishops and monks were the promoters of David's kingship and royal authority throughout 12th century Scotland, but this development was piecemeal and his reign was not without rebellions of which there were four: 1124, 1130, 1134 and the last in 1151. The Church in Scotland greatly helped the process of unification and preached peace and care for the poor.

One of King David's greatest satisfactions was his son Henry; David was devastated when he died in 1152.

On 24th May 1153 King David became ill at Carlisle and died so peacefully that his passing went unnoticed by his attendants. So ended what was probably the most important reign in the history of Scotland. Future generations would refer to him as 'St David' but he was never canonised.

Appendix

Some Closes and Wynds of Bygone Days

Many old tenements with their Closes and Wynds in the Royal Mile have been demolished to make way for new buildings and new streets. The names of some of these old closes have their own stories of people and events in these bygone days.

Castle Hill

On the site of Castle Hill Reservoir stood the **Town's Yards** with its fire station, a depot and a cistern which controlled the water intake from Comiston Springs, installed in 1681 by Dutchman Bruschi, and was demolished to make space for the new reservoir in 1851 which made provision for new wells at various intervals down the Royal Mile.

Cockpen Mansion was immediately west of Ramsay Lane, it was owned by the grandparents of Lord Cockburn (ref. No. 24. Cockburn Street); his grandmother, Lady Cockpen, lived here from 1761

The Palace of Mary of Guise (mother of Mary Queen of Scots) was situated on the site of the General Assembly Hall, built in 1845-50. She took up residence in the palace when she was forced to flee from the Palace of Holyroodhouse when the Earl of Hertford (Protector Somerset) sacked Holyrood in May 1544. He burned most of Edinburgh on the orders of Henry VIII. This was the 'Rough Wooing' and was in revenge for the broken marriage treaty between his son Prince Edward and young Mary who would become 'Queen of Scots'. Other Closes demolished were Tod's, Nairn's and Blyth's.

Blair's Close was demolished to build Castlehill School (now The Scotch Whisky Heritage Centre). The mansion of the Bairds of Saughtonhall was situated here and its name was changed to Baird's Close when the family of Sir David Baird (1757-1829), the victor of Seringapatam took up residence. Sir David was born there.

Rockville Close, east of Boswell's Close, was the residence of Lord Rockville, Alexander Gordon (1739-92) a judge.

Coalstoun's Close or Kennedy's Close was the residence of the Earl of Cassillis whose family name was Kennedy. Another judge, Lord Coalstoun (d 1776) was characterised in Stevenson's *Catriona* as Sheriff George Broun, the defending counsel in the Appin Murder Trial. The house became an asylum for the blind in 1794 at the instigation of Dr. Blacklock, the blind poet who encouraged Robert Burns to come to Edinburgh on 15th November 1786.

Stripping Close was one of the closes on the site of the Tolbooth Church. Its name signifies the place where prisoners from the Tolbooth were brought to strip to the waist before being marched downhill to one of the nine whipping centres in the Royal Mile. In this close was the printing office of James Donaldson (1751-1830) who published the *Edinburgh Advertiser* and who founded Donaldson's School for the Deaf opened in 1850 in West Coates.

Lawnmarket

Donaldson's Close was situated in a building which was demolished in 1825 to make way for Johnston Terrace (named after Sir William Johnston, Lord Provost 1848-51, the famous map-maker). Donaldson's Close led to a court where the house of Lord Provost Archibald Stewart was visited by Prince Charles Edward Stuart during his occupation of Edinburgh in 1745. The house was bought by Alexander Donaldson who founded the *Edinburgh Advertiser*. His son, James, inherited the business and on his death in 1830 left £210,000 to found Donaldson's School in West Coates.

Baxter's Close was demolished to make way for Bank Street. It takes its name from baxters or bakers. A plaque near the entrance to Lady Stair's Close is inscribed:

> *In a House on the East Side of this Close ROBERT*
> *BURNS lived during his first visit to Edinburgh in 1786.*

He lodged with his friend John Richmond of Mauchline at 1/6d (7p) per week.

Lady Elgin, the wife of the 7th Earl of Elgin and only daughter of William Hamilton Nisbet of Dirleton lived in this Close. She was governess to Princess Charlotte, daughter of Princess Caroline and the Prince of Wales who became George IV. As Governess Lady Elgin kept open the communication between Charlotte and her estranged parents.

High Street

Galloway's Close was immediately below (east) of Bank Street on the site of the Sheriff Courthouse which was opened in 1937. An advertisement of 1782 in the *Caledonian Mercury* announced: 'Mrs Waterston, Wax Chandler in Galloway's Close, has now opened a shop on the North side of Lawnmarket.' Recently widowed she took over the running of her husband's business, now George Waterston & Sons Limited.

Libberton's Wynd, opposite the Sheriff Courthouse, was demolished in 1834 when George IV Bridge was built. It was the site of Johnnie Dowiels Tavern, a favourite haunt of poets Robert Fergusson and Robert Burns. Henry Mackenzie, author, Crown Attorney of the Scottish Court and Comptroller of Taxes, known as the 'Man of feeling,' was born here in 1745.

Dunbar's Close, west of Bank Street, was thought to take its name from Oliver Cromwell's victory at the Battle of Dunbar (3rd September 1650); one of Cromwell's old guard-houses was situated there but the close is probably named from a glover named Dunbar who lived in the Close. William Waterston's sealing wax workshop was here in 1764 (the company still flourishes at Warriston as George Waterston and Sons Limited). The property was sold to the Bank of Scotland for its Head Office.

Byres Close was east of St Giles Street and was the residence of John Byers (1569-1629), a rich merchant who bought the Coates estate about 1610 and on which St Mary's Episcopal Cathedral in Palmerston Place was built between 1874 and 1917. Byers was City Treasurer, Bailie, Dean of Guild and Lord Provost. His son Sir John Byers built the L-shaped old East Coates House in 1615 which is now St Mary's Music School. The house of Adam Bothwell, Bishop of Orkney, who died in 1593, is situated on the right of the close. His sister was the mother of Lord John Napier the inventor of logarithms. The mottoes over the dormer windows are *Exitas acta probat* (Ovid) - The end justifies the deeds. *Nihil est ex omni parte beatum* (Horace) - There is no such thing in the world as unmixed happiness.
The house of Sir William Dick of Braid who died in 1655 was situated between Byres Close and Advocates' Close. He lent money to James VI and as Lord Provost of Edinburgh he gave large sums of money to

the Covenanters and later he supported Charles II's Royalist cause and advanced £20,000. For this he was fined £65,000 by the Parliamentary Party. After Charles II came to the throne Dick left for London hoping to recover £160,000 but instead he found himself in severe debt and was imprisoned on more than one occasion for petty debts. He died in poverty at Westminister without sufficient funds to give him a decent burial. The entrance to his house in the Royal Mile came to be called **Kintyre's Close** after the house was bought by the 1st Earl of Kintore whose mother removed the Regalia of Scotland from Dunotter to Kineff and spread the rumour that her son had taken the Regalia abroad so that Cromwell could not get his hands on the Scottish crown, sword and sceptre.

The Tolbooth stood at the north-west corner of St Giles Church. It was built about 1561 and demolished in 1817. Its main entrance door was situated on the spot where the stone setts in the shape of a heart are to be found on the ground just east of the Buccleuch statue - the "Heart of Midlothian", as it was named by Robert Louis Stevenson. The Tolbooth was the meeting place of the Scottish Parliament and was the Town Hall, its chambers being used by the Privy Council. It accommodated the College of Justice and was a prison after 1640. Here many criminals met their end on the scaffold; the notorious Deacon Brodie was hanged here on 1st October 1788 on a scaffold of his own design.

Luckenbooths were small shops or locked booths situated on the north side of St Giles. George Heriot, the King's jeweller, and Allan Ramsay had their booths here; the latter set up his lending library here in 1726, the first in Scotland.

Krames, or "Creams" as it was known locally, was the narrow passageway between the Luckenbooths and St Giles. Lord Cockburn in his *Memorials of his Time* describes it 'like one of the Arabian Nights bazaars in Bagdad'.

Warriston Close takes its name from Lord Warriston, Archibald Johnston, a Lord of Session in 1641 (ref.17)

In **Writers' Court** Writers to the Signet had their library in 1699.

The Royal Exchange, now the City Chambers, was built in 1753-61 for the merchants of Edinburgh and initiated by Lord Provost

Drummond (ref. 20); he insisted that he merely executed that which the Duke of York (who became James VII) had proposed in 1680. The building was enlarged in 1901 when many old Closes were demolished.

New Bank Close, on the south side of the High Street, almost opposite the Royal Exchange (The City Chambers), was the site of the New Bank, which became the Royal Bank and was founded in 1727 with stock which exceeded that of the Bank of Scotland. Alexander Donaldson, the bookseller, had his shop here and was succeeded by his son, James Donaldson, who left money for the building of Donaldson's Hospital.

Allan's Close was immediately east of the City Chambers. Here Deacon Brodie, Edinburgh's *Jekyll and Hyde*, hid the tools of his nefarious trade - burglary (ref.10)

Craig's Close, next to Allan's Close, was the home of several printers: Andrew Hart who died in 1621 printed a 1610 edition of the Bible. James Watson produced his *Choice Collection of Comic and Serious Scottish Poems* from which Robert Burns learned of earlier Scottish poets. William Creech (1745-1815) published Burns' 1793 Edinburgh Edition of his poems and Archibald Constable (1774-1827) published Sir Walter Scott's Waverley novels. Scott, with young Prince Gustavus of Sweden, witnessed the proclamation of George IV's accession to the throne at Mercat Cross in 1820 from a window of this house.

Old Post Office Close was next to Craig's Close and was the site of the post office during the reign of George I. There was one letter-carrier for the city. In Matthew Thomson's Tavern in this close the Wagering Club was founded in 1775.

Kennedy's Close was situated immediately west of the Tron Church. George Buchanan (1506-82) was classical tutor to Mary Queen of Scots and he lived here after resigning his Principalship of St Andrews University to accept the tutorship of the four year-old Prince James, son of Mary Queen of Scots who became James VI after she was forced to abdicate in 1567. Buchanan turned against Mary after the murder of her husband, Lord Darnley. Buchanan attested that the handwriting of the 'Casket Letters' was hers but historians now agree that Buchanan himself may have fabricated them. Tradition has it that students of Edinburgh University are capped with 'Geordie Buchanan's breeks'. Before he died in 1582 at his house in this Close he completed his *History of Scotland.*

Milne Square was immediately opposite the Tron Church. The tall, three-sided grey building which formed the square was built by Robert Milne in 1689. Seven generations of his ancestors were Master Masons to the Crown (ref.7 Mylne's Court). The building was purchased in 1695 by William Paterson for The Company of Scotland Trading to Africa and the Indies. This was Paterson's cherished scheme for Scotland which challenged the English trading monopoly - the East India Company. Paterson, an intelligent, fast-talking man, had already founded the Bank of England and had fallen out with his co-directors and resigned. He placed his considerable energies into what was to become the Darien disaster in which about half of Scotland's wealth was to be lost. The meetings of the Council, the directors and their numerous committees were held in Milne Square.

Cap and Feather Close was demolished when the North Bridge was built in 1763-72. In fact, the public notice submissions for the design of the bridge make specific reference to the line of the bridge from the Cap and Feather Close. One of the numerous clubs, the Knights of the Cap and Feather Club, met there and Robert Fergusson, the poet so admired by Robert Burns, was born here on 5th September 1750.

The **Netherbow** was a gate or port at the entrance to Edinburgh and was finally demolished in 1764 having been seriously damaged during the 'Rough Wooing' when the Earl of Hertford invaded Edinburgh in 1544. Bonnie Prince Charlie's Jacobites had no trouble gaining entrance through the Netherbow in 1745 when they occupied the city; the guard had opened the gates to allow a coach to leave and the Highlanders simply pushed their way in.

Canongate

Boyd's Close took its name from its owner, James Boyd who changed the name of his coaching inn from Boyd's Inn to the **White Horse Inn** as a mark of his gratitude to his race horse which won him many races. It was situated just east of St Mary's Street on the south side of the Canongate. It was here that the boorish Dr Samuel Johnson (1709-84), the great lexicographer, critic and poet, threw his lemonade out of the window in angry remonstrance against a waiter who had put sugar lumps into his glass using his greasy fingers. Later that day, 14th August 1773, Johnson and James Boswell (1740-95), who hero-worshipped

Johnson, walked up the Royal Mile arm-in-arm to Boswell's house in James's Court.

Gibb's Close, east of Boyd's Close, was the home of the brother of the infamous William Burke who murdered Mary Paterson there in 1828. He, with his partner-in-crime Hare, sold dead bodies to Dr Knox, the anatomist, for £10 each. Hare turned King's evidence and Burke was hanged.

> 'Up the close and doun the stair,
> But and ben wi' Burke and Hare.
> Burke's the butcher. Hare's the thief.
> Knox the boy that buys the beef.'

Coull's Close was demolished when Cranston Street was broadened. In this close was Paul's Work where the Ballantyne Press produced 145,000 copies of Scott's Waverley Novels. Walter Scott and James Ballantyne were school friends in Kelso.

Little Jack's Close was named after a slater. In her house here Susanna, Countess of Eglintoun, entertained Prince Charles Edward during his occupation of Edinburgh in 1745. David Hume wrote most of his *History of England* between 1753 and 1762 in this close. Behind Jack's Land stood the house of General Thomas Dalyell of the Binns. Having been appointed Commander-in-Chief in Scotland by Charles II, Dalyell commanded the army which defeated the Covenanters at Rullion Green in 1666. He was so dismayed by the execution of Charles I that he refused to cut his beard in his lifetime; it grew to an enormous length.

Callender's Entry, between Golfer's Land and Whitefoord House, takes its name from blacksmiths under Royal patronage called Callender. The Entry became famous for Janet Hall's alehouse where the finest claret was served to such as poet Allan Ramsay (1685-1758) (ref. 6.) and poet and dramatist John Gay (1685-1732) the author of *The Beggar's Opera* under the patronage of the 3rd Duke and Duchess of Queensberry.

Thomson's Court on the north side of the Abbey Strand was the Sanctuary for aristocratic debtors - "the Abbey Lairds" who were allowed to cross the paved girth on Sundays. The Sanctuary ceased to be needed when imprisonment for debt was abolished in 1880.

Chancellor's Court, east of Queensberry House, was named from the site of the Lord Chancellor's house. He was James Drummond (1648-

1716), the chief administrator during the reign of James VII and was created Duke of Perth. It was he who invented an instrument of torture - the thumbscrew.

Horse Wynd was the entrance to the Royal Stables and **Lothian Hut**, built by the 3rd Marquess of Lothian, was the home of the University's Professor of Moral Philosophy, Dugald Stewart before he moved to Whitefoord House.

References

1. Old and New Edinburgh, Vols I-III, by James Grant. Pub Cassell & Co. Ltd.

2. Statistical History of Scotland, 1853, by J.H.Dawson. Pub. W.H.Lizars.

3. Anecdotes and Facts of Scotland and Scotsmen, by James Mitchell LL.D. 1825.

4. Traditions of Edinburgh, by Robert Chambers LL.D. Pub. W & R Chambers Ltd.

5. Memorials of His Time, by Lord Cockburn. Pub. Robert Grant & Son Ltd.

6. A Small Country, by Neil McCallum. Pub. James Thin, The Mercat Press.

7. Edinburgh in the Age of Reason, a commemoration by The Hon. Lord Cameron, G.E.Davie, Duncan Forbes, Allan Frazer, Douglas Young and A.J.Youngson. Pub. Edinburgh University Press. 1967.

8. The Scottish Enlightenment by David Daiches. Pub. The Saltire Society. 1986.

9. A Hotbed of Genius, The Scottish Enlightenment 1730-90, Ed. Daiches, Jones and Jones. Pub. Edinburgh University Press.

10. Edinburgh, a Travellers Companion, by David Daiches. pub. Constable & Co. Ltd.

11. Scotland's Story in her Monuments by David Graham-Campbell. Pub. Robert Hale. 1982.

12. A Short History of Scotland, by P. Hume Brown. Pub. Langside Publishers.

13. Scotland, A New History, by Michael Lynch. Pub. Century Ltd. 1991.

14. Scottish Kings by Gordon Donaldson, Pub. Book Club Associates.

15. The Lives of Kings and Queens of England, Ed. Antonia Fraser. Pub. Macdonald Futura Publishers.

16. A History of Scotland by J.D.Mackie. Pub. Penguin Books Ltd.

17. Great Contemporaries by Winston Churchill. Pub. The Reprint Society.

18. Edinburgh, The Buildings of Scotland by John Gifford, Colin McWilliam and David Walker. Pub. Penguin Books Ltd.

19. History and Derivation of Edinburgh Street Names. Pub. Edinburgh Corporation, City Engineers Department. 1975.

20. Civic Survey and Plan for Edinburgh by Patrick Abercrombie LL.D. and Derick Plumstead ARIBA. Pub. Oliver & Boyd.

21. Edinburgh, The Third Statistical Account of Scotland. Edited by David Keir. Pub. William Collins Ltd. 1966.

22. 101 Great Scots, by Allan Massie. Pub. W & R Chambers Ltd. 1987.

23. Edinburgh Portraits by Michael Turnbull. Pub. John Donald Publishers Ltd.

25. The Lord Provosts of Edinburgh 1296-1932, by Marguerite Wood. Pub. T&A Constable at the University Press.

26. The Strange case of Deacon Brodie, by Forbes Bramble. Pub. Hamish Hamilton, London.

27. Lord Provost George Drummond 1687-1766, various authors. Pub. Scotland's Cultural Heritage, University of Edinburgh. 1987.

28. Robert Burns, The Letters of the Poet, printed for the Ninety Burns Club, Collins Clear-Type Press, London.

29. Dictionary of National Biography, Pub. Smith Elder & Co. Ltd.

30. The Complete Peerage. Pub. St. Catherine's Press, London, 1912.

31. Edinburgh 1329-1929. Oliver & Boyd. 1929.

32. John Knox and the Scottish Reformation, by G Barrett Smith. Pub. The Religious Tract and Book Society of Scotland.

33. Capital Walks in Edinburgh - The New Town, by David Dick. Pub. Neil Wilson Publishing Ltd., Glasgow, Scotland.

34. On the Psychology of Military Incompetence, by Norman F. Dixon. Pub. Futura Publications (a division of MacDonald & Co. (Publishers) Ltd., London. 1976).

35. The Interpreter Geddes, by Amelia Defries.

36. Memorable Edinburgh Houses, by Wilmot Harrison. Pub. Oliphant, Anderson and Ferrier, Edinburgh 1893.

37. Literary Landmarks of Edinburgh by Laurence Hutton. Pub. James R. Osgood, McIlvaine & Co. 1891

38. Cockburn's Millenium by Karl Miller, Pub. Gerald Duckworth & Co., Ltd.

39. Mary Queen of Scots by Antonia Fraser, Pub. Panther Books

40. The Last Will and Testament of George Heriot and the Original Statutes of his Hospital, 10th December 1623 by Dr Balcanquall. Printed by Neill & Co. 1835.

41. The Edinburgh Literary Guide by Andrew Lownie. Pub. Canongate Press.

42. A Diary of Edinburgh by Trevor Moyle. Pub. Polygon Books.

43. Edinburgh the Golden Age by Michael Joyce. Pub. Longmans Green & Co.

44. Edinburgh by Allan Massie. Pub. Sinclair-Stevenson.

45. Edinburgh edited by Owen Dudley Edwards and Graham Richardson. Pub. Canongate Publishing Ltd.

46. Eccentric Edinburgh by GK Gillon. Pub. Moubray House Publishing.

47. Close Encounters in the Royal Mile, by Alastair M.R. Hardie. Pub. John Donald Publishers Ltd.

Index